GINGER BLISS
AND THE
VIOLET FIZZ

GINGER
BLISS

AND THE

VIOLET
FIZZ

A COCKTAIL LOVER'S GUIDE
TO MIXING DRINKS USING
NEW AND CLASSIC LIQUEURS

A.J. RATHBUN

THE HARVARD COMMON PRESS
BOSTON, MASSACHUSETTS

THE
HARVARD
COMMON
PRESS
5   3   5
ALBANY
STREET
BOSTON,
MASSACHUSETTS
0   2   1   1   8

WWW.HARVARDCOMMONPRESS.COM

PRINTED IN CHINA | PRINTED ON ACID-FREE PAPER

· · · · · · · · · · LIBRARY OF CONGRESS · · · · · · · · · ·
· · · · · · · CATALOGING-IN-PUBLICATION DATA · · · · · · ·
· · · · RATHBUN, A. J. (ARTHUR JOHN), 1969- · · · ·
· · · · GINGER BLISS AND THE VIOLET FIZZ : · · · ·
· · · A COCKTAIL LOVER'S GUIDE TO MIXING · · ·
· DRINKS USING NEW AND CLASSIC LIQUEURS / ·
· · · · · · · · · · · · · A.J. RATHBUN. · · · · · · · · · · · · ·
· · · · · · · · · · P. CM.   INCLUDES INDEX. · · · · · · · · · ·
· · · · · · · · · · · ISBN 978-1-55832-665-1 · · · · · · · · · · ·
· · · 1. COCKTAILS. I. TITLE.   TX951.R167 2011 · · ·
· · · · · · · · 641.8'74—DC22   2010048160 · · · · · · · ·

SPECIAL BULK-ORDER DISCOUNTS ARE AVAILABLE
ON THIS AND OTHER HARVARD COMMON PRESS
BOOKS. COMPANIES AND ORGANIZATIONS
MAY PURCHASE BOOKS FOR PREMIUMS
OR RESALE, OR MAY ARRANGE A CUSTOM
EDITION, BY CONTACTING THE MARKETING
DIRECTOR AT THE ADDRESS ABOVE.

· · · · BOOK DESIGN BY MODERN GOOD · · · ·
· · · · PHOTOGRAPHY BY JERRY ERRICO · · · ·
· FOOD/DRINK STYLING BY HELEN JONES ·
AUTHOR PHOTOGRAPHS BY NATALIE FULLER

10   9   8   7   6   5   4   3   2   1

FOR KAISER AND COEN:
YOU CAN'T COMPLETELY ENJOY THIS
BOOK FOR A FEW MORE YEARS, BUT THANKS
FOR THE LAUGHS AND INSPIRATION.

CONTENTS

ACKNOWLEDGMENTS

To travel to and within the dimension of the *Ginger Bliss and the Velvet Fizz* (as well as their many beauteous brethren) without assistance, aid, and companionship is not only dangerous, but not nearly as much fun. It's a journey I'd never take alone, let me tell you. Because of this, I'd like to raise a toast of thanks and praise to the many who helped me put this book together. But a few intrepid ones deserve a special shout-out and holler, starting with editor Valerie Cimino. Once again (she's resilient), Valerie helped me create a book from the initial idea to the last strained drink, adding her wit, wisdom, and good cheer to every page. A big cheer must also be given to Bruce and the entire Harvard Common Press crew, who are boisterous, bouncy, and incredibly helpful and talented. Special thanks to editor Dan Rosenberg, who wasn't afraid to get poetic in naming the book.

Of course, I wouldn't even take a drinking trip such as this without the constant and consistent aid of my agent, Michael Bourret, who is always ready to pitch in, answer questions, listen, and give advice and who is, well, awesome. He deserves a *Salut!* at full volume (as does his partner, Miguel, who moved with him to the West Coast, making it easier, at least in theory, for us to get together for drinks). Now, though, back away from your desk and make yourself a cocktail, Michael, 'cause you're working too hard.

A booming toast—*Prost!*—needs to be given up in addition to copy editor Karen Wise, for her keen-eyed help with the book and for her aid with my dubious translations, and to photographer Jerry Errico and his team, whose lovely pictures of the drinks contained within brighten up the ride and bring the book to full-color life.

As mentioned above, traveling solo just isn't as jolly. Because of that, a huge shout-out (*Cinghiale!*) to a few more specific folks is in order, because they helped make everything possible. This toast encompasses a bit of a wide range but starts with the fantastic bartenders of both the pro and home varieties, who provided recipes and inspiration for this volume, as well as the amazing modern drink scribes (check out some of my favorite reads on page 182) whose delectable drinks I borrowed from their delectable books. You all rule! Thanks for making this book, and the drinking world, a tastier place to reside within—the next drink's on me when we're in the same town. A special glass has to be raised to two bar geniuses in particular: My local bartender, Andrew Bohrer, who isn't afraid to don a curly wig on video or let me in early when I need a snazzy cocktail, and my former local bartender, Jeremy Sidener, who isn't afraid to host afternoon book signings. Speaking of local drinkers and drink makers, I wouldn't even be able to make it through writing a book, much less make it through a week, without the support (and by "support" I mean "drinks") from those I imbibe with the most:

Double Taker Jeremy, wife Megan, and Beatrix; poet and drink designer Ed and wife Jill; Mark, Leslie, and Alex; Shane; Christy; Andrea S. (thanks for the editing help, too) and Eric; the Amazon Kitchen team past and present; Rebecca, Eric, and Meg; Andy and Deena; the Thirteenth Street basketballers; Philip, Mimi, and Yuki; Jon and Nicole; Joel and Alexis; Jesiks and Koes near and far; Erika; Becks and Drew; Nichole; Brad and Erin; Ame and Ron; Tasha and Keith; Brett and Chelsea and Nevia; Braiden and Spencer; and the world's most amazing video and film director, Brad K., wife Christy, and Cash and Harley. Big props also to the Lisa Ekus crew for their help getting the drinking word out, to anyone who's stopped by my blog Spiked Punch (www.ajrathbun.com/blog) or my Italy blog Six Months in Italy (www.sixmonthsinitaly.com), to Andrew and Marianne for making my Italy pre-tirement possible (start your own Italy dream trip at www.amicivillas.com), to the bands that keep things rollicking (specifically old-schoolers TSL, DG, GFB, MVG, SB, AD and the HFs, Bs of O, Malinks, Withholders, Tales from the Birdbath, The Table of Contents, Zoom, and Tom Waits, the inspiration for The Hounds They Start to Roar, page 204, and many evenings of drinks), and to anyone else who's made me a drink in the last 21 years.

Three final toasts are in order before the voyage (and the liqueur pouring) begins. First, to my wonderful family, who haven't yet seem shocked that I write so much about cocktails. For all the Rathbun, James, DeMaranville, Fuller, and Davis family members, you're the best family anyone could ask for. Thanks again, always, for the support and love—and for bringing extra snacks to parties whenever they're needed.

The penultimate toast goes to you, dear reader and home bartender. Thanks a whole case of liqueur bottles for not being afraid to take this expedition into the realm of liqueurs and vermouths, and for expanding the cocktail revolution into your homes.

But the final toast goes to those nearest and dearest to me, Sookie and Rory (the best, and sometimes nuttiest, dogs anyone ever could want to have, even when they knock over a bottle of booze or a glass that's just been poured), and, last and loudest, to Natalie. Thanks again, dear, for putting up with my cocktail and liqueur obsession (even when it takes us overseas for six months) and for not being shocked at the number of liqueur bottles in the dining room. Here's to many more evenings spent together cocktail testing, party throwing, and drink sipping as the sun goes down.

INTRODUCTION

Shhh . . . I have a secret. Come closer, because this is something that you can't tell anyone, a series of rituals and whispered words, a bunch of formulae and unknown ingredients, a matter of great importance that must be kept hush-hush. Follow me, and we'll unlock one of the most masterful mysteries that the world (or, at least, the drinking world) has ever known. Don't be scared—by unlocking this clandestine curiosity, you'll be going on the liquid ride of your life, which will change everything you ever thought about throwing parties. We'll go through the padlocked oak doors, around the maze of tables and chairs, and past the row of stools standing like sentinels guarding our destination. We won't even stop to stare at the wondrous words printed and scrawled across the coasters, because we're going to the dimension of the *Ginger Bliss and the Violet Fizz.*

Which actually isn't a scary or secretive place at all, even with the array of enchanting bottles that stand on shelves in a manner that seems to taunt, "Look at me but don't touch, because you don't have the expertise to unlock the delicious enigma that is me."

But first, let's step back for a minute and give some context to our sleuthing. In the beginning, there was man and woman (we're stepping *way* back). How they got to that way-back place, I'm leaving for others to discuss, but they were thirsty, I know ('cause I'm thirsty just typing this, and they were working harder than I am). This thirst led to water, sure, but then to the discovery of more spirited beverages, including wine and clear alcoholic spirits, and then more aged and flavored mixtures built off of those bases (yes, we're rushing through history rapidly here because I don't want to delay you from the book's real contents for too long). But every palate is different, and our imbibing ancestors, like us, were drinking for taste as well as for the divine freeing of the mind that the drinks bring along. So they also started sweetening their spirituous combinations here and there, and experimenting with flavors, and maturing them, until they reached a point where what they had was so delicious that they started distributing it to others in their tribe, and then farther afield. This made these liqueurs and vermouths (as they started to be called) more and more available, and more and more beloved, and more and more used in cocktails, highballs, and other drinks.

Now, in the modern age, a growing number of these liqueurs and vermouths and their ilk are becoming available worldwide, and even more are being created (or re-created in the case of a few that were lost along the way) than ever before. This liqueur globalism is one of the many drivers behind the modern cocktail revolution, a revolution that we are lucky be able to take part in as it happens. There are so many new and newly available bottles out there, in physical liquor stores and via the magic of Internet liquor stores, that at times it becomes over-whelming, and it can confuse even the most intrepid of home entertainers.

There are really three (because three is a magic number) categories making up this new availability. First are those items that are brand-new to the cocktail landscape, such as VeeV Açaí spirit and Loft Lavender Cello liqueur. Next up are the classic ingredients that were once on most bar shelves but that disap-peared from production for decades—swell little numbers such as crème Yvette and absinthe. And finally there's a whole host of ingredients that over time have become underappreciated (here we're looking at venerable names like Chartreuse and Bénédictine) or saddled with stereotypes that just didn't fit (for instance, delicious-but-often-pigeonholed charmers like amaretto and Cointreau).

The availability quotient is, definitely, one driver of this revolution. Another is the emergence of modern professional bartenders, who are on the front lines reclaiming the bartender's place as craftsman, artisan, and artist. To do this, these honorable women and men are rediscovering and using classic techniques, unearthing classic recipes, and using the wide range of now-available ingredients to create new mixtures—with an eye toward enriching your drinking experience when out and about. This is why, when you meet any of these true bartenders, you should be happy, trust to their expertise, and always tip well.

But what about when you throw a party at home? I mean, you like to make drinks too, right? And you're intrigued by what you see when out at a bar, that twinkling rainbow of bottles and the magic that you know they contain. Maybe you tried a new small-batch vermouth recently while out with friends, and you want to seek out a bottle for home use. And when you go into your local liquor store or are surfing online and see a new and unknown bottle, you want to know you're making a good investment when you buy it. You want to ensure that once you get that bottle of Czech herbal liqueur home, you will be able to use it in a way that will assuredly set your next party amongst the stars (or at least on a level above every other party being thrown that month, or season, or year, even). This book, my adventurous one, is for you.

GINGER BLISS, PAGE 198

CHAPTER 1

HOW TO ENTER THE WORLD OF
LIQUEURS
AND VERMOUTHS

. . . .

The answer to the question of how to expand your usage of liqueurs and vermouths is not, in this instance, to flirt with a bunch of bartenders (though by and large they are incredibly pleasant people). Because we're talking about usage at home bars now, the place where *you* do the pouring, shaking, and stirring, the spot where *you* become the drink dispenser, the arena where *you* make the secret mixes that delight guests—and, most important, delight you. Because you have to enjoy the drinks first and foremost or your guests probably won't be so delighted, and you won't have as much enjoyment at your own party, which would be a crying shame.

This is why I've designed *Ginger Bliss and the Violet Fizz* in a very particular manner. There are numerous awe-inspiring classic and modern cocktail tomes available that break out chapters by base spirit (gin, vodka, brandy, whiskey, tequila, and sometimes Champagne), and this can be handy. Other fine volumes are alphabetized by drink, which can, again, be useful (especially when you're looking for a specific drink you've heard of). And then other worthy reads (including a few by yours truly) organize chapters by theme, which is helpful when you're planning a party around a particular occasion or season. Here, however, we're talking about integrating specific liqueurs and vermouths into your cocktailing life, about changing your get-togethers from being solely gin-and-tonic and rum-and-coke deals, about using those many bottles you see out and about but don't know how to use, even when you know what tastes you tend to enjoy most.

For these reasons, the chapters of drinks in the following pages are grouped around liqueurs that share a flavor profile. By "flavor profile" I'm talking about the flavor of a particular liqueur that's responsible for the personality and taste of a drink. This doesn't mean that in every recipe the liqueur in question is the main ingredient. On the contrary, it is often the second most-used ingredient (after the base spirit), and sometimes it's even farther down the list. The liqueur, though, and the many qualities it imparts, is the key to that particular drink's existence. It's what makes the drink a successful and delicious addition to your day, and that's why it's in the book.

So, for example, there's A Liquid Citrus Circus, containing recipes highlighted by the vast panoply of fun citrus liqueurs, and a chapter that reminds you to Take Your Herbal Medicine, which contains the darker, more intense herbal liqueurs that are popping up regularly these days. There's also a chapter detailing The Justice League of Vermouths—though they aren't specifically liqueurs, vermouths and their cousins figure prominently as some of those curious bottles you might have glimpsed when out drinking or shopping.

One intriguing thing to remember when going through the chapters (and one of the things that makes trying new recipes so much tasty fun) is that there are certain liqueurs that by their very complex natures can show up in multiple chapters. Chartreuse is a historically perfect example. Made from a secret recipe known to only two monks at a time (for the full history, see page 58), it has a flavor profile that is layered and intricate, with both floral and herbal accents that show up on the tongue when sipped solo (which isn't a bad thing to try, and a drink of choice in some spots). Different parts of its multifaceted personality shine more brightly when it is combined with other ingredients, which means that you'll find drinks highlighting Chartreuse in both A Bouquet of Lovely Liqueurs (drinks such as the Triomphe Cocktail on page 76) and Take Your Herbal Medicine (drinks such as the Last Word on page 137). So, don't get thrown off if you see a key ingredient in multiple spots: Just be glad our drinking world is rarely boring for your palate.

By breaking out the chapters in this flavor-oriented way, it makes it easier to plan a party around a few signature drinks. You can go about it two ways. First, if you're out drinking or shopping and you see something intriguing, pick up a bottle and check where it fits as far as "flavor profile," and then flip to that chapter to find an enticing way to use it. For example, if you know already that you tend to favor fruit flavors, then, before the festivities, skip to the chapter called If You're Feeling Fruity, pick out a few intriguing drinks, and stock up on their ingredients. In the same manner, if you're looking for a cocktail to serve as an after-dinner dessert, turn the pages to the Here's to You, Sweets chapter, which is full of sweeter numbers, and pick out the perfect match for that after-dinner moment. The idea is to make it easier for you to pick out a few signature drinks to make any gathering sparkle—from parties of many people to those that consist of just you and a significant other.

Stocking Your Home Bar

One of the hardest parts of knowing how to stock your home bar is the uncapping—or knowing where to start. No one becomes a superstar home bartender overnight, so don't fret about it to the point where you end up standing in the kitchen gritting your teeth to nubs. That's not going to be enjoyable for anyone. Really, there's no need to worry about throwing a successful party, as long as you remember that the answer to the question "How do I throw a successful party?" comes mainly down to one word: preparation. Being prepared makes everything go more smoothly. It means having the right ingredients, tools, glassware, and more, which we'll discuss soon, but it also comes down, at heart, to this idea of having a signature drink or two, so you can focus on a few quality offerings instead of trying to anticipate what possible combination of ingredients every single attendee might want.

First, you'll be able to stock up on the ingredients for the drink, ensuring that you don't run out of that one liqueur that makes the drink shine. Second, you'll be able to prep needed garnishes and squeeze juice in advance, making it breezy during the party to make drinks for folks and leaving you time to revel in the party instead of spending hours cutting, juicing, and swearing. Third, when you're trying to get people excited about a party with clever invitations, exhilarating emails, and bright banners pulled by airplanes, you can drop the names of your signature cocktails, thereby stirring excitement and a little buzz, which never hurts. And having a delish couple of cocktails makes your party one that people will continue to talk about long after that last sip is swallowed.

Looking at the bigger picture, having signature drinks also helps you to build your home bar in an organic, and festive, fashion. Here's what I suggest: You decide to throw a soirée next Saturday (I'll watch for my invite), and then pick out two signature drinks from this very book. When shopping for the liquors and liqueurs and bottled ingredients involved in the drinks, pick up a little extra. This covers the bases in case anyone brings extra guests (which they always do), but it should also leave you with something in the way of liquid leftovers. Then, when deciding on drinks a few days later to go with dinner, or for a Sunday brunch the following weekend, look for different recipes that contain those very bottled leftovers, then go shopping just for the ingredients you don't have yet. And while shopping, get a little extra. You see where this is going: Soon you'll have a well-stocked bar of bottles that you know the flavor profiles for, and that go in drinks you're already familiar with, and that you like for certain occasions. Running low? Start the cycle again.

Before I begin unveiling the other, more basic necessities for the bar, some words about the stars of this book, the many liqueurs and vermouths. I'll do this chapter by chapter, to help you understand and decide on what flavors and signature cocktails appeal most. I'm not, of course, going to suggest that every single liqueur or vermouth available worldwide today is in this book. Because I would never lie to you, friend. There are so many varieties available, and so many new ones coming out even as you read, that it would be impossible to cover each, and would also dilute the book so much that it wouldn't be helpful. *Ginger Bliss and the Violet Fizz* does cover a wide variety, though, enough to keep you in signature cocktails and flavors for parties from January 1 until December 31 and every rollicking reason for revelry in between. So, let's open the first bottles.

CHAPTER 2: A LIQUID CITRUS CIRCUS

In this chapter, you'll find those drinks that derive their flavor profile from liqueurs that are primarily citrus-based, though in many cases they also have spice overtones. Many of these drinks have a tropical quality coming from ingredients such as orange curaçao, a liqueur made from the laraha fruit (a relative of the Valencia orange) that's cultivated on the island of Curaçao. Other well-known citrus liqueurs featured in this chapter include Cointreau, which is made in Saint-

Learn More with Liqueur Spotlights
....

ABSINTHE (PAGE 225)

AMAROS (PAGE 148)

ANISETTE (PAGE 275)

APEROL (PAGE 145)

BÉNÉDICTINE (PAGE 162)

BITTERS, BITTERS, EVERYWHERE (PAGE 27)

CAMPARI (PAGE 126)

CHAMBORD (PAGE 84)

CHARTREUSE (PAGE 58)

CHERRY HEERING (PAGE 87)

COINTREAU (PAGE 49)

CRÈME YVETTE (PAGE 61)

CYNAR (PAGE 134)

FERNET-BRANCA (PAGE 155)

GALLIANO (PAGE 200)

GETTING VERY VERMOUTHY (PAGE 244)

GRAND MARNIER (PAGE 36)

KIRSCH (PAGE 101)

KÜMMEL (PAGE 216)

LILLET (PAGE 239)

MARASCHINO (PAGE 104)

RHUM CLÉMENT CREOLE SHRUBB (PAGE 45)

SAMBUCA (PAGE 197)

ST-GERMAIN (PAGE 68)

STREGA (PAGE 222)

TIA MARIA (PAGE 169)

TUACA (PAGE 189)

WHAT DOES "CRÈME DE" MEAN? (PAGE 265)

Barthélemy-d'Anjou, France, from a combination of bitter and sweet orange peels grown in places such as Spain and Haiti; Grand Marnier, which combines Cognac with a specific Caribbean orange, the *Citrus bigaradia*; and limoncello, the Italian sun god of liqueurs, which can be found in various commercial varieties but might just be best when homemade (see A Note, page 44). On the newer side are recipes calling for liqueurs such as the recently available Rhum Clément Creole Shrubb, which has an orange-based flavor mingling with vanilla, cloves, cinnamon, nutmeg, grapefruit, and a slight peppery finish.

CHAPTER 3: A BOUQUET OF LOVELY LIQUEURS

When building your garland of cocktails in this chapter, you'll find an assortment of liqueurs that offer floral and botanical qualities. Not only a delight to the mouth, they also bring blooming aromas that add to the drink's overall aesthetic sensibility. Here you'll find liqueurs that are flowering at first glance, such as newer numbers Loft Lavender Cello, which has a delicate taste achieved by using only organic lavender grown on a particular Washington State farm, and St-Germain elderflower liqueur, which is made from 100 percent hand-picked elderflowers (as the story goes) once a year in late spring. We'll revisit more renowned liqueurs, such as the violet-heavy crème de violette and the recently re-released crème Yvette, which has violet flavors backed by berries, vanilla, and spices. This chapter also contains liqueurs that have a personality on the botanical side of floral and that bring out their floral-ness when combined into certain mixes—liqueurs such as Chartreuse, which comes in four varieties, contains 130 secret ingredients, and has a history that goes back almost a thousand years; and Elisir M.P. Roux, a French botanical liqueur created by combining flowering herbs and spices including marjoram, fennel, cinnamon, coriander, lemon peel, star anise, and ginseng.

CHAPTER 4: IF YOU'RE FEELING FRUITY

As you might expect from a fruit liqueur chapter, the flavors contained within are as wide (almost) as the flavors of the fruit world itself—though remember, you won't find citrus-based drinks here because they're back in Chapter 2. You will find drinks based on landmark fruit liqueurs such as cherry Heering, which has been made by Peter Heering since 1818. Cherry Heering is built on cherries and brandy, but it isn't as dry as cherry brandies such as kirsch or Kirschwasser (also featured in this chapter), which is made using sour Morello cherries. You'll also find fresh fruit liqueurs like VeeV Açaí spirit, the first liqueur made with açaí, the national fruit of Brazil; and the ruby-colored and berry-ific PAMA pomegranate liqueur, crafted out of pomegranate juice, vodka, and a smidge of tequila. Of course, a fruit chapter wouldn't be complete without cocktails containing Chambord (which descends from a liqueur that was crafted in the late seventeenth century in France's Loire Valley of black raspberries, blackberries, and spices), and its cousins framboise (which is usually made from red raspberries and has a bit more kick than Chambord) and crème de cassis (which is made from black currants).

CHAPTER 5: TAKE YOUR HERBAL MEDICINE

The drinks in this chapter tend to be on the complex side, can be strong and bold in flavor, and have a bit of an unfortunate reputation for being enjoyable only after a long apprenticeship program (where you take a teensy sip here and there) or if you're insane. This is a shame, because the liqueurs used in this chapter are both some of the most fun and some of the most rewarding in flavor. The liqueurs I'm convincing you to cuddle up to here include some internationally well-known ones like Campari, whose history of love traces back to the 1800s in Cassolnovo, Italy, where Gaspare Campari was born; Bénédictine, which goes back to the Renaissance, when a monk named Dom Bernardo Vincelli mixed a healing assortment of 27 spices, plants, and herbs together with a spirituous liquid and sweetener; Pimm's No. 1, which is still created following James Pimm's original recipe; and Chartreuse, which boasts enough layers of flavor that it can fit into both this chapter and A Bouquet of Lovely Liqueurs, depending on how it's mixed. You'll also find lesser-known but still international (those herbal liqueurs tend to travel) liqueurs such as Amer Picon, a French apéritif with a slightly bitter presence and a touch of orange (it isn't as readily available as it once was; see page 248 for more info and a substitute), and Becherovka, which has been a hit since 1807 in the Czech Republic and is created via a secret recipe using 32 herbs and spices. Finally, you'll meet the amaro family of Italian after-dinner digestivos, a family that contains numerous herbal members traveling the road from slightly sweet and barely bitter liqueurs like artichoke-based Cynar all the way to muscular numbers such as Fernet-Branca, whose history goes back to 1845, and which is an amalgamation of herbs, spices, and roots gathered from the far corners of the world.

CHAPTER 6: IT'S A NUTTY, NUTTY WORLD

Those folks who tend to never leave the bowl of mixed nuts at parties will find much to love in this chapter, as it contains cocktails and drinks using an assortment of liqueurs that have flavors falling on the nutty side. This includes a variety of liqueurs based on specific nuts, such as nocino, made from green walnuts in Italy's Emilia-Romagna region, and Castries Peanut Rum Crème, which has strong peanut flavor and a rum bite and is a bit creamy (which helps it be at home in cocktails in this chapter as well as in the Here's to You, Sweets chapter, depending on what it's mixed with). You'll also find liqueurs that have a nutty taste, if not an allegiance to a particular nut, such as Tia Maria, which is nutty with coffee and vanilla flavors (as well as carrying a legend that goes back to the seventeenth century), and amaretto, which when mixed right delivers a solid almond flavor that actually comes from apricot or peach pits. You'll meet nutty favorites here like Frangelico, the Italian hazelnut liqueur whose bottle looks like a Franciscan monk and whose history goes back 300 years, alongside liqueurs more recently made available on a wide scale, such as delicious Dumante Verdenoce pistachio liqueur, crafted with love and all-natural ingredients on the slopes of Mount Etna in Sicily.

CHAPTER 7: THE SPICE OF THE DRINKING LIFE

In this chapter, you'll find an amusing, entertaining, and varied grouping of liqueurs that hold in common their allegiance to a particular spice or collection of spices. The list starts with absinthe—a liqueur that was out of circulation for a long time—which is distilled from wormwood, anise, and fennel. Absinthe's anise-based relatives Pernod and pastis also show up in the chapter, as does anisette, which is sweeter than those mentioned above and which uses anise seed for its flavoring rather than star anise. You'll also find pals like Galliano, named for Giuseppe Galliano, who, with 2,000 Italian soldiers defended a fort against an army of 80,000 during the Abyssinian war; kümmel, whose caraway, cumin, and fennel flavors made the news first in 1696 when Russian leader Peter the Great fell for them; Tuaca, whose recipe, legends say, was created by Lorenzo de' Medici, ruler of Florence, Italy, during the Renaissance; and another Italian favorite, Strega, the saffron-hued magical liqueur made since 1860. You'll also find new spicy favorites like St. Elizabeth Allspice Dram, an allspice-flavored liqueur made with Jamaican allspice berries and rum; and Navan vanilla liqueur, which is made from Madagascar vanilla merged with Cognac.

CHAPTER 8: THE JUSTICE LEAGUE OF VERMOUTHS

Regular vermouth does play a key role in many of the most classic of cocktails, so you might wonder what there is to learn about vermouth. Well, the drinks in this chapter let vermouth play more of a key role, and the recipes expand into using vermouth's cousins as well. Which means you'll see regular sweet and dry, or Italian and French, vermouths as well as Dubonnet, the French aromatized wine spruced up by the addition of herbs, spices, and quinine (there are two Dubonnets used today, red wine–based Rouge, which is spicy and sweeter, and white wine–based Blanc); and Lillet, which was first created in 1887 by Paul and Raymond Lillet and which includes the better-known Blanc and the lesser-known-but-worth-tracking-down Rouge. You'll also find drinks here that call for some vermouths that have recently become more available, such as Punt e Mes, a rich Italian-style vermouth whose name means "point-and-a-half"—the story goes that the company was founded after the stock market jumped a point and a half in one day, making one man a good amount of money.

CHAPTER 9: HERE'S TO YOU, SWEETS

In this chapter you'll find a collection of dessert drinks and sweeter combinations that often provide a liquid accompaniment to those more romantic moments between two people. Because of this chapter's embracing nature, you will find some liqueurs used here that also show up in other chapters, such as crème Yvette, the violet and spice liqueur used in the floral chapter, and its slightly-more-violet-y cousin, crème de violette, as well as Strega, that saffron-scented star from the spice chapter. But we'll also explore liqueurs specific to sweeter drinks. For instance, we'll revisit cream liqueurs such as Irish whiskey–based Baileys Irish cream; Crema de Alba, a brandy-based cream liqueur featuring a coffee, nutty, and sherry flavor; and Amarula cream, which is made from the fruit of the African marula tree, yielding a nutty, caramel flavor. You'll also find drinks using the well-known chocolate liqueur crème de cacao, which comes in light and dark varieties; Scotch treat Drambuie, which is crafted carefully from whisky, honey, and a variety of herbs; and Parfait Amour, a violet-hued liqueur that has floral tinges combined with vanilla and sugar—it was once thought to be a love potion, making it perfect for this chapter.

A Base Spirits Refresher

While *Ginger Bliss and the Violet Fizz* is, at its boozy heart, about using specific personalities (and tastes) of liqueurs and vermouths in creative cocktails, most of these drinks are also built upon one of the seven base spirits. Here, I'm talking about brandy, gin, rum, tequila, vodka, whiskey/whisky, and Champagne. (Some might disagree on that last bubbly base, but I believe so strongly in sparkling wine cocktails that I would be ashamed to leave it off the list. If some want to argue, they can go into the other room and argue while we're sharing drinks in here.) We aren't going to dwell on these too much, because I know that many of you are already versed in the base spirits and have a number of them in your home bars, but let's at least make some friendly reintroductions.

Starting alphabetically, we begin with brandy, a base that has been sadly underemployed lately, though many top drink slingers are working hard and happily to reverse the trend. The name comes from *brandewijn*, or brandywine, and it originally meant "burnt wine." There are today three types of brandy: grape brandy (which is the "basic" brandy, such as Cognac and Armagnac), fruit brandy (which we touch on more throughout this book, as it has lots in common with liqueurs and is sometimes treated as such), and pomace brandy (which is constructed from what some might see as leftovers: grape skins, seeds, and pits, and which includes the mighty Italian digestivo grappa).

Our bubbly base spirit, Champagne (and its sparkling wine siblings), adds a touch of class and effervescence to a host of hopping drinks. True Champagne, by law and various regulations (and some historically significant treaties), comes from the Champagne region in France and must be created from a secondary fermentation of a wine using yeast and rock sugar inside the bottle, which then increases carbon dioxide levels and creates bubbles. Other sparklers use this same method—look for the phrase *méthode traditionnelle* on the bottle. Five levels of sweetness are used to classify Champagne from driest to sweetest: brut, extra-dry, sec, demi-sec, and doux. Champagne is mostly made with the white Chardonnay grape or the darker-skinned Pinot Noir or Pinot Meunier grape, though the wine itself ends up clear and elegant. This elegance often leads to true Champagne being more expensive than other sparkling wines, which is why, unless specifically called for (and sometimes even then), you should feel okay about subbing in a quality sparkling wine for Champagne in recipes, as long as you get one that is in the appropriate sweetness range. You shouldn't sub, though, when a recipe calls for another variety of sparkler. For example, if a recipe calls for rosé Champagne or rosé sparkling wine, find a true rosé.

Tracking Down the Latest in Liqueurs
. . . .

As mentioned, the range of new liqueurs (both newly created and new to the U.S. market) and vermouths is expanding rapidly. I'm bringing this up for two reasons: First, to say that this book, while awfully helpful and full of creative and delicious cocktails, doesn't in any way claim to be the be-all and end-all collection of every liqueur and vermouth available. It's just a great cross-section of current hits, organized in a manner that helps you add a flavorful spark to your home cocktail creating. Second, so that I can point you in the direction of five online locales, including stores and research spots, that you should browse occasionally, to find out what new liqueurs and vermouths are out there:

Internet Wines and Spirits (www.internetwines.com) was one of the first online liquor and liqueur sellers. It is reliable and offers a good selection.

DrinkUpNY (www.drinkupny.com) was one of the first online spots to offer a wide range of absinthes. When browsing, I almost always find something here that I haven't yet seen.

Haus Alpenz (www.alpenz.com) is an importer with an interesting and expanding profile of liqueurs from around the world, including a number of exquisite small-batch beauties. But it's not a seller, so go here to research rather than to buy.

Preiss Imports (www.preissimports.com) is also an importer, with a strong reach into European liqueurs and spirits. Again, you can't buy from this site, but browsing sure is informative.

Wikipedia's Liqueur List (www.en.wikipedia.org/wiki/list_of_liqueurs) is a large and ever-changing list. Yes, it is in the sometimes-wild Wiki land, which can feel like a boozy jungle. But just scroll through until you find something intriguing you've never heard of, and click it or paste it into your search engine of choice.

A top-forty favorite in cocktails from yesteryear and today, with an explosion in brands available in recent years, gin is at its core a juniper berry–flavored grain spirit, which gets its name from an English shortening of *jenever*, the Dutch word for "juniper," or (as some have started to think) *genièvre*, the French counterpart. It's hard to determine exactly when gin was discovered, though stories point to Dutch doctor Franciscus Sylvius (aka Franz de le Boë), which helps to highlight gin's medicinal side—like many liquors and liqueurs, gin was thought to have restorative and curative powers. It became an incredibly popular cocktail ingredient in the first cocktail blossoming, pre-Prohibition, when multiple styles of gin were used. Lucky for us modern consumers, some gin styles have been revived, and today you can get classic London dry gin (with a bright juniper taste, often augmented by citrus or spice undertones) as well as the Dutch- or Holland-style genever/jenever, which tends to offer a strong juniper style, and Old Tom gin, which is a sweeter gin made famous as the crucial ingredient in the original Tom Collins.

Rum has a colorful history and has had a number of names on its passport to prove it, including hydra-monster, cursed liquor, kill-devil, and that demon rum. Because rum isn't as regulated as some base spirits, it has a more free-spirited personality, and maybe because of that it is hard to pin down. We do know that there are white and dark rums, with the former being clear and the latter covering a wide range of shades from amber to almost pitch black. All rum, though, begins clear as distilled sugarcane juice or molasses. Then it's fermented and aged in different manners that alter the shade and the taste of the rum. When "white" rum is called for in the following pages, you should go for one of the clear rums, and when "dark" rum is used, try one that's a rich amber color like light brown sugar; use the really dark, more aged (and more expensive) varieties only if specifically called for. With rum's laissez-faire personality, it's no wonder that flavored rums have started entrenching themselves on shelves. Unless called for by name, shy away from using these varieties in drinks, as it can be hard to tell which are flavored using natural ingredients and which using chemicals and evil.

Tequila remains at heart a local spirit. To be true tequila, it has to be made close to the town of the same name in Jalisco, Mexico (which is, if you're traveling, about 65 kilometers from Guadalajara). Tequila is actually a type of mescal, the name for any spirit distilled from the agave plant; however, there's a Tequila Regulatory Council, whose guidelines the spirit must follow to be classified as true tequila. These guidelines ensure that a tequila is made in the geographical area described above and that it is at least 51 percent blue agave (a particular type of the plant, which just so happens to grow well in the red volcanic soil of the region). There are five types of tequila: *blanco* or "white" (sometimes called *plata*, or "silver") is not aged, or is aged only a smidge, and is stored in stainless-steel or plain oak barrels; *oro* or "gold" (sometimes called *joven*, which means "young") refers to a blend of *blanco* with caramel or food coloring (if cheaply made) or one of the last three types (if made with more care); *reposado* ("rested"), which is aged for at least two months but not more than a year in oak barrels; *añejo* ("aged"), which is aged for at least one year but not more than three years in oak barrels; and *extra añejo*, the newest category, established in March 2006, which refers to tequilas aged for a minimum of three years in oak barrels. Though *blanco* is the type used most in cocktails, and the others are usually sipped solo, you do see some crossover in specific drinks.

With a jump in popularity from the 1950s onward, vodka is currently beloved by many for its malleability and kick. A usually colorless spirit crafted from grain, potatoes, soybeans, grapes, and/or other ingredients, vodka made its first popularity push in the United States in the 1950s via an advertising campaign dreamed up by the Smirnoff distributor and the owner of Los Angeles–based bar the Cock and Bull. They decided to focus on a cocktail instead of the spirit itself, and pushed the drink the Moscow Mule out into the world. Today flavored versions of vodka (from citrus to pepper to chocolate and every other flavor occurring in nature and not) have become very popular, with some brands delivering deliciousness and some a liquid that tastes like chemically altered lighter fluid. Don't use the flavored versions unless the recipe specifically calls for one.

Whiskey (or whisky, if your bottle is from Scotland or Canada) is more of a base spirit family than a single base spirit. It's a host of relatives that sometimes argue at the table but that are each worthy of inclusion. To start unwrangling this spirited family tree, let's talk through some of the regulations, starting in the United States. American straight whiskey must be made from a grain mash that contains between 51 and 79 percent of a single grain (corn for bourbon, rye for rye) and must be aged in charred oak barrels. (Corn whiskey is an exception, as it must be at least 80 percent corn.) Moving north, Canadian whisky must be aged in oak barrels in Canada for at least three years, and must be mashed and distilled there too, using wheat, corn, rye, barley, or barley malt—usually blended, as most Canadian whiskies are blends. Irish whiskeys come in three forms: single malt (pure malted barley), pot still (malted and unmalted barley), and blended (malted and unmalted barley, as well as corn or other grains), with every type aged for three years in oak casks and triple-distilled. Scotch whiskies have to be made in a distillery in Scotland and contain water and barley (different grains are sometimes included), and they must be aged in oak casks for at least three years and a day, be double-distilled, and have their malt dried over a peat fire. Scotches are either single malt (100 percent malted barley) or blended, with the stated age of the blend being the youngest part. This brings up a good point: There are many blended whiskeys and whiskies available, which may have to follow strict guidelines depending on country and type, and which shouldn't be frowned upon. Within this book, the type of whiskey/whisky, if not the brand, will be called out in the ingredients, and the drink in question has been structured for that particular type, so please follow the ingredients list and you'll end up with a better-balanced drink.

Revealing the Mixer Mantra

While liqueurs and vermouths are crucial to our mission, and base spirits are the foundation from which the liqueurs and vermouths shine, a host of other ingredients make the cocktails inhabiting the following pages (and, eventually, homes and parties) sing in luscious tones. These are the mixers, those sometimes overlooked ingredients. Too often, someone decides to spend the weekly take on a particularly high-priced bottle of gin, and picks just the right liqueur to pair it with, but then brings both down by grabbing a can of frozen juice. Or takes them down ten pegs by introducing them in the glass to some club soda that hasn't had a boogie-ing bubble in it for weeks. Argh! It's enough to make a grown cocktail lover cry. But you, *you* can avoid these mixer monstrosities by following one simple mantra: the fresh rule.

The fresh rule (it almost needs capitalizing, but I don't want to seem like I'm screaming at you, just taking it very seriously) is one important rule. It covers most of what you might think of as "mixers" and so is easy to remember (we'll cover the three outliers below). Simply put: Fresh is better. Always. If you want superior drinks, use fresh mixers. Isn't simplicity wonderful? It's easiest to remember, I think, when dealing with fruit juices. Fresh juice takes a drink from lackluster to legendary, which then also takes a party from tedious to tremendous (and again, that's what we're aiming for).

Juicing isn't tough (we'll go over the juicer options in the section on tools), and it is well worth it. It starts with picking out the right fruits, though. When at the grocery store or farmer's market or orchard, be sure to look for fruits that are

Simple Syrup

 GINGER BLISS & THE VIOLET FIZZ

Makes about 4½ cups

3 CUPS SUGAR

2½ CUPS WATER

1. Add the sugar and water to a medium-size saucepan. Stirring occasionally, bring the mixture to a boil over medium-high heat. Lower the heat a bit, keeping the mixture at a low boil for 5 minutes, stirring occasionally.

2. Turn off the heat and let the syrup cool completely in the pan. Store in an airtight container in the refrigerator for up to 1 month.

A NOTE: I tend to use my simple syrup all the time, but if you're going to use only a bit here and there, you can add ½ ounce of high-proof neutral grain spirits or vodka to the bottle and it will last for many months.

lacking in blemishes and that have a crisp aroma—get right up close and personal with them to find out. Don't be ashamed to talk to your fruit, knowing that the dubious looks from other shoppers are going to be balanced by smiles once you're serving the right stuff. When juicing, don't juice more than a day or two before serving time. Here's a lively hint to make citrus juicing easier, too: Before juicing, run fruits under warm water, or wrap them in a damp towel and microwave them for 20 seconds, and then roll them under your palm with steady pressure. This helps to get the juice flowing. If (because of a great fruit famine, perhaps) you find it impossible to use fresh juice, then pick drinks that don't use it. Or, pick up some fresh juice at a local juice bar. Or, as a last resort (say you're stranded on an island for a month with only three pieces of fresh fruit), use frozen juice concentrate, but at least get a couple whole fruits so you can have a squirt or so of fresh juice and fruit for garnishes to give a fresh burst.

The fresh rule, as mentioned, travels beyond juice to other mixers. It should go without saying (but, hey, reminders don't hurt) that if using dairy products (most often cream, which adds a smooth sexiness to many sweet drinks), don't trot out something that's been in the hinterlands of your fridge and expect to get applause. Even if it's within the "use by" date, if it's been hanging in there for some time, cream and other products pick up scents from the fridge—and you sure don't want a Cara Sposa (page 262) to taste radish-esque. This is especially true for drinks that use eggs (and don't be scared by these drinks—eggs add amazing mouth feel and texture). Always use the freshest eggs, organic if possible.

Also, follow the fresh rule with bubbling mixers. This means that the ginger ale you're using to craft a Tuscan Mule (page 219) shouldn't enter the event with ambiguity and a faint *pfff*. It should come onto the scene like a knight of carbonation, with a brisk effervescent nature and bubbles galore. The same goes for club soda and other bubbling favorites. If they've even started to go flat, they'll take any drink down with them when falling on their drinky faces. When picking out bubblers, be sure to get reputable brands and not knock-offs. These top-shelf items won't set you back excessively, but they are going to be more reliable and vivacious. If you have your own CO2 dispenser and it roars, then feel free to use it when applicable, too.

The last three mixers I'm going to touch on may, as mentioned, go slightly against the fresh rule. The first and second are somewhat related, as they're items you'll want to make yourself if possible. The first is simple syrup. A basic sugar and water syrup, this is used to add a slight sweetness and to smooth the rough edges out of many drinks. It's easy to make and keeps in the fridge for a month. You'll find that having it at arm's length comes in handy for cocktailing, sure, but also for making nonalcoholic drinks such as lemonade and home-crafted sparkling fruit drinks—there's really no reason not to always have some on hand.

The second mixer that you can, and should, make yourself, is grenadine.

Now, I know you're thinking "I can get grenadine in any store." But most of what's out there passing for grenadine is chemically sweetened dyed-red syrup. Real grenadine should have a sweetness in it but should also have a serious pomegranate-y tang, and it should add that flavor to drinks it's contained within. You can make it very simply (which I am fond of), or add a few other accents. Beyond being enjoyable in drinks, it's also handy if you have kids, or cousins, or rockingly cool nephews or nieces, because it's used to make the classic Shirley Temple and Roy Rogers. If you somehow can't find the time to make grenadine, at least pick up a brand that has some serious flavor, such as Scrappy's or Stir-rings. The grenadine recipe below is a version I picked up from one of Seattle's best bartenders, Andrew Bohrer. You can learn more about him and check out a few of his recipes on pages 130, 194, and 204, and you should definitely visit his blog Cask Strength (www.caskstrength.wordpress.com), where he writes in charming style about cocktails and life behind the professional bar.

The final mixer we're going to touch on also skirts around the fresh rule, and it is a mixer that was, sadly, somehow misplaced for a while but that has recently made a welcome comeback. I'm talking here about those champions of

Grenadine

GINGER
BLISS &
THE VIOLET
FIZZ

Makes about 4 cups

4 CUPS UNSWEETENED POMEGRANATE JUICE

1 PINT FRESH RASPBERRIES

4 CUPS SUGAR

2 OUNCES ORANGE FLOWER WATER

1. Add the pomegranate juice and raspberries to a large saucepan and place over high heat. Cook for 15 minutes.

2. Let the mixture stay at a steady boil, stirring occasionally, for 15 minutes longer, reducing the heat if needed to prevent burning.

3. Slowly stir in the sugar, stirring continuously. When the sugar is completely dissolved, remove the pan from the heat and stir in the orange flower water.

4. Let cool, and strain into bottles. Refrigerate in an airtight container for up to 1 month.

A NOTE: Serving the grenadine to adults only? Add 2 cups of brandy in step 1, and an extra 2 cups of sugar in step 3.

the dash or two: bitters. Bitters are, basically, a bitter flavoring agent for drinks (and also a medicine, or at least they were thought of that way for years and are still a precious prescription when taken with a glass of club soda after eating too much). Created with care and craft, they contain a base spirit infused or altered or enchanted with a bundle of herbs, fruits and fruit peels, spices, roots, leaves, love, flowers, long-lost magical items, and much more. Each type of bitters is different, which means that you can't substitute one for the other in drinks without changing the drink's character. This isn't to say that one won't be good subbed in for another—it'll just be a different drink. So, if you kick off your Kick-Off (page 238) with Peychaud's bitters instead of Angostura, you probably should call it a Kick Return. There are currently, and thankfully, many bitters now available, including the Peychaud's and Angostura just mentioned, revisions of classics such as Regan's Orange Bitters No. 6, and brand-new models such as Bittermens Xocolatl Mole Bitters. You can learn even more about bitters on page 27, but one thing to remember is that they keep for a year at least—though you'll probably use them more quickly than that.

Unearthing the Right Ice

Isn't it nice that we no longer have to chip ice off of glaciers? Though, that would probably teach us from an early age to respect ice in ways that we now don't. Anyhow, it's not too late to discover some key facts about ice in order to upgrade the chilly side of cocktails. To begin with, though it may sound funny, the fresh rule should also apply to ice as much as possible when you're entertaining at home. Unless you have a dedicated ice freezer or ice machine plugged in, you'll want to watch the ice you use, to make sure it hasn't been in the freezer too long, as it could pick up aromas and scents from its freezer roommates. Since you don't want your ice, and thus your drinks, smelling of the cod you caught two Junes ago, be sure to use fresh ice whenever possible.

There are a few types of ice you'll want to be aware of as well. First off, ice cubes, which should be of the 1-inch variety and as square as you can get. Second is cracked ice, which you can either buy or make yourself, by cracking those cubes into smaller pieces with a muddler or smallish mallet of some sort. I like to crack it myself, because I have more control over the ice, and because, well, it's a kick to do. You don't want to pulverize it, just crack it into a few irregular pieces. These pieces melt more quickly and thus chill a drink more rapidly, which is why cracked ice is ideal when you're stirring a drink to combine it. Cubes are used most often when shaking a drink, because they won't melt so fast (if they did, a shaken drink might get watery).

This, of course, invites the question "When to shake and when to stir?" There are some rules to follow, outside of the ice choices. Always shake and never stir a drink with fruit juice or fruit, cream, or eggs, because you have to have a more violent combining, an emulsifying of sorts. Stir when those ingredients aren't involved, as stirring can deliver chilly results without clouding the drink up. One thing to remember, though, is that you can shake most cold drinks (if you don't feel like stirring or feel uncomfortable with stirring). They might not look as clear and might be a bit frothier than when stirred, but they'll turn out dandy.

There are also third and fourth ice types: crushed ice and ice rings. Crushed ice is used to make a drink agreeably frothy, or even rustic, as with the Bruja Smash (page 194) or the classic Daiquiri. You can purchase crushed ice, or crush it yourself, using a Lewis bag (a canvas bag made for the job) or other bag and a mallet—with crushing, as opposed to cracking, you really want to go to town on the ice. Ice rings, or ice molds, are used within punch bowls, both because they'll keep it cold longer and because they look dashing. There are no recipes in this book calling for ice rings, but you can make your own ice mold using a ring mold or even a regular round or square baking pan.

Divulging Garnishing

After stocking up on bottles and bases and migrating to fresher mixers, you might believe that you're completely set on ingredients, but stop! You wouldn't go out without accessories, would you? In the same way, and even more important, you shouldn't send certain cocktails and highballs and slings and such out to waiting guests without proper garnishing. And they are for far more than appearance, as most garnishes also add essential flourishes of flavor to a drink, without which the drink is as plain as a princess without a proper tiara. Because of this prime role that garnishes play, they too need to follow (as you might guess) the fresh rule. For garnishes, this applies to most everything, including raspberries, mint and basil leaves, freshly grated nutmeg, and many more.

While the array of garnishes mentioned above is as important as the drinks they live with, there is one garnish group we'll need to gather round a little more closely, because of how often they come to the forefront. I'm talking about our old pals, the citrus garnishes. Again, pick your garnish-destined citrus fruits with care, getting up close and personal to be sure of ripeness and loveliness. And then cut them to pieces—specifically, twists, wheels (and half-wheel slices), and wedges. To make a citrus twist, start by cutting off the bottom of a (freshly washed, preferably organic) fruit in a straight line—don't cut off too much, just enough to give you a flat bottom. Then place that flat side down on a cutting board. Using a sharp knife and a keen eye, cut ½-inch-wide strips of peel going from top to bottom, trying to get as little of the white pith as possible. The strips you cut are your twists, which should be sturdy enough to actually twist over the top of a drink. When doing so (making sure you're over the glass), notice how the fragrant oils rocket off the twist's outer side and into the drink and onto the glass's edge. Those oils are the treasure within the twist, because of the massive flavor burst they provide for the nose and mouth while drinking. Too often bartenders at large just flop a twist in a glass, or twist it to make it look pretty but twist nowhere near the glass, thus losing those essential oils. Don't make this mistake, cocktail-loving friends. Here and there you'll see a recipe suggesting a wider twist—say, 1½ to 2 inches wide. You may want to use a wide, sharp peeler for this. There are a couple of drinks that get fun with flaming twists, too, and instructions are included in those recipes.

Our other crucial citrus garnishes are wheels, their sibling slices, and wedges. These are a snap to make. For the wheel and slice family, first slice off the top and bottom ends of the fruit in a straight line with a sharp knife, and then cut the fruit into equal-size wheels, from ⅛ to ¼ inch in size. If you want slices, cut the wheels in half, or cut the fruit in half before slicing. If you're eager to quickly perch slices on a glass's edge when serving, cut notches in the slices. Wedges are also a breeze, and also start by cutting off the fruit ends. Then, with the fruit on a cutting board, cut it in half lengthwise, and put each side cut side down on the board. Make two length-of-the-fruit cuts, top to bottom. Then cut each of the three pieces in half. This should leave you with six equal-size wedges per half, or twelve total.

Don't Have a Bare Bar: Exposing Crucial Bar Tools

Learning to pick the proper ingredients for a drink is indeed important, but if the proper cocktail-creating tools are missing, you'll have a hard time serving anything but booze straight out of a bottle (which is both unhygienic and lacking in the class department).

The bar tool assortment starts with one main item: the cocktail shaker. You get to choose between two time-honored types, the cobbler-style shaker and the Boston-style shaker. The cobbler shaker is an old classic that's as easy to use as tying your shiny shoes (well, more or less). It comes with three pieces: a big bottom cup, a top cup with a built-in strainer, and a top cap for the top cup. To use, just add ice and ingredients to the big cup, put the top cup with top cap on, shake that thing, and then remove the top cap and strain it. You should pick one that's 18/10 stainless steel to resist rusting, and be sure it fits well in your hands, because comfort is essential. The second shaker type, the Boston shaker, has two pieces, a bottom cup made of glass and a top cup made of metal (you'll want 18/10 stainless here too). To use, add ice and ingredients to the bottom cup and then position the top cup so it nestles over the bottom one. Then, holding that bottom cup firmly and thinking about steadiness, give the top cup a bit of a thump. Your goal is to create a seal between the shakers, so that there will be no spillage. Once that's accomplished, hold both pieces and shake. Then, place the shaker, metal side down, on a sturdy surface. Giving the side of the shaker a tap if you need to, break the seal, and then using a separate strainer, strain the drink into a glass. No matter which shaker you choose, shake drinks for 10 to 15 seconds to deliver frosty results, unless a recipe suggests you do it less or more.

Once your shaker is shining in its glory atop the bar, there are some more tools to invest in for maximum bar-osity. First, if you have a Boston shaker— and maybe even if you have a cobbler shaker—you'll need a strainer. There are three styles of strainers out there. The most prevalent is probably the Hawthorn strainer, which is a strainer with a spring around the edge, to help it cuddle up to the mixing glass or shaker. It tends to do that especially well when used with a metal cup, such as the bottom of a cobbler shaker or the top of a Boston shaker. The Julep strainer is usually more of a round shape with holes in it, a shorter handle, and no spring. The Julep strainer fits better into a glass (whereas the Hawthorn slips more), and so is a good choice if you have a separate mixing glass for stirring drinks or are using the bottom piece of a Boston shaker for straining. The fine strainer is just what you'd expect: a fine-mesh strainer. It's generally used in concert with one of the other types when a drink features fruit juice or herbs. The fine-mesh strainer ensures that no solid bits make their way into the drink.

When using a shaker and strainer, you'll want to be shaking and straining the right amounts, so also invest in a jigger for measuring. Even if the shaker's top cap doubles as a measuring device (as with many cobbler shakers) it still doesn't hurt to have a second 18/10 stainless-steel jigger to ensure accuracy. I find that a double-sided jigger with 1 ounce on one side and 1½ or 2 ounces on the other side comes in handy in most situations. If you're scaling up to make multiple drinks, then be sure to keep the ratios intact, and always get measurements right to achieve bar mastery.

The next tool I couldn't live without is my trusty muddler. Shaped a bit like a tiny baseball bat, with one end tapering into the other (and with the tapered end often having a knob), the muddler is used for muddling, the process by which you lovingly and not wackily beat up fruit or herbs or other things in a shaker or mixing glass to get them to release those juices and essential oils that bring so much harmony and flavor to drinks. As with the shaker, find a muddler that feels comfortable in your hand. There are many to choose from, including metal and plastic models, but I like a sturdy wooden muddler that doesn't have a lot of varnish on it, one that I can use for muddling but that also has enough heft for cracking ice.

Another tool that you'll use a lot is a dedicated bar spoon for stirring drinks, as some cocktails want to be stirred rather than shaken. Find one that's long, thin, and elegant, and that you're happy to twirl around in a glass, alone or in front of a crowd of people.

Now, I'm hoping you haven't yet forgotten the fresh rule—and our wonderful talk about fresh juices. To get those fresh juices, invest in a juicer as well, one that's brawny enough to be used regularly. There are lots and lots of handheld juicers to choose from (want a green one? yellow? not a problem) in department stores, online stores, and various other spots. But if you're going to be juicing a decent amount, a lever-model juicer, one that can sit firmly on the counter and that you can use without straining arm muscles, works best. There are many sizes to fit various counters and bars. You can invest in an electronic juice extractor as well, for massive amounts of juicing, but I find that with citrus fruits, the juice comes out tasting a little pithy.

One final tool might be pushing some folks' definition of "bar tool," but I believe it can really make many merrymaking moments easier. I'm talking about a good pitcher, one to make drinks for masses within and also to serve said drinks to said masses—so, a creation device as well as a serving device. I find pitchers so helpful that I like to have two, a sturdy plastic one for outdoor picnics, hayrides, and barbecues, and a sparkling glass one for more classy indoor affairs.

A Second Exposé on Secondary Tools

Once the main tools are in place, there are other items that you may find somewhat or even incredibly helpful (but always enjoyable), depending on the situation. To start with, a steadfast 18/10 stainless-steel ice bucket can keep you from having to delve into the freezer every time a new drink is created, and of course you'll want an ice scoop to go with it. A spice grater can be very relevant when you're grating nutmeg and other spices. A few colorful (or black and white, depending on your color scheme) bar towels are always going to be useful, because spills happen whether we plan for them or not. Likewise, having a set of decorated or plain (again, depending on your style and party personality) bar napkins ready to roll out isn't a bad idea either. For garnishing with more panache, some outlandish toothpicks might be nice; and for letting guests get in on keeping their own drink in motion, some snazzy swizzle sticks can be clever additions. Your bar, like your party, should be a reflection of you and your own style, so go as deep or as shallow into these extra tools as you see fit.

Unveiling the Glassware Enigma

Much like not having tools to create the drinks, without glassware to serve the drinks, a bar seems to be missing something (or everything, because without something to serve in, it's hard to, well, serve drinks). But you don't need every single glass type known to history. A few key additions and you'll be glass-efficient for the drinks in this book.

Perhaps the most recognizable glass found in bars is the basic cocktail glass (which here and there is called the martini glass after its most famous occupant). It's a graceful situation, with a longish stem and a slightly curved bowl. Today, you can find a much wider size range than in classic cocktail days past, with some cocktail glasses having bowls the size of Boise, 12 ounces and larger, as well as smaller models going down to 3 ounces. Many of the drinks in this book (a good percentage, actually) tend toward fitting better into the smaller versions, with the drinks themselves around 3 ounces. This is a pour that again harkens back to those cocktailing days past, when the great bartender Harry Craddock said you should be able to consume the cocktail "while it's laughing at you"—that is, while it's still at the optimum chilled temperature. I'm not going to get on any sort of high horse about giant glasses, though, or even larger cocktails, because I sure don't want to cause offense at some future date when I'm at a home or local bar and someone thinks I have a distaste for certain drinks. As long as the drinks are consumed while still good and cold, count me in as a consumer.

The next pieces of glassware to invest in for your bar are the highball and the old-fashioned glass. These glasses are a bit like the odd couple of the bar, opposites that probably still have a lot of friendliness toward each other. Highballs are the taller, slightly more glamorous, and more slender of the pair, holding between 10 and 12 ounces. Old-fashioned glasses (also called rocks glasses) are shorter, squatter, and tougher, looking like they could handle themselves in a bar fight. They tend toward being in the 6- to 10-ounce size, with thick bottoms that keep them from wobbling. Double old-fashioned glasses that run 15 ounces and thereabouts are also available.

A few more worthy glasses include the larger Collins glass, which holds 12 to 16 ounces and is taller than the highball and usually a touch wider, and a set of tulip-style beer glasses (which taper outward as they get taller) that tend to be in the 15-ounce range.

Both white wine glasses, which are delicate and with smaller bowls, and red wine glasses, which tend to be more goblet-y in shape and manner, are useful additions, because multipurpose wine glasses are suggested for serving some of the drinks here. When thinking of wine glasses, don't forget about wine's more vivacious cousin, Champagne, and the current vessel of choice for serving it and drinks containing it, the flute glass. Willowy and trim, the flute glass helps to focus the bubbles, but keep an eye out for coupe glasses, the older style of Champagne glasses (antique stores and estate sales are fantastic places to look for these and other glassware). Coupe glasses have a much wider bowl, and you can go ahead and feel happy about using them for Champagne, Champagne drinks, and even drinks that would usually use a cocktail glass (as long as your coupe's bowl isn't too wide or deep). According to a legend (which is probably untrue but so much fun to tell), the coupe-style glass was originally based on a mold of Marie Antoinette's breasts.

Our last core piece of glassware is the largest, and perhaps my favorite. I'm talking about a glittering punch bowl for making larger batches of drinks and for those larger parties where you'd rather not make every drink by hand. Get one that has decently thick walls so there's no fretting over inadvertent cracks, either a crystal one that has classic class to it and comes with crystal punch cups so there can be some cross-glittering going on, or a sleek modern number that demonstrates that you are a true artist of the party-throwing.

There are many, many other glasses that might catch your fancy, including the vast horizon of cordials available. From tiny-bowled and long-stemmed varieties to those with mini-stems and short fat bowls, from those that come in matching sets to those that come in rainbow sets featuring many colors, cordials are lovely for sipping individual liqueurs out of, for serving smaller cocktails within, and for turning a home bar into a fantasy world that transports visitors in ways they hadn't imagined. Other glasses out there that you may want to indulge in include portly brandy snifters, curious shot glasses, specific glasses for pousse café–style drinks, glasses made solely for grappas, and so forth. Don't let glassware run the bar, however. If you come across a drink that makes your mouth water, a drink you know would be ideal for an occasion happening in a few hours, and the only thing holding you back is that it's supposed to be served in a cocktail glass and you have only white wine glasses, well, use white wine glasses and don't worry about it. Your glassware, like everything else behind the bar, should never become a hassle.

One Last Word Before the Adventure Begins

Okay, you've stocked up on vital liqueurs and vermouths, discovered what's needed in the way of base spirits, had the fresh rule unveiled in front of your very eyes and so are ready to keep the mixers in mighty fine form, learned about the ins and outs of garnishing, and checked off tools and glassware needed and wanted. But before taking that last step, one more ingredient is needed to become a home-entertainer supreme: fun. Sure, I've thrown it in here in dribbles, but I want to underline it one last time before the shaking and sipping starts: Drinking with friends and family, and making drinks for these and other folks whom you enjoy being with, should always be a fantastic time for all. The drinks on the pages that follow are meant to add to the fun, to make the memorable moments spent with folks while conversing and cocktailing more momentous. In today's world, the pace is almost always at 100 miles per hour, with most communications between people happening at a distance, rapidly, and in truncated fashion. Occasions when care has been taken to serve delicious and intriguing drinks to be consumed amid catching up, laughter, and affection are some of the few times we slow down and really enjoy those folks we care about, whether in a big group or a twosome. That's really what this book is about: making it possible for you to create the cocktails that accompany these shared moments and make them better. But don't dawdle here any longer—turn the pages and enter the realm of the *Ginger Bliss and the Violet Fizz.*

BLUE TRAIN COCKTAIL, PAGE 30

CHAPTER 2

A LIQUID

CITRUS

CIRCUS

. . . .

The bar's big top is a welcoming one, with many different acts happening at once. You've got people cheering, and shakers bounding about like acrobats, and glasses balanced on elephants (or trays, let's say), and little garnishes trotting around like small dogs in bowties. This particular circus features a ringmaster with a bit of an orangey hue, or a lemony one, because this is a circus where citrus takes the stage, keeping other ingredients on their toes, while always, always, entertaining the crowd.

It's not so surprising to see citrus liqueurs as ringmasters in a number of circuses, for a couple of scrumptious reasons. Citrus liqueurs have been standout performers in cocktails for many, many years, and so they are understood to carry a certain weight (not in pounds, but in force of character and reputation and respect) and can be relied upon not to wilt in the spotlight. Also, citrus liqueurs have a certain playfulness, a certain amount of inherent joy, that fits the circus association like a white glove. I attribute this frolicking manner and history to the fact that many of the ingredients in citrus liqueurs come from tropical climes, with sand and sun and surf, with bikinis and cutoffs, with volleyball and swimming. I realize I've made a move from an indoor form of entertainment to an outdoor one, but the school's-out nature of the circus and the summertime nature of the beach are related and, in a way, pulled together by citrus liqueur–based drinks.

Which is why the Gloom Chaser is an ideal accompaniment for a run toward the beach on the first sunny day after many weeks of gray, and why the Nothing Up Her Sleeve goes like a line of colorful scarves with a by-the-pool party hosted by a minor magician, or with an evening watching TiVo'd episodes of the sadly canceled genius comedy *Arrested Development*, where the exploits of woeful magician Gob play a central role. If more examples are needed to point to the good-time nature and wonder of citrus liqueurs and the drinks they play within, then raise the curtain on the classic Harvey Wallbanger, which is perhaps the best drink to have with a bubble bath and rubber duckie (at least that's my take), or the Golden Gleam, which glistens like the bejeweled tiara on the head of a knife-thrower's blonde model, or the Three Wishes, because so many of us have wished that we could run away to the circus or to the beach—or, best of all, a circus on the beach.

These wishes still apply, even though we've grown up (at least past 21), especially after a particularly long week (or day) at work, when repetitive tasks, or a too-small cubicle, or having to sit on the bus next to a strident cell-phone talker lead to nothing more than the desire for an entertaining escape. While responsibilities may make becoming a full-time circus clown or surfer impossible, there's no reason not to turn the page and enter the citrus circus. So take a ride on the Blue Train Cocktail or another one of the drinks contained in this chapter, and get away from the everyday for a few hours with a few friends.

14 JUILLET

When sipping the simple but luscious number called the 14 Juillet, I often find myself desiring to slip a few French phrases into the conversation. It could be the Armagnac (Cognac's cousin from the Armagnac region of France, which is distilled in a single copper still and usually aged for ten years) mingling with my bloodstream, or the Cointreau, which is made from bitter and sweet oranges and crafted in Saint-Barthélemy-d'Anjou. I say this as a way of warning: You might want to start speaking French after a few of these, too. The fact that you may not know French makes no difference at all (I admit deficiency in this, too). *Mais parfois, la puissance du 14 Juillet réussit bien.*

ICE CUBES

1½ OUNCES ARMAGNAC

1 OUNCE COINTREAU

½ OUNCE FRESHLY
SQUEEZED LEMON JUICE

1. Fill a cocktail shaker halfway full with ice cubes. Add the Armagnac, Cointreau, and lemon juice. Shake well.

2. Strain into a cocktail glass cheerfully.

The Drinker's Blogosphere: 10 URLs to Visit

While I'm a big proponent of drinking most times (if not all times) with folks whose company you enjoy (while the folks are in the room), in this modern world it can also be oodles of electronic fun drinking with people, or talking about drinking with people, who aren't in the room. I'm talking mainly about those great cocktail-and-drinking-related blogs that are out there, a grouping I like to call The Drinker's Blogosphere. It's a vast and wide e-bar, for sure, with lots of enjoyable conversation happening in a really wide range of places, but these ten are certainly good ones to start your exploration with:

1. Cask Strength
http://caskstrength.wordpress.com

2. The Cocktail Chronicles
www.cocktailchronicles.com

3. Underhill Lounge
http://underhill-lounge.flannestad.com

4. LUPEC Boston
http://lupecboston.blogspot.com

5. Pegu Blog
www.killingtime.com/Pegu

6. Jeffrey Morgenthaler
www.jeffreymorgenthaler.com

7. Oh Gosh
http://ohgo.sh

8. MXMO, or Mixology Mondays
http://mixologymonday.com

9. Alcohology
http://alcohology.wordpress.com

10. Scofflaw's Den
www.scofflawsden.com

THE ANACAONA APÉRITIF

A drink crafted by the cocktail countesses of LUPEC Boston (for more about these cocktail dream girls, see the Bourbon Belle on page 90, as well as www.lupecboston.com), this is a slightly citrusy, slightly herbal, bubbly, classy, and feisty cocktail that has a history behind it (and I always love a history, because it gives me much to talk about when serving a drink—I sure don't want to start boring folks I'm trying to entertain). Here's what the LUPEC-ers tell us about this drink: "Ingredients from France, Haiti, and the Caribbean mingle in the glass. We've named it for Queen Anacaona, one of the earliest Taino leaders to fight off Spanish conquest of Haiti in the late 15th century. She resisted in vain but is revered to this day as one of the nation's founders."

. . . .

CRACKED ICE

1 OUNCE DUBONNET ROUGE

¾ OUNCE COMBIER L'ORIGINAL LIQUEUR D'ORANGE

1 TEASPOON ST. ELIZABETH ALLSPICE DRAM

3 DASHES ANGOSTURA ORANGE BITTERS

2 OUNCES CHILLED BRUT CHAMPAGNE OR SPARKLING WINE

WIDE ORANGE PEEL, FOR GARNISH

1. Fill a cocktail shaker or mixing glass with cracked ice. Add the Dubonnet, Liqueur d'Orange, St. Elizabeth, and bitters. Stir well.

2. Strain into an attractive apéritif glass or flute. Top with the Champagne.

3. Squeeze the orange peel over the drink to release those fragrant and essential oils, and then gently rub the peel around the rim of the glass. Discard the peel, and drink happily.

A NOTE: Combier L'Original Liqueur d'Orange is a French orange liqueur that is seen by some as the original triple sec. This may be the case, as it's been available and going through its triple-distillation process since 1834. It uses all-natural ingredients (including bitter Haitian and sweet Valencia oranges) and is becoming more and more available.

ONE OF MY FAVORITE PARTS (AND YOURS, TOO, I'LL BET) OF THE MODERN COCKTAIL REVOLUTION IS THE REEMERGENCE OF BITTERS.

At one point in our cocktail history, from the first real flowering of cocktails in the late 1800s through around the 1950s, bitters were considered key components of many cocktails, with an awareness that the type of bitters being used completely changed the flavor of a drink—to the point where a change in bitters meant a change in name. Which makes sense, as drinks with different flavors should have different names (and not just have "-ini" tacked onto the end of them).

What happened to bitters, then, in the middle and late part of the last century? Well, basically, outside of reliable Angostura bitters, and in a few wonderful bastions of bartending, Peychaud's bitters, they faded off bar menus and liquor store shelves, and then, sadly, out of the minds of many, many drinkers. This was an amazing shame, because bitters add key spice, herb, and other flavors and aromas to drinks—those hints, layers, and accents that turn mundane mixtures into mighty liquid marvels. Basically, we've let our drinks be dumbed down by the lack of bitters. I, for one, don't want anyone dumbing down my drinks.

This is why I'm so glad that lately there's been a bitters explosion. Not only is Angostura still available (and the company has come out with a few wrinkles on the original, like an orange bitters), but earthy, dreamy Peychaud's is now not an afterthought, but a true essential. The Fee Brothers (www.feebrothers.com) line of bitters, including peach, mint, a whiskey barrel–aged type, and more, can be found in many places nationwide, and the cocktailian professor himself, Gaz (aka Gary) Regan has his own traditional orange bitters, called Regan's Orange Bitters No. 6, available in better gourmet stores as well as online.

But this is just the bitters beginning. As more people have discovered how important bitters are in cocktails, more and more bartending folks are making their own, and there are increasingly more new varieties and brands available online and in stores. Some notables include the German brand The Bitter Truth (www.the-bitter-truth.com), whose bitters (including celery bitters) and cocktail flavorings are now available in the United States, Seattle-based Scrappy's (www.scrappysbitters.com), whose bitters and tinctures come in flavors like cardamom and lime, and Bittermens (www.bittermens.com), whose chocolate bitters are beloved by bartenders nationwide. If you aren't already versed in the bitters landscape, I recommend checking out their websites to learn more about them, and then visiting a reputable online bar store like the Cocktail Kingdom (www.cocktailkingdom.com).

BIG SPENDER

W hen drinking one of these, it's hard for me not to start singing in a bawdy Broadway voice, "Hey, big spender!" while twirling a white boa around my head. This drink is a doozy, and you really don't have to roll out the greenbacks (or multicolored bills, if in another country) to make it. You do have to pay homage to the King—King Cocktail, that is, meaning Dale DeGroff himself, as this drink comes from his book *The Essential Cocktail* (Clarkson Potter, 2008). As he says in that illuminating and illustrious book, "You don't need to use Cristal—although, hey, it is the Big Spender—but it should be some type of sparkling rosé, such as Billecart-Salmon Brut Rosé." Valuable advice indeed. For more info on Rhum Clément Creole Shrubb, see page 45.

CRACKED ICE

1 OUNCE GRAN CENTENARIO AÑEJO TEQUILA

1 OUNCE RHUM CLÉMENT CREOLE SHRUBB

1 OUNCE FRESHLY SQUEEZED BLOOD ORANGE JUICE

CHILLED ROSÉ CHAMPAGNE

WIDE ORANGE TWIST, FOR GARNISH

LONG THIN ORANGE PEEL, FOR GARNISH

1. Fill a cocktail shaker or mixing glass halfway full with cracked ice. Add the tequila, Creole Shrubb, and blood orange juice. Stir well.

2. Strain into a flute glass, and then fill the flute almost to the top with Champagne.

3. Flame the wide orange twist over the drink (see A Note) and discard. Drape the long thin twist over the glass in a spiral fashion.

A NOTE: For a flaming twist, be sure you have an oval-shaped twist about 1½ inches long. First, light a match, holding it in one hand about 4 inches above the drink. With the other hand, hold the twist, peel side facing the drink, above the match. Twist the twist quickly, so that the oils shoot out, flaming as they pass through the flame into the drink.

BLUE RIBAND➤

I found this in *Chesterfield Cocktails* by Anthony Hogg (a book I was lucky enough to unearth when browsing a dusty bookstore in London). Mr. Hogg says, "The 'Blue Riband' was awarded to the liner making the fastest Atlantic crossing; variously held by British, French, German, and U.S. ships, this cocktail must have originated in one of them." Which means you should shake this up when wearing seafaring garb, either a white admiral's yachting cap and white trousers or a pea coat and a Greek fisherman's cap. There's no need to actually get on a boat. I believe that having boat races in the bathtub is an even better idea.

ICE CUBES

2 OUNCES GIN

1 OUNCE ORANGE CURAÇAO

½ OUNCE BLUE CURAÇAO

LEMON SLICE, FOR GARNISH (OPTIONAL)

1. Fill a cocktail shaker halfway full with ice cubes. Add the gin, orange curaçao, and blue curaçao. Shake well.

2. Strain into a cocktail glass. Garnish with the lemon slice if that will make your voyage more enjoyable.

BLUE TRAIN COCKTAIL

This is a shaker that'll make people sing. Why, you might ask (being a questioning type)? It could be the beautiful balance between orange-flavored Cointreau, tangy lemon juice, and violet-hued-and-imbued crème de violette, traveling together on sturdy rails of gin (if you don't mind the metaphor). It could be the lovely color of this cocktail, a vision that adds an artistic note to Sunday afternoon soirées. It could be the name, which lends itself to travels while the taste frees the mind. I think it's all of the above, combined within a single glass.

ICE CUBES

1 OUNCE GIN

½ OUNCE COINTREAU

½ OUNCE FRESHLY SQUEEZED LEMON JUICE

½ OUNCE CRÈME DE VIOLETTE

1. Fill a cocktail shaker halfway full with ice cubes. Add the gin, Cointreau, lemon juice, and crème de violette. Shake briefly.

2. Strain into a cocktail glass.

A VARIATION: There is another drink, called just the Blue Train, or the Blue Train Special, which shakes together 1½ ounces brandy and 1 ounce fresh pineapple juice over ice, and then tops it with Cap Classique or other sparkling wine and a pineapple chunk in a flute glass.

BRANDY CHAMPARELLE

B ack in the olden days, sexy was a swatch of bare ankle seen across a room, or a glimpse of the inner part of the elbow, a flash of a smile and a laugh heard with the knowledge that it came in response to a gently off-color story. I like to feel that the recipient of the raised eyebrow was wearing, under several layers, a wickedly intricate lacy garment with a host of ties, snaps, hooks, and other fasteners—much like this drink, which is in the pousse family of layered drinks and so takes a steady hand to construct. And, like our imaginary garment, this drink is wonderful to deconstruct, too.

1 OUNCE ORANGE CURAÇAO

1 OUNCE YELLOW CHARTREUSE

1 OUNCE BRANDY (OR COGNAC)

1. Add the curaçao to a cordial or other lovely glass that's not overly large. Carefully (pouring over a spoon if you need to) float the Chartreuse on top of the curaçao.

2. Float the brandy on top of the Chartreuse, again pouring it over a spoon if need be.

VARIATIONS: I've seen this made with the addition of 1 ounce of anisette, layered between the curaçao and the Chartreuse. And I've also seen it with a few drops of Angostura bitters sprinkled on the top at the very end. I'm not as fond of the former but am never sad to see the latter.

"We had finished our coffee and were sipping our Chartreuse when Sergent Heath, looking grim and bewildered, appeared at the door leading from the main dining room to the veranda, and strode quickly to our table."

—S.S. VAN DINE, *THE SMELL OF MURDER*, 1938

BRANDY CRUSTA

The key to this creative traditional drink is a two-parter: First, be sure the lemon rind is long and unbroken and between the ice and glass (because it both adds a sculptured look to the drink and ensures that a lemon whiff accompanies each sip), and second, don't forget the orange curaçao, which brings an additional citrus hint to the party. As the Crusta is a family, as well as a member of said family, there are some variations. The easiest is achieved by changing up the base liquor: rum, gin, and whiskey sub in swell for brandy. And, as long as you're following the full-rind rule, switching to an orange rind, and orange juice instead of lemon juice (as long as it's freshly squeezed), is dandy.

SUGAR, FOR GLASS RIM

ORANGE SLICE, FOR GLASS RIM AND GARNISH

1 LEMON

ICE CUBES

1½ OUNCES BRANDY

1 OUNCE SIMPLE SYRUP (PAGE 12)

½ OUNCE ORANGE CURAÇAO

¼ OUNCE FRESHLY SQUEEZED LEMON JUICE

2 DASHES ANGOSTURA BITTERS

MARASCHINO CHERRY, FOR GARNISH (OPTIONAL)

1. Pour a thin layer of sugar onto a saucer or small plate. Wet the outside rim of a chilled wine glass with the orange slice. Holding the glass by the stem, rotate it through the sugar, so that the sugar coats only the outside of the rim.

2. Using a vegetable peeler or one of the garnish-focused peelers out there, very carefully peel the rind off half of the lemon, in one long spiral strip, working to get as little of the white pith as possible. Place the spiral in the cocktail glass.

3. Fill a cocktail shaker halfway full with ice cubes. Add the brandy, simple syrup, orange curaçao, lemon juice, and bitters. Shake well.

4. Add about 5 small ice cubes or 1 large ice cube to your wine glass. Make sure the lemon rind encircles the ice and is positioned between it and the glass.

5. Strain the mix from the cocktail shaker over the ice. Garnish with the orange slice (or use a second slice if you feel that first one is too tapped out) and a cherry.

FROTHY DAWN

H ere comes the Frothy Dawn, here comes the Frothy Dawn, and I say, it's rummy fun, it's rummy citrusy fun. Three things to remember, if you don't want dawn to be a dud: First, always use freshly squeezed orange juice; second, maraschino liqueur is not the same as that syrupy stuff found in a jar of maraschino cherries (it's a dry, flavorsome liqueur made from the flesh and pits of Marasca cherries); third, crushed ice brings the froth, so try to track some down. This recipe probably could have gone into the fruity or spicy chapter as well, but it's here by virtue of the OJ.

CRUSHED ICE

1½ OUNCES WHITE RUM

1 OUNCE FRESHLY SQUEEZED ORANGE JUICE

½ OUNCE FALERNUM

½ OUNCE MARASCHINO LIQUEUR

1. Fill a cocktail shaker halfway full with crushed ice. Add the rum, orange juice, falernum, and maraschino liqueur. Shake well.

2. Strain the dawn into a cocktail glass.

A NOTE: I first saw this made a tad differently and called solely Frothy Cocktail. Without the dawn, though, where's the sunshine?

---

5 Drinks for First Dates

GINGER BLISS & THE VIOLET FIZZ

Sure, first dates can be a little nervy, but it should be an enjoyable kind of nervous. I mean, the possibilities are endless—and isn't getting to know someone new a good time nine times out of ten? But if you're feeling the butterflies, one thing to remember is that the other side of your date is feeling it too. Calm those butterflies for you and your date with one of the following cute and date-worthy drinks.

1. French Connection (page 171)

2. Friar Untucked (page 270)

3. Hanky Panky (page 135)

4. Great Secret (page 234)

3. First Loves (page 64)

GLOOM CHASER

ere's an idea: Invite the ol' gang over (an aside: Does anyone say "the ol' gang" anymore? Even Archie? If not, let's bring it back, okay?) on a cloudy, nasty, rainy, yucky Saturday, and have them show up bundled from the top of the head to the bottom of the big toe in wicked-weather gear: rubbery rain suits, woolen caps, galumphing galoshes, gloves, and thick scarves. Then, once the outdoors is shut away out-of-doors, crank up the heat, turn on some disco lights, put 1990's fave Deee-Lite song "Groove Is in the Heart" on the stereo, and have a whole platterful of Gloom Chasers ready to be consumed. You might want to warn everyone to pack a pair of shorts or a swimsuit, though, because once that gloom is shucked off, the heavy clothes won't be far behind.

ICE CUBES

¾ OUNCE GRAND MARNIER

¾ OUNCE ORANGE CURAÇAO

¾ OUNCE FRESHLY SQUEEZED LEMON JUICE

¾ OUNCE GRENADINE (PAGE 14)

1. Fill a cocktail shaker halfway full with ice cubes. Add the Grand Marnier, orange curaçao, lemon juice, and grenadine. Shake well.

2. Strain into a cocktail glass. Sip, and watch that gloom run.

A VARIATION: In certain spots, this is seen made as a dry Martini, with a few dashes of grenadine and a few of absinthe (a drink also called the Gloom Raiser—you can see how the confusion might set in).

A NOTE: In this drink (if not in all drinks), please shy away from commercial grenadine in favor of the homemade version, otherwise your cocktail will be so sweet that the gloom may just return.

Grand Marnier

In my mind, it was a sunny day in April 1827, with flowers blooming and the promise of a delicious summer full of fruit trees blooming big, when Jean-Baptiste Lapostolle decided to start a fruit liqueur distillery in Neauphe-le-Château, France. And (this is also in my mind) it was another beautiful spring day when Jean-Baptiste's granddaughter married Louis-Alexandre Marnier, combining two fabulous families into the one Marnier Lapostolle. Louis-Alexandre, combining his love of Cognac with the Lapostolles' love of liqueurs—specifically combining Cognac with *Citrus bigaradia*, an orange from the Caribbean— produced a secret recipe that we know today as Grand Marnier.

A type of (or at least a relative of) triple sec, Grand Marnier has an illustrious history, winning many awards and becoming a favorite of folks from classic French chef Auguste Escoffier (who used it in a soufflé) to those who just like to drink it over ice on a hot summer day when sitting in the backyard to those who enjoy it in cocktails like the Gloom Chaser (page 35) and the Red Lion (page 45). A number of varieties are made by the same family. The original is Grand Marnier Cordon Rouge, but there's also Louis-Alexandre, named after the creator; and Cuvée du Centenaire, made in 1927 to celebrate the company's hundredth anniversary, using rare petite and grand Cognacs. The Cuvée du Cent-Cinquantenaire was launched in 1977 in honor of the 150-year anniversary and features aged Cognacs. There's even a Cherry Marnier.

GOLDEN GLEAM

S weep guests off their feet and into some lawn chairs the moment before the sun goes down during an Indian summer evening, tell them to relax, and then go inside and make up a round of this brandy, fruity, Grand Marnier–infused mix. Bring it out on a big tray (being careful to watch your balance, because you sure don't want to spill even a drop), and pass a drink to each guest—saving one for yourself, of course. Then stretch out on the last remaining lawn chair, smile, and take in the kudos while everyone sips the golden-brown drink as the last lingering moments of daylight, and summertime, fade beneath the horizon.

. . . .

ICE CUBES

1½ OUNCES BRANDY

1 OUNCE GRAND MARNIER

¼ OUNCE FRESHLY SQUEEZED LEMON JUICE

½ OUNCE FRESHLY SQUEEZED ORANGE JUICE

LEMON TWIST, FOR GARNISH

1. Fill a cocktail shaker halfway full with ice cubes. Add the brandy, Grand Marnier, lemon juice, and orange juice. Shake well.

2. Strain into a cocktail glass. Garnish with the twist.

A NOTE: I think that if you have a fine-mesh strainer, you should strain this drink (even if it means you're straining it twice), because it's awfully pretty when clear (it helps with the gleaming).

HARVEY WALLBANGER

One story goes that this drink was created in 1952 for a surfer who used to hang out in a bar owned by genial bartender Donato "Duke" Antone, who himself was the brother-in-law of New York state senator Carlo Lanzillotti. Duke's bar was the Blackwatch, and he may have also created a few other classic or almost-classic or at least well-liked drinks such as the Rusty Nail and the Godfather. Is it all true? I'm not sure, but I like the legend, and so here's a toast to Duke, and to surfers, and to well-named drinks that highlight the prowess of Italian liqueurs such as Galliano. Herbal, golden, and a smidge sweet, Galliano has a legend as well, as it was created in 1896 and named after Giuseppe Galliano, a hero of the Italian-Ethiopian war. For more info on this luscious liqueur, see page 200.

ICE CUBES

2 OUNCES VODKA

5 OUNCES FRESHLY SQUEEZED ORANGE JUICE

½ OUNCE GALLIANO

1. Fill a highball glass three-quarters full with ice cubes. Add the vodka and the orange juice, and stir briefly.

2. Float the Galliano on top of the vodka-juice mixture.

A NOTE: To repeat (or proclaim for the first time, for those who haven't heard this before): I think a Harvey Wallbanger is best sipped in the bathtub.

LOCOMOTIVE

Chugga-chugga-chugga, whoo whoo! Can you hear the train a'coming, coming round the bend? It's a winter train, and when the smoke flows from the smokestack, it seems to hang in the air like a thick cloud of cotton tacked to the bright blue sky. And the train rolls on, through the snow-covered hills, with windows slightly steamed from the warmth inside. It's lovely watching the locomotive roll down the chilly tracks, but even better to be inside where it's warm, sipping a steaming Locomotive. And if you can't actually be on a winter train, or watching one, while having your Locomotive, then know that it's also a fine accompaniment to putting together a model train set with friends or family or watching *The Great Train Robbery*.

. . . .

1 TEASPOON SUGAR

1 EGG YOLK, PREFERABLY ORGANIC

2 OUNCES ORANGE CURAÇAO

4 OUNCES FULL-BODIED RED WINE (SUCH AS CABERNET SAUVIGNON)

LEMON SLICE, FOR GARNISH

1. Add the sugar and the egg yolk to a small bowl. Whisk to combine.

2. Add the sugar-egg mixture, orange curaçao, and wine to a small saucepan and place over medium-high heat.

3. Cook, while stirring, until it's warmed through—but don't let it boil.

4. Pour into a heatproof mug. Garnish with the lemon slice.

A WARNING: As this drink contains nearly raw egg, it shouldn't be served to the elderly or to those with compromised immune systems.

. . . .

"She had had a Mandarine–Curaçao in front of her, and now she had drunk it down thirstily. Latimer had cleared his throat."

—ERIC AMBLER, *A COFFIN FOR DIMITRIOS*, 1939

LUCIEN GAUDIN

S ometimes the very name of a drink dictates what should occur on an evening or an afternoon when you're consuming said drink. As cocktail historian Dr. Cocktail (also known as Ted Haigh) tells us, this drink was named for a gold medal–winning Olympic fencer. This doesn't mean you should be handling sharp objects while consuming these, but a little play-acting with plastic swords or feathers, and a point system that involves sips of the drink and then indicates who constructs the next round of Lucien Gaudins? Seems like a good way to commemorate a champ.

CRACKED ICE

1 OUNCE GIN

½ OUNCE COINTREAU

½ OUNCE CAMPARI

½ OUNCE DRY VERMOUTH

ORANGE TWIST,
FOR GARNISH

1. Fill a cocktail shaker or mixing glass halfway full with cracked ice. Add the gin, Cointreau, Campari, and dry vermouth. Stir well.

2. Strain into a cocktail glass. Garnish with the orange twist.

A NOTE: Campari does tend to shine out, but in this case the Cointreau holds the Campari and vermouth at bay and so deserves center stage, hence the drink's placement in this chapter. But bear in mind that this is an herbal concoction as well.

NOTHING UP HER SLEEVE

I think this drink couples nicely with close-up magic—tricks as simple as the Gypsy Thread, the Haunted Hank, and the Linking Rings, tricks that I'm theorizing all magicians know. But, I'm also thinking of those tricks we regular folks know that might lead to magic, such as the Bare Elbow Brush, the Sultry Gaze Across the Room, the Cozy Bumping Into, the Drinks Appear, and the Sliding Past While Putting a Hand on the Back. Weighing it over, the latter may in fact be more magical—and more likely to lead to finding out what is actually up someone's sleeve.

ICE CUBES

1½ OUNCES COGNAC

1 OUNCE GRAND MARNIER

½ OUNCE ANISETTE

BRANDIED CHERRY, FOR GARNISH

1. Fill a cocktail shaker halfway full with ice cubes. Add the Cognac, Grand Marnier, and anisette. Shake well.

2. Add the brandied cherry to a cocktail glass. Strain the drink into the glass while saying "Abracadabra!"

A NOTE: No need to go overboard on the Cognac price here—and feel free to sub in a good brandy.

The Taste's the Thing
. . . .

Individualism is what makes us grand, right? Can we all agree on this and still be seen as individuals? If everyone were the same, wearing the same red boots as I do, and the same white boa, and the same Rich Fulcher (dancing as Bob Fossil, from the Mighty Boosh) T-shirt, wouldn't it be, well, boring? Individual taste is, on some level, the same thing. If everyone had the same taste, I suppose bartending might be easier, but it would also be a little less fun. But when taking individual taste into account, I'm not suggesting that it's an excuse for going pie-wacky and starting to disregard recipes and proven drink ideas or some such nonsense. Just the opposite, in fact. I (and many helpful bartenders, modern and throughout history) spent lots of time testing and trying and balancing the recipes contained within this book, and we got them to a point where we think they're pretty darn grand and bound to become a hit with the majority of those who try them. However, if you feel that a drink doesn't have quite enough fresh lemon juice for you, then slowly add a little more (maybe ¼ ounce at a time), until it achieves your desired level of taste and takes you to another realm of drinking satisfaction. You may want to change the name of the drink a bit, 'cause you'll probably be drinking something wholly new, in a way. As long as the result is an enjoyable drink, though, I won't complain about you altering a little, to taste.

PEGU

T he Pegu is a memorable cocktail, one whose bread-crumb trail starts at the first Pegu Club, a British hot spot in Rangoon in the 1920s. The exact date of the house cocktail creation isn't narrowed down, but it's at least before 1927, when it appeared in the book *Barflies and Cocktails* (which you can read more about on page 281), and the trail leads all the way to the modern Pegu Club in New York City's SoHo. Happily, since this cocktail's trail continues, you can order a Pegu (or Pegu Club, as some refer to it) when walking into any reputable cocktail house and rest assured you'll get something close to this recipe. (You might see Cointreau or Grand Marnier stepping into the spot usually held by orange curaçao, but hey, when traveling, you sometimes have to give other customs a try.)

ICE CUBES

1½ OUNCES GIN

¾ OUNCE ORANGE CURAÇAO

½ OUNCE FRESHLY SQUEEZED LIME JUICE

DASH OF ORANGE BITTERS

DASH OF ANGOSTURA BITTERS

1. Fill a cocktail shaker halfway full with ice cubes. Add the gin, orange curaçao, lime juice, and both bitters. Shake well.

2. Strain into a cocktail glass, and dream of days when this classic was (according to Harry Craddock in *The Savoy Cocktail Book*) a drink "that has traveled, and is asked for, round the world."

PRINCESS

A truly regal rejuvenator, the Princess wears her title because of two facts. First, the key ingredient, limoncello, is an Italian lemon liqueur that is, itself, a reigning monarch in the world of liqueur, one that seems distilled from pure sunlight, spun gold, and summer afternoons. Second, the drink was concocted by my wife, Natalie, on a July day when we were picking raspberries from a patch that was in our then-backyard. And Natalie is herself a princess, one who makes a fine drink and who makes a fine day even finer. Be sure to serve this, then, to your prince or princess, whenever the temperature demands a cold, tall, royal mixture.

ICE CUBES

1½ OUNCES LIMONCELLO

CHILLED CLUB SODA

5 OR 6 FRESH RASPBERRIES

1. Fill a Collins glass three-quarters full with ice cubes. Add the limoncello.

2. Fill the glass to about ½ inch from the top with the club soda. Add the fresh raspberries. Stir regally, but seriously, perhaps busting up the raspberries a bit, until everything is well combined.

A VARIATION: You can also sub in other small members of the berry family, such as blueberries, as long as they're fresh.

A NOTE: If possible, use homemade limoncello, because it's tasty and not tough to make. Just add 1 liter grain alcohol or vodka and the peels of 14 lemons to a large glass container with a tight-fitting lid and place in a cool, dry spot away from sunlight. Let sit for 2 weeks. Add 3 cups Simple Syrup (page 12), stir, and reseal. Let sit for 2 more weeks. Strain the liqueur through a double layer of cheesecloth into a pitcher or other vessel. Strain again through 2 new sheets of cheesecloth into 1 large bottle or a number of smaller bottles or jars. Bellissima!

RED LION

Roarrrrr! Can you hear the roaring? That's the crowd at this episode of Cocktail Challenge. Here it is: Is this drink named after a robot cat from the cartoon *Voltron*, a chain of hotels, the Elizabethan playhouse outside of cheery London, or a colorful name for the cougar? Mull it over, put the answer in an envelope (roaring the whole while), and send it to me. If you get it right, I'll pick up the next Red Lion, right after I take a time machine back to the early 1900s to discover where the name did in fact come from.

. . . .

ICE CUBES

1½ OUNCES GIN

¾ OUNCE GRAND MARNIER

½ OUNCE FRESHLY SQUEEZED LEMON JUICE

½ OUNCE FRESHLY SQUEEZED ORANGE JUICE

1. Fill a cocktail shaker halfway full with ice cubes. Add the gin, Grand Marnier, and lemon and orange juices, and shake well.

2. Strain into a cocktail glass.

VARIATIONS: Throughout history, there have been other Red Lions, including one that reduces the lemon juice to ¼ ounce and adds 3 dashes of grenadine, and another that flip-flops the amounts of gin and Grand Marnier; that one I'm not as prone to pet behind the ears.

LIQUEUR SPOTLIGHT
. . . .

Rhum Clément Creole Shrubb
. . . .

Becoming very popular recently in cocktails such as Big Spender (page 29), Rhum Clément Creole Shrubb has a clear taste that's orange-based but also features hints of vanilla, cloves, cinnamon, nutmeg, grapefruit, and a slight peppery finish. The story begins way back in 1852, when Homère Clément was born in Trinité, Martinique. Originally a physician, he made a fortuitous career change after doing a little research into Cognac and Armagnac distillation processes, and he decided to start distilling rum in a different way—using sugarcane instead of the predominant molasses. He crushed and fermented the sugarcane into a sort of sugar wine, which was then distilled and made into the well-respected line of Rhum Clément rums. Aged and white rums then provide the base for the Creole Shrubb, made after combining the rums with bitter white curaçao, orange peels, and a variety of mysterious ingredients.

SCOTTISH BLUSH

Made in Leith, Scotland, Glayva liqueur mingles aged Scotch whiskies, citrus fruits, anise, clove, herbs, a whisper of heather honey, and more. If you can't easily track it down somewhere within driving distance, look for it online, because it's the crucial ingredient in this particular cheek-warmer. And, if you're more than a wee bit romantic and perhaps prone to blushing, you'll be tickled to serve up a Blush when looking to enchant another as you're blushing at his or her slightly suggestive remarks.

ICE CUBES

1½ OUNCES GIN

1 OUNCE GLAYVA

½ OUNCE CRANBERRY JUICE

½ OUNCE FRESHLY SQUEEZED ORANGE JUICE

LIME WHEEL, FOR GARNISH

1. Fill a cocktail shaker halfway full with ice cubes. Add the gin, Glayva, cranberry juice, and orange juice. Shake well.

2. Strain into a cocktail glass and garnish with the lime wheel (I suggest squeezing it over the glass, too).

THEY SHALL INHERIT THE EARTH

Morley Callaghan was a Canadian writer, known in the last century for penning everything from novels (including the one that this drink is named after) to memoirs. He was also known for palling around in Paris with Ernest Hemingway, F. Scott Fitzgerald, and the rest of the rowdy Americans there, and especially for a certain sparring match with Hemingway, in which he knocked Papa H down and out (seems Mr. Callaghan was quite the pugilist, though Hemingway blamed Fitzgerald, who was refereeing the match). What I didn't know, until reading it in the "Drinks of Famous People" section of the 1962 book *The Art of Mixing Drinks* (which is based on the *Esquire Drink Book* and which is not to be confused with David A. Embury's *Fine Art of Mixing Drinks*), is that Mr. Callaghan developed a taste for French liqueurs between boxing bouts, as demonstrated in the recipe below, adapted from one attributed to him.

ICE CUBES

½ OUNCE COINTREAU

½ OUNCE BÉNÉDICTINE

1 OUNCE BRANDY

1 OUNCE FRESHLY
SQUEEZED LEMON JUICE

1. Fill a cocktail shaker halfway full with ice cubes. Add the Cointreau, Bénédictine, brandy, and lemon juice. Shake like a boxing novelist.

2. Strain into a cocktail glass, and drink while reading.

LIQUEUR SPOTLIGHT

Cointreau

One of the most well-known orange-flavored liqueurs (a cousin to, if not an extension of, triple sec), Cointreau gets its flavor from a combination of bitter and sweet orange peels, acquired from a wide range of locales such as Spain and Haiti. All of these oranges and their peels are brought to Saint-Barthélemy-d'Anjou, outside of Angers in France, where they are combined and added to a base spirit and introduced to a few other key elements. The recipe itself is, naturally, a secret, but we do know it was originally designed by Adolphe Cointreau, a confectioner, and his brother Edouard-Jean. The brothers, after lots of testing and tasting, started the Cointreau Distillery in 1849 but didn't sell their liqueur to the public until 1875, after more testing and tasting, at which point the recipe reached perfection to their palates. Cointreau is now available worldwide (in more than 200 countries, they say) and is used in many cocktail recipes such as the Flash (page 93) and They Shall Inherit the Earth (page 48), as well as being sipped on its own, still beloved for its balance. The current reach of Cointreau would definitely make Adolphe happy, since he spent so much time laboring "to combine crystal clear purity with the subtlety of tastes obtained from the perfect harmony of sweet and bitter orange peels." Now that's a goal worth aspiring toward.

THREE WISHES

And the djinn appeared in smoke and orange fire and a thunderclap and a ringing in the ears, as if the beach had been rent in two and the skies were wrung by giant hands. It wore jewels that glittered like amber eyes on its thick fingers, golden bands across massive wrists, and robes that reflected nothing out of their black depths. And though its eyes could cause madness if looked into for long, the truly fearful aspect of this otherworldly being was the row of darkly liquid bottles attached to a belt of rope around its waist. Was it the corporeal representation of the many souls it had captured in the bottles? A series of heavenly or demonic philters designed to end the world? Or the makings of a drink usually reserved for mythological beings? Only by making the right wishes will you find out for sure.

. . . .

CRACKED ICE

2 OUNCES DARK RUM

1 OUNCE RHUM CLÉMENT CREOLE SHRUBB

1 OUNCE AMARETTO

1. Fill a cocktail shaker or mixing glass halfway full with cracked ice. Add the rum, Creole Shrubb, and amaretto. Stir like a djinn.

2. Strain into a cocktail glass.

A NOTE: I think cracked ice is crackingly good for stirring here, but if you have only ice cubes and don't feel like cracking, they'll work too.

VIOLET FIZZ, PAGE 77

CHAPTER 3

A BOUQUET

OF LOVELY

LIQUEURS

hough there have been some remarkable floral and floral-esque liqueurs, they don't tend to have the strong reputa-tion of some of the other liqueur categories, in the same way that daisies don't have the same sort of reputation as a giant sombrero. While daisies look as pretty as a French picture and are never frowned upon when you show up with them at a soirée, they sure don't have the same impact, the same stop-'em-in-their-tracks fascination, the same oh-my-golly exclamations as a giant sombrero. And how many people do a dance around daisies at a party?

On the flip side, though, if you show up for an evening date with just one special person, that favorite person in your eyes, the one you want to demon-strate your more refined, graceful, artistic, and appreciative nature to, then the daises are always going to elicit a little gasp at your thoughtfulness (especially if they're arranged in an artfully careless manner and are extra-fresh, and the picture of spring, which is indeed the picture of romance blossoming). And the giant sombrero? Though it has a place in romance, on those more intimate evenings it's only going to raise a lot of doubt about intentions and their seriousness.

Want to know what shows intentions even more artistically and gracefully than a handful of flowers? One of the following cocktails or highballs that are, in essence, liquid bouquets, imbibables highlighting liqueurs known for their floral essences. This heralded position of being a perfect present for showing off a classy-but-sexy side is why the following concoctions, even though they don't have the flamboyant reputation of some of the drinks in other chapters, get their deserved kudos.

So the next time you're thinking, "I'll bring daisies," instead show up bearing the ingredients for a Chartreuse Daisy. When thinking about wildflowers, round up the necessaries for an Eve's Garden. Instead of buying a dozen roses at the corner store, serve up an Elderthorn and ensure that you don't end up getting pained by what you bring (as you might with those prickly roses). There are also some other perfectly romantic numbers in the following pages that don't sound like flowers—such as the Luminous Angel, First Loves, and the Haute Toddy—and if you're wondering, these are a bigger hit than a box of fancy chocolates (though having both cocktails and sweets isn't a bad idea). And if your relationship does involve giant hats, well, none of these go down badly when wearing a substantial sombrero, either.

ACCISMUS BLOSSOMS

F lirtatious moments should be approached with tact, strategy, and smarts as opposed to the hammer manner many use. One strategy for a more-witty-and-less-annoying pickup moment is using a feigned indifference. This is when you meet a person you'd really love to know better, but act a little standoff-ish (not jerk-ish, just not falling-all-over-yourself-trying-to-impress-ish). The next time you find yourself in one of these moments, with another person you really have a hankering for, then I suggest making the move from acting uninterested to revealing that first pinch of interest with this drink in hand. It'll serve as the perfect opener while providing that potentially special someone with an enticingly distinctive drink.

· ·

CRACKED ICE

1½ OUNCES HANGAR ONE MANDARIN BLOSSOM VODKA

1 OUNCE CRÈME DE VIOLETTE

½ OUNCE APEROL

DASH OF FEE BROTHERS PEACH BITTERS

EDIBLE FLOWERS, SUCH AS ORANGE BLOSSOMS, NASTURTIUMS, OR ROSES, FOR GARNISH

1. Fill a cocktail shaker halfway full with cracked ice. Add the vodka, crème de violette, Aperol, and bitters. Stir well.

2. Strain into a cocktail glass. Garnish with a few edible flowers.

AVIATION

This is one high-flying cocktail. It dates back to about 1916 and was probably a hit then, considering how it takes the aerodynamics of gin to the altitude of maraschino liqueur and into the clouds of crème de violette before banking down through lemon juice to land on a cherry. The question is—and this is a question asked far too often about far too many drinks—what caused the crash landing for the Aviation in the middle of the last century? It dropped off the map into some boozy Bermuda Triangle for a while, before rising on the updrafts back into the communal cocktail consciousness. And I, for one (hopefully you are for two), am happy to see it take off again.

ICE CUBES

2 OUNCES GIN

½ OUNCE FRESHLY SQUEEZED LEMON JUICE

2 TEASPOONS MARASCHINO LIQUEUR

1 TEASPOON CRÈME DE VIOLETTE

MARASCHINO CHERRY, FOR GARNISH

1. Fill a cocktail shaker halfway full with ice cubes. Add the gin, lemon juice, maraschino liqueur, and crème de violette, and shake well.

2. Strain the mixture into a cocktail glass and garnish with the cherry.

A NOTE: For a long time, crème de violette went MIA in the United States, so much so that in many recipes for the Aviation, it's dropped entirely. While the cocktail can still be tasty that way, it won't be the same. Luckily, you can now find crème de violette without too much of a layover. If it's not in your neighborhood liquor store, try online. Its floral flavor is really what makes this drink fly, in terms of both taste and aesthetics.

CHARTREUSE DAISY

The Daisy (which is closely related to the Fix, though they sound like opposite ends of the spectrum) is a classic old family of drinks that employ a little sweet, a little citrus, and a spirit to make their way in the world. The materfamilias (I think the Daisy family has to be matriarchal) is the basic Gin Daisy, which is darn close to what we have here, except I've upped the proportion of Chartreuse enough that I decided to give it top billing. (For more on Chartreuse, see page 58.) You can add different fruit as garnish if you have something special and ripe in your orchard or garden (cherries or berries would be lovely). As David Embury reminded me in his essential book, *The Fine Art of Mixing Drinks* (Doubleday, 1948, which means, sadly, he reminded me of it only on the page and not in person), one thing to remember about both the Daisy and Daisy's above-mentioned cousin the Fix is that "these are drinks of the Mid-Victorian Era. Put on your hoop skirt and bustle and wax your mustache, and sip them to the dream rhythm of a Viennese waltz." And now you know why this drink, and his book, are so essential.

CRACKED ICE

2 OUNCES GIN

½ OUNCE FRESHLY SQUEEZED LEMON JUICE

¼ OUNCE GRENADINE (PAGE 14)

1 OUNCE YELLOW CHARTREUSE

STRAWBERRY, FOR GARNISH

ORANGE WHEEL, FOR GARNISH

1. Fill a cocktail shaker halfway full with cracked ice. Add the gin, lemon juice, and grenadine. Shake very well, until the shaker gets frosty.

2. Fill a goblet three-quarters full with cracked ice. Strain the mixture over the ice. Stir briefly. Float the Chartreuse over the ice, and stir again briefly. Garnish with the strawberry and the orange wheel.

Chartreuse

Glowing, floral, herbal, vegetal, magical, healing, otherworldly, and darn delicious, Chartreuse is one of a kind, even though there are four varieties. With this said, you'd expect it to have quite a history—and it does: a history that goes back to the year 1084, to the start of the Chartreuse order of cloistered monks, or Carthusians. In 1605, the Chartreuse monastery in Vauvert, France, was visited by the marshal of French King Henry IV, Francois Hannibal d'Estrées, who brought with him a great gift: a manuscript with a recipe for "An Elixir of Long Life." The manuscript was a bit shabby and hard to transcribe, but the monks didn't give up on it. Sadly, it took a lot of work, so the elixir wasn't ready for consumption until 1737. At this point, the monks began making it available to the public, under the name Chartreuse Elixir.

The recipe is still made by the monks, and it still contains 130 secret ingredients, including herbs, roots, leaves, spices, sunshine, and more, all combined in oak casks, with exact quantities, assortments, and levels known to only two monks at any time. While the secret has been passed down throughout history, it has also been modified here and there to expand the line from one elixir to the following four: Elixir Végétal de la Grande-Chartreuse, extra aged V.E.P. Chartreuse, and the primary green and yellow varieties (the green being the more muscular of the two, and the yellow a bit sweeter). Today, both main varieties are consumed solo over ice by many during spring and fall afternoons as the sun shines, and they're also favorite ingredients for bartenders looking to add flavor to cocktails, including the Tipperary and the Triomphe Cocktail, both found on page 76.

CYCLAMEN

This fragrant head-turner comes from friendly bar artiste David Shenaut, who tends bar in Portland, Oregon; whose cocktails are masterfully crafted; and whose cocktail talk is always welcoming. David was one of the founders—and is the current president—of the Oregon Bartender's Guild (www.oregonbarguild.org) and has his own professional bartending service, On the House (www.onthehouse.biz). He originally suggested dry shaking each and every ingredient except the simple syrup (and without ice, naturally) with the spring-like coil taken off of a Hawthorne strainer, but also says the below method works dandy. He says of the drink itself that it is "a very soft and feminine style drink," which I think makes it ideal for spring afternoons when you and yours are lounging around as flowers and romance bloom.

- -

ICE CUBES

1½ OUNCES SQUARE ONE CUCUMBER VODKA

¾ OUNCE APEROL

½ OUNCE YELLOW CHARTREUSE

¾ OUNCE FRESHLY SQUEEZED LIME JUICE

½ OUNCE RICH SIMPLE SYRUP (SEE A NOTE)

1 EGG WHITE, PREFERABLY ORGANIC

FRESH MINT SPRIG, FOR GARNISH

1. Fill a cocktail shaker halfway full with ice cubes. Add the vodka, Aperol, Chartreuse, lime juice, rich simple syrup, and egg white. Shake exceptionally well.

2. Strain the drink into a small coupe-style glass, a pretty cordial glass, or a not-gigantic cocktail glass. If possible, strain through both a regular and fine-mesh strainer.

3. Garnish with the mint sprig, after slightly spanking it. Not because it's been naughty (though those mint sprigs sometimes are), but to get the fragrance flowing.

A NOTE: To make rich simple syrup, follow the recipe on page 12, but increase the sugar to 5 cups.

A WARNING: As this drink contains raw egg, it shouldn't be served to the elderly or to those with compromised immune systems.

ELDERTHORN

T his sounds like a sticky wicket at first—as though it involves crawling through a thicket of very prickly trees, trees that have been around since the proverbial dawn of time, to get to a drink. Well, it'd be worth it, but instead of the struggle, let's flip this over and think of it in a different way. Instead of "prickly and old," think "wise and worthy," which matches both the ingredient list (with wise Cognac alongside St-Germain elderflower liqueur and Cynar, the Italian artichoke digestivo) and the drink's history. See, this drink comes from the fruitful and wise cocktail mind of Robert Hess (aka DrinkBoy), whose book *The Essential Bartender's Guide* (Mud Puddle Books, 2008) is, well, essential for anyone contemplating a cocktail-making career, and whose website (www.drinkboy. com) is essential for anyone wanting to know more about cocktails and spirits.

CRACKED ICE

1 OUNCE COGNAC

½ OUNCE ST-GERMAIN ELDERFLOWER LIQUEUR

½ OUNCE CYNAR

1. Fill a cocktail shaker or mixing glass halfway full with cracked ice. Add the Cognac, St-Germain, and Cynar. Stir well.

2. Strain the mixture into a cocktail glass.

A NOTE: If you can't find St-Germain elderflower liqueur but can find Pür Spirits' Pür-Likör Blossom elderflower liqueur, you should feel sunny about substituting (check www.purspirits.com to see if it's available in your area). They do taste different, but both go well in this drink.

Crème Yvette

There have been many sad occasions for cocktail lovers in the past 100 years, including the disappearance of many kinds of bitters (luckily, this has been remedied recently—see page 27 for more), the appearance of the letters "-ini" appended to numerous drink titles instead of the creation of original interesting titles, the preponderance of chemical flavorings, and more. One sad occasion that happened in 1969 was when crème Yvette (aka crème d'Yvette) stopped being made. But we can unleash the confetti, because as of the fall of 2009, this intriguing, painterly, and delish ingredient is back on the market. Made from Parma violet petals, spices, berries, and vanilla (and love, one hopes), crème Yvette adds a lush purple color to many drinks, as well as a layered floral flavor with a soupçon of sweet on the end of a sip. Its ability to delicately alter a cocktail's taste and hue makes it a key ingredient in drinks such as the Blue Moon (page 260).

Crème Yvette's history goes back to 1890, when it was originally made and distributed by the Sheffield Company out of Connecticut. Soon after, in 1900, Charles Jacquin et Cie (America's oldest cordial company) purchased the recipe and right and began distributing it around the world. That is, until 1969, when it stopped being produced—I'm guessing due to a case of mass hypnosis blanking out how good it is from people's minds. For its reintroduction into the market, we owe our thanks to Charles Jacquin et Cie's Rob Cooper (who is also responsible for St-Germain elderflower liqueur, which you can read more about on page 68), who after some persistent requests unburied the recipe, tracked down new French sources for ingredients, and began producing crème Yvette once again.

EVE'S GARDEN

C harles H. Baker, Jr., was the Grand Funk Railroad of his time. The author of two indispensable books of drinking and culinary lore—*An Exotic Drinking Book* and *An Exotic Cookery Book*—first released in 1939 as *The Gentleman's Companion,* Mr. Baker basically traveled round the world gathering recipes and writing about them in a most entertaining fashion. Or, to put it in another vernacular, he came to your town and helped you party down.

This particular delicacy from Mr. Baker's drinking volume is within a section titled "Ten More which Are Not Called Angels," right after a section called "First a Brief Company of Six Angels." Damiana, a traditional Mexican liqueur made with the leaves of the flowering and fruiting damiana shrub, is said to have aphrodisiac qualities, so be sure to always have enough to make this for two. But since it's ticklish to prepare, I suggest making only one at a time.

1 OUNCE DAMIANA

1 OUNCE CRÈME YVETTE

1 OUNCE COGNAC

¼ OUNCE HEAVY CREAM

1 SOUR CHERRY, FOR GARNISH

1. Add the Damiana to a cordial or other similar attractive glass. Slowly top it with the crème Yvette, pouring over a spoon if needed—you don't want them to mix, because layering is desired.

2. Pour the Cognac on top of the crème Yvette, again pouring over a spoon if needed so that they don't mix.

3. Slowly spoon the cream on top of the cognac, and gently place the cherry on top of the cream.

A NOTE: Crème Yvette went out of circulation from 1969 to 2009, but it's now available again. See more on page 61.

A SECOND NOTE: In Mr. Baker's book, this is garnished with a green cherry, but I like the sour cherry (and am a bit wary of the green cherry). But if you want to substitute the green for authenticity, I won't stop you.

"This sort of thing only goes to show what grown men will do to keep from devoting their time to something constructive in life."

—CHARLES H. BAKER ON EVE'S GARDEN, *THE GENTLEMAN'S COMPANION,* VOLUME II, 1939

FIRST LOVES

Ah, first loves. Do you remember yours? The winks, the giggles, the hold-ing hands in the back of the bus, the nervous moments alone, the trading of jackets (if your first love was in winter, that is), the slow dances, the colorful birds flying above, the whispers outside lockers or in hallway corners, the sharing of lunches, the brightly colored afternoons on the swing set or slippery slide, the gin drinks. Wait, you didn't shake any gin drinks with your first love? Well, maybe you should track that person down and make up for the missteps. Or, if that seems too stalker-like, why not make this gin drink for your current love and go through the whole loveliness a second time?

ICE CUBES

2 OUNCES GIN

1 OUNCE LOFT LAVENDER CELLO

¼ OUNCE APEROL

¼ OUNCE FRESHLY SQUEEZED LEMON JUICE

LEMON SLICE, FOR GARNISH

1. Fill a cocktail shaker halfway full with ice cubes. Add the gin, lavender liqueur, Aperol, and lemon juice. Shake well.

2. Strain into a cocktail glass. Garnish with the lemon slice and a longing glance.

A NOTE: Loft liqueurs were the first to be certified organic in the United States, and they use only fresh ingredients that are as local as they can get them. Loft liqueurs come in an array of intriguing flavors, including lemongrass, ginger, and the lavender used here. To achieve its delicately sweet taste, only lavender from a specific farm in Washington State is used.

GARLANDED GALLIMAUFRY

Thre are almost enough ingredients in this to be called a kitchen-sinker, but that might be confused with a dangerous baseball pitch thrown only in the final inning of the final game in a playoff series. However, don't be thrown off by the baseball metaphor, the ingredient list, or the multisyllabic moniker. This mellifluous floral cocktail isn't hard to make (and, thanks to the Internet, the ingredients aren't hard to find), and it is better suited to first dates than baseball games because of its light, intriguing, and sylvan personality. The name, while a tongue twister, is also enjoyable to say and a good conversation piece. Just say that *gallimaufry* comes from the Middle French *galimafree*, meaning "stew," which descends itself from *galer* (a party word meaning "to make merry") combined with *mafrer* ("to gorge"). So, basically, it means to indulge in making merry, which is something I suggest doing as often as possible.

ICE CUBES

1½ OUNCES LOFT LAVENDER CELLO

¾ OUNCE ELISIR M.P. ROUX

½ OUNCE FRESHLY SQUEEZED LIME JUICE

DASH OF PEYCHAUD'S BITTERS

DASH OF ANGOSTURA BITTERS

2 OR 3 EDIBLE FLOWERS, SUCH AS HIBISCUS, HYSSOP, OR LILAC, FOR GARNISH

1. Fill a cocktail shaker halfway full with ice cubes. Add the lavender liqueur, Elisir M.P. Roux, lime juice, and both bitters. Shake well.

2. Strain into a cocktail glass or curvy cordial glass. Garnish with the edible flowers.

A NOTE: Elisir M.P. Roux is a French botanical liqueur made from an assortment of flowering herbs and assorted spices, including (but not limited to) marjoram, hyssop, fennel, cinnamon, balm, coriander, garden balsam, wild angelica, lemon peel, star anise, ginseng, and damiana. With such a lineup, you can imagine that recipes made using this beautiful bottle could also find a home in the Take Your Herbal Medicine chapter.

HAUTE TODDY

I f you drink (since you've picked up this book, I'm going to go out on a limb and say you do), then you'll want to *Imbibe*. In this case, though, I'm referring not to the general meaning of the word but to the magazine of the same title. *Imbibe* (the magazine) is a monthly publication full of "liquid culture," which deliciously equals articles about drinks, drinking spots, drinking ingredients, and drinkers, as well as lush photography, commentary, and good cheer. There's also an *Imbibe* website (www.imbibemagazine.com), which is where I found this winter weather beater.

½ OUNCE HOT WATER (SEE A NOTE)

¾ TEASPOON CLOVER HONEY

1 OUNCE ELISIR M.P. ROUX

LEMON SLICE, FOR GARNISH

1. Add the hot water to a small mug. Add the honey, and stir to combine.

2. Add the Elisir M.P. Roux to the mug, and stir briefly. Garnish with the lemon slice.

A NOTE: You want your water hot in this fashionable number, but not rapidly boiling—burnt tongues are never stylish.

A SECOND NOTE: For more on Elisir M.P. Roux, see page 65.

LUMINOUS ANGEL

I s she an indicator of destiny, of what the fates might have in store, of the glow of the future? Like a liquid version of the fortune cookie, or the midway's mechanized turbaned soothsayer who delivers what is to come on a small white piece of paper when the right amount of spare change is deposited, does the Luminous Angel deliver words of providence and chance through the voice of anyone consuming her melodious mix? Perhaps not always (though who knows, really, what the fates have in store?), but one future event can be predicted by the Luminous Angel: Make it properly, and you'll serve a drink that will convince pals you have the ability to control their destinies—by making them a second round, that is.

ICE CUBES

2 OUNCES COGNAC

½ OUNCE ELISIR M.P. ROUX

½ OUNCE FRESHLY SQUEEZED ORANGE JUICE

2 DASHES SCRAPPY'S CARDAMOM BITTERS

1. Fill a cocktail shaker halfway full with ice cubes. Add the Cognac, Elisir M.P. Roux, orange juice, and bitters. Shake well.

2. Strain into a cocktail glass and let the glowing begin.

A NOTE: Scrappy's bitters (and tinctures and syrups) are made with care and dedication in Seattle. If your local liquor store doesn't yet have them, see if you can get them to order some. Otherwise, try online at a place like Cocktail Kingdom (www.cocktailkingdom.com).

"And why is my head so heavy? Is it the cognac, or all this being so queer? Anyway, I fancy I've done nothing unsuitable so far."

—LEO TOLSTOY, *ANNA KARENINA*, 1877

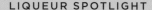

St-Germain

Released in 2007, St-Germain elderflower liqueur has become widely popular in a short amount of time, and it is now found on bar shelves from Portland, Maine, to Portland, Oregon, and many, many places in between. It's used in a wide range of cocktails (such as the Elderthorn on page 60 and the Rive Gauche Rickey on page 70) and highballs, or served on its own with a little lemon and ice. With a subtle and delicate range of flavors, St-Germain comes across the palate with a floral overview backed by hints of citrus, pear, and tropical fruits. The key is that it's made from elderflowers hand-picked (as the legend tells us) once a year in the dwindling days of spring, which is when they're at the peak of their ripeness; and they're picked by groups of French bicyclists, riding bicycles that have baskets created specifically to cradle and not bruise the blossoms. With that care in preparation, it's no wonder that St-Germain has bloomed into such a favorite.

MEXICAN BOUQUET

The modern landscape of creative cocktail writers, cocktail makers, and cocktail consumers is varied, bright, and blooming, much like a bouquet of fresh, boozy flowers. One of those blooms happens to be Meaghan Dorman, the creator of this particular Mexican Bouquet. Meaghan's not only a dandy freelance drinks-and-spirits writer for publications like *Penthouse* magazine, but she also writes the packed-with-boozy-goodness blog Spirit Me Away (www.spiritmeaway.com) and is as of right this very minute the head bartender at the speakeasy-licious Raines Law Room, a New York City spot with a Renaissance romance vibe and a "bar without a bar" layout. Stop on by the next time you hit the big city and order up your very own bouquet.

ICE CUBES

1 TEASPOON MYMOUNÉ ROSE SYRUP

¾ OUNCE ST-GERMAIN ELDERFLOWER LIQUEUR

¾ OUNCE FRESHLY SQUEEZED LEMON JUICE

2 OUNCES WHITE TEQUILA

LEMON ZEST, FOR GARNISH

1. Fill a cocktail shaker halfway full with ice cubes. Add the rose syrup, St-Germain, lemon juice, and tequila. Shake in a blooming fashion.

2. Strain into a cocktail glass (chilled if you're not actually in a Mexican desert). Garnish with the lemon zest.

A NOTE: Meaghan says, "I prefer to use Mymouné brand rose syrup, which is natural and delicious. It's found in a lot of natural foods and ethnic shops." Follow her advice is what I say.

RIVE GAUCHE RICKEY

T he Rickey is beloved for its ability to rise to great refreshing heights, making it a reliable favorite for taking the edge off of sweaty summer days and nights for well over a hundred years. It seems a Civil War veteran from the proud state of Missouri—an honorary colonel, a lobbyist with an especially silver tongue, and a self-taught biochemist—developed this basic but graceful and thirst-quenching drink, which in its most recognized version contains ice, lime juice, gin, and soda. His name: Joe Rickey. The Rickey's connection to our capital city has led to this darn appealing updating of the classic by Chantal Tseng of D.C.'s Tabard Inn (www.tabardinn.com). It may have sparkling wine instead of club soda, and the addition of the St-Germain elderflower liqueur, but you should still feel good about serving it at your next Civil War reenactment or any party where the dress is strictly late 1800s.

½ OUNCE FRESHLY
SQUEEZED LIME JUICE
(KEEP HALF OF A LIME
SHELL AFTER SQUEEZING)

CRACKED ICE

1¼ OUNCES GIN

¾ OUNCE ST-GERMAIN
ELDERFLOWER LIQUEUR

DASH OF ABSINTHE

4½ OUNCES CHILLED BRUT
SPARKLING WINE

LAVENDER SPRIG,
FOR GARNISH

1. Add the lime shell to a Collins glass, and then fill the glass with cracked ice.

2. Add the lime juice, gin, St-Germain, and absinthe. Stir briefly.

3. Fill the glass with the sparkling wine, and stir again briefly. Garnish with the lavender sprig.

A NOTE: Chantal suggests Aviation for the gin and Charles de Fère Blanc de Blancs for the sparkling wine. These are the kinds of choices that get you elected to office, people, so pay attention.

"Morning was hot and slightly sour in Big Dan Malloy's mouth. He lay on his back for long minutes listening to the intimate feminine splashing in the bathroom, wondering why he ever combined Champagne and Lobster Thermidor."

—DAY KEENE, *NAKED FURY*, 1952

ROLAND GARROS

This flowery-but-strong cocktail is for serving after the neighborhood's local pro-am tennis tournament (or even just "am"), when the mixed doubles teams are pairing off for a little post-tourney romancing. As it does boast that whiff of a kick, it's probably not good for serving before the matches have begun, even though that's when everyone is Love-Love. The name, bouncing off that of the French Open (which itself was named for a famous aviator who flew the first nonstop flight over the Mediterranean), is in honor of the key ingredient, Elisir M.P. Roux, a French apéritif containing hand-selected herbs such as marjoram, hyssop, garden balsam, wild angelica, and more.

ICE CUBES

1 OUNCE COGNAC

¾ OUNCE ELISIR M.P. ROUX

½ OUNCE GRAND MARNIER

¼ OUNCE FRESHLY
SQUEEZED LEMON JUICE

ORANGE SLICE,
FOR GARNISH

1. Fill a cocktail shaker halfway full with ice cubes. Add the Cognac, Elisir M.P. Roux, Grand Marnier, and lemon juice. Shake well.

2. Strain into a cocktail glass, and garnish with the orange slice. Drink while wearing tennis togs.

SEASON FINALE

Is a poor end of the season (or—intake of breath 'cause it's even worse—a poor end of the final season) for a grand TV show even worse than a show that wasn't any good to begin with? And, for that matter, to stretch the point, is a poorly made great drink even worse than a drink that was never going to be more than alley water? Here's a way out of both dilemmas: Make the following drink whenever you're watching the coup de grâce of a particularly prized program and you can avoid both, because the drink is delish and, even if the actual finale episode isn't another *Dallas*, Episode 54 (sometimes known as the "Who Shot J.R.?" season finale), you'll be having too much fun to let it bother you for long.

ICE CUBES

2 OUNCES COGNAC

1 OUNCE DAMIANA

½ OUNCE FRESH PINEAPPLE
JUICE

1. Fill a cocktail shaker halfway full with ice cubes. Add the Cognac, Damiana, and pineapple juice. Shake well.

2. Strain into a cocktail glass.

SWEET PEA

A drink for the gardener in your life, or to swill when chilling in the garden, or to accompany a meal made to eat while watching a gardening show on TV, the Sweet Pea is adapted from Paul Abercrombie's healthy (and hopping) book *Organic, Shaken and Stirred* (for more from this tasty topical tome, see page 182). You can find organic versions of all the ingredients below except for the elderflower liqueur. Please don't skip the organics, or Paul may hunt you down and pluck the drink away from you like he'd pluck a rotten pea off the vine. And no one wants that kind of trouble.

9 FRESH ENGLISH PEAS

10 SEEDLESS GREEN GRAPES

1 TEASPOON BROWN SUGAR

ICE CUBES

1 OUNCE GIN

½ OUNCE ELDERFLOWER LIQUEUR (SEE A NOTE)

¼ OUNCE FRESHLY SQUEEZED LIME JUICE

1. Add 6 of the peas, all of the grapes, and the brown sugar to a cocktail shaker. Using a muddler or wooden spoon, muddle well.

2. Fill the shaker halfway full with ice cubes, and add the gin, elderflower liqueur, and lime juice. Shake well.

3. Strain through a fine-mesh strainer into a cocktail glass (chilled if possible). Garnish with the remaining 3 peas.

A NOTE: If possible, I suggest Pür Spirits' Pür-Likör Blossom elderflower liqueur (check www.purspirits.com to learn more) in this mix.

TEMPORARY GETAWAY

T here are bad days and then there are bad days. The former are manageable. The latter, well, they're a different story. They're days when your manager again does little all day and then refuses to trumpet your name loudly when presenting the work you slaved over, days when the bus driver pulls away with an evil sneer as you sprint to the bus stop two seconds too late, days when the slice of pizza you brought for lunch gets squished to a ball of dough in your backpack. I'm not a doctor or pharmacist, but my prescription for overcoming the bad days? Take a Temporary Getaway (or maybe more than one) and watch the day slip into the past—and look to the future, which is bound to be a whole lot brighter.

3 APPLE SLICES

½ OUNCE FRESHLY SQUEEZED ORANGE JUICE

½ OUNCE FRESHLY SQUEEZED LEMON JUICE

ICE CUBES

1 OUNCE ST-GERMAIN ELDERFLOWER LIQUEUR

4 OUNCES CHILLED BRUT SEKT

1. Place 2 of the apple slices, the orange juice, and the lemon juice in a cocktail shaker or mixing glass. Using a muddler or wooden spoon, muddle well.

2. Fill the cocktail shaker halfway full with ice cubes. Add the St-Germain and, using a long spoon, stir well.

3. Pour the chilled Sekt into the cocktail shaker. Using that same reliable spoon, stir briefly, being sure to bring up the fruit on the bottom when stirring.

4. Strain into a flute glass or cocktail glass (in this instance I like the way the latter breathes, but a flute's more traditional). Garnish with the remaining apple slice, putting a little notch in it if needed for rim balancing.

A NOTE: Sekt is a German sparkling wine that tends to be a tiny bit sweet. If you can't track down a bottle, try the Italian sparkling wine Prosecco—at least you'll be staying within Europe on your getaway.

TIPPERARY

I t's a long way to Tipperary, says the World War I song. There have been many versions of a Tipperary cocktail, including a not-bad one with gin, dry vermouth, grenadine, orange juice, and mint. But other Tipperary cocktails are missing one crucial component: They aren't Irish. How can you have a non-Irish Tipperary? You can't, in my mind. That's why I choose this version, highlighted by Irish whiskey combined with sweet Italian vermouth and that flower of French liqueurs, Chartreuse.

CRACKED ICE

1 OUNCE IRISH WHISKEY

1 OUNCE YELLOW CHARTREUSE

1 OUNCE SWEET VERMOUTH

1. Fill a cocktail shaker halfway full with cracked ice. Add the Irish whiskey, Chartreuse, and sweet vermouth. Stir well.

2. Strain into a cocktail glass, and garnish with a small Irish flag.

TRIOMPHE COCKTAIL

T here are those devoted to investigating classic cocktail books and writing about those drinks in newer books, and there are those who have blogs where they touch on classic drinks, and then there is Erik Ellestad of the Underhill-Lounge blog (www.underhill-lounge.flannestad.com). Erik has delved deeply into the classic *Savoy Cocktail Book* by Harry Craddock in an "ongoing effort to make all of its cocktails." Then there's the fact that Erik also writes about other cocktails, and also tends bar at San Francisco's fantabulous Heaven's Dog restaurant and lounge and during Savoy nights at the Alembic. With all that said, the Triomphe Cocktail is one of his own creations and is, as he says, "a variation on the Savoy cocktail, Champs-Élysées, made with vodka instead of brandy. And to be honest, I kind of prefer it to the original brandy version."

ICE CUBES

1½ OUNCES VODKA

¾ OUNCE FRESHLY SQUEEZED LEMON JUICE

½ OUNCE YELLOW CHARTREUSE

½ OUNCE SIMPLE SYRUP (PAGE 12)

LEMON TWIST, FOR GARNISH

1. Fill a cocktail shaker halfway full with ice cubes. Add the vodka, lemon juice, Chartreuse, and simple syrup. Shake well.

2. Strain into a cocktail glass. Twist the twist over the glass and add it to the drink.

VIOLET FIZZ

Not everyone can be the main character in a comic strip. For every Spider-Man, there has to be at least one Mary Jane, and for every Wonder Woman a Steve Trevor, not to mention those characters even farther from the spotlight, like Otto the dog in *Beetle Bailey*. Without these characters, though, the strips and comic books (and, to stroll down the literary lane, the stories, novels, and narrative poems) would be much less interesting places to visit. Because of that, I'm saying we should raise a Violet Fizz in honor of each and every one of these less-than-major characters, on June 17 and January 28, two days that were used as birthdays (in comics, sometimes birthdays change) for Violet Gray, the underutilized dark-haired girl in *Peanuts*. Here's to you, supporting characters, here's to you.

ICE CUBES

2 OUNCES GIN

½ OUNCE CRÈME DE VIOLETTE

¼ OUNCE FRESHLY SQUEEZED LEMON JUICE

¼ OUNCE SIMPLE SYRUP (PAGE 12)

CHILLED CLUB SODA

1. Fill a cocktail shaker halfway full with ice cubes. Add the gin, crème de violette, lemon juice, and simple syrup. Shake extrawell.

2. Fill a highball glass three-quarters full with ice cubes. Strain the mixture into the glass.

3. Fill the glass with chilled club soda, stir well, and drink quickly, before those bubbles have a chance to fade.

A NOTE: Have a reliable soda siphon? Use it here instead the club soda. And to make it even prettier, garnish with a fresh violet.

A SECOND NOTE: Looking for another Fizz? See the Springtime Fizz on page 113.

GRADUATE, PAGE 95

CHAPTER 4

IF YOU'RE

FEELING

FRUITY

....

L ife is like an orchard—if you choose the right path, that is. No worry about Frostian less- or more-traveled paths here; all that's needed is to follow some straightforward advice and directions. First, spend some time with the lofty liquid gentleman in the corner, the one with the many medals, that's right, the Admiral, who is dancing with the fluid Anna Lovely—and, at a second glance, I think their whirling around means that they're dancing and drinking the Ballets Russes. Don't interrupt them, but don't skip out, either.

Now, the military man alluded to is going to direct traffic toward some Blood and Sand, but hopefully it's teamed up with at least one Desert Healer to keep stuff cool, and don't forget for a minute to bring along a Corkscrew or two in case it's necessary (and I think it is). Of course, this pouring and traveling along rainbow roads may end with spending some time in La Jolia, which isn't a penitentiary—indeed, it's where doing time is a dream. Once passing back outside, spend some time taking dips and sipping up and traveling alongside the Allegheny, being sure to get caught enjoying The Reef for at least time enough to make memories, and then ring the pomegranate-y Gong that is on the table.

That delicious noise is a cue to begin a serious escape into International Relations. Now, maybe spending time traveling alone along the path is disheartening, so I suggest pairing with the Bourbon Belle, and then (because no one should restrict themselves too much along the road) the Rebecca and its raspberries. Such a large amount of cooing while traipsing here and there, from one liqueur shelf to another, might start to make heads spin, might even demand a new guide to ensure that the orchard doesn't slip out of view or that a wrong turn into rottenness ensues. With this in mind, go no further without George's Special pathfinder.

The path can be long and full of potentially thirsty moments, as well as moments where the trees themselves seem to be alive with their fruits talking, and the bushes seem to twinkle with multicolored juicy lights, and you may question your sanity, but really, you should experience the Lunacy when in this chapter. However, if it becomes too much, then don't stop, experience Persephone's Exiliar, and soon you'll be skipping to the Silver Jubilee under a Shooting Star.

At this point, you may want to Graduate, and that's okay, as long as it doesn't imply that the journey's end is near—because there are still more fruit liqueur liquid delights worth trying (not to mention places like Xanthia and personages as renowned as the Singapore Sling). The trip doesn't stop when going through the pages and drinks contained within this orchard, because these are paths—and drinks—you'll want to explore again and again.

ADMIRAL

A hoy—want to be the one looked up to as being in charge on your shindig ship? Your gala gondola? Your bash boat? Then let me suggest three things: Serve up a great number of glasses of this cheery cherry and gin coalescence to guests, use freshly squeezed lime juice to ensure tip-top flavor, and finally, don't even have the party if you aren't going to wear an admiral's hat. Without the hat, it's another run-of-the-deck occasion, and you're just another guy or gal shaking drinks. Become the admiral while shaking the Admiral, and the salutes will be aimed at you.

. . . .

CRACKED ICE

2 OUNCES GIN

½ OUNCE CHERRY HEERING

½ OUNCE FRESHLY SQUEEZED LIME JUICE

1. Fill a cocktail shaker halfway full with cracked ice. Add the gin, cherry Heering, and lime juice. Shake well.

2. Strain into a cocktail glass. Return the salutes. Drink.

A NOTE: Feel this needs a garnish to be five-star? In that case, I suggest a cherry–lime slice combo.

ALLEGHENY

The cocktail is quite the coming together of a host of intriguing and seemingly distant elements. This makes a certain sense, if you consider that the Lenape tribe living along the Allegheny River called their land *Alligewinenk*, which means "a land into which they came from distant parts," at least according to one missionary in the late 1700s. Holding this thought in mind, you should serve up the shaken Allegheny when dressing up in traditional tribal or missionary garb. Or, if that seems too labor intensive, serve it whenever you have a picnic beside a river.

. . . .

ICE CUBES

1½ OUNCES BOURBON

1 OUNCE DRY VERMOUTH

½ OUNCE BLACKBERRY BRANDY

½ OUNCE FRESHLY SQUEEZED LEMON JUICE

DASH OF ANGOSTURA BITTERS

LEMON TWIST, FOR GARNISH

1. Fill a cocktail shaker halfway full with ice cubes. Add the whole Allegheny (isn't that a kick to say?) to the cocktail shaker. Shake well.

2. Strain into a cocktail glass and garnish with the lemon twist.

A NOTE: Be sure to get blackberry brandy made with real blackberries (and not some sort of chemical blackberry flavoring). If you can't find it, one option is to make your own. I would suggest adding 1 pound fresh blackberries and the peel of 1 lemon to a large glass container with a tight-fitting lid. Muddle well, and then add 1 pint brandy and place in a cool, dry spot away from sunlight. Let sit for 2 weeks. Add 3 cups Simple Syrup (page 12), stir, and reseal. Let sit for 2 more weeks. Strain the liqueur through a double layer of cheesecloth into a pitcher or other vessel. Strain again through two new sheets of cheesecloth into one large bottle or several smaller bottles or jars.

ALQUIMISTA

The dreary room is barely lit by a candle in the corner, and all sorts of tarnished apparatus lie like lifeless dolls on tables and chairs. In the corner, draped in a black cloak that may have been made from the wings of bats, mutters a crooked man (or is it a woman?), assembling a potion from ingredients rarely found in nature. The toenail of a death-defying dog? The legendary fruit of the açaí? And what is the figure mumbling about . . . changing lead to gold? Taking over the world? Wait, it's turning our way!

And then you realize that person is merely flipping the light switch, and suddenly the dreariness is cheerful, the apparatus a shiny cocktail shaker, and the shady figure is balancing a tray on which are placed glasses full of this cocktail, which is made by a transformation of açaí spirit, pear simple syrup, lemon juice, and pomegranate seeds.

ICE CUBES

2 OUNCES VEEV AÇAÍ

1 OUNCE PEAR SIMPLE SYRUP (SEE A SECOND NOTE)

½ OUNCE FRESHLY SQUEEZED LEMON JUICE

4 OR 5 POMEGRANATE SEEDS, FOR GARNISH

1. Fill a cocktail shaker halfway full with ice cubes. Add the VeeV, pear simple syrup, and lemon juice. Shake well.

2. Place the pomegranate seeds into a cocktail glass, and strain the mixture into it.

A NOTE: VeeV Açaí is the first açaí-based liqueur, with açaí being not only an antioxidant-packed superfruit (according to some, that is) but also the national fruit of Brazil.

A SECOND NOTE: To make the pear simple syrup, add 2 cups peeled chopped pear to the saucepan when making the simple syrup recipe on page 12. Be sure to strain the syrup through a fine-mesh strainer (twice, if needed) to remove the pear pieces before bottling.

ANNA LOVELY

Sadly, I have no idea who Anna is, though if she's as lovely as this well-mixed number, she's lovely indeed. I discovered this attractive gin-based cocktail in the gin-tastic book by Gaz (aka Gary) Regan, *The Bartender's Gin Compendium (Xlibris, 2009)*. If you're a gin lover who's looking to learn more about gin, searching for a whole host of recipes using gin, or you just enjoy reading about spirits and cocktails, then this is the book for you. Gaz is a charmer and one of the most knowledgeable cocktailians around (learn more at www. ardentspirits.com). This recipe is adapted from one by Timothy Lacey, who can be found (according to this fine book) in the Drawing Room at Le Passage in Chicago.

½ **OUNCE GREEN CHARTREUSE**

ICE CUBES

2 OUNCES DISTILLER'S GIN NO. 6

1 OUNCE CRÈME DE PÊCHE

½ **OUNCE FRESHLY SQUEEZED LEMON JUICE**

1 OUNCE SIMPLE SYRUP (PAGE 12)

1. Add the Chartreuse to a highball glass. Rinse it around the inside of the glass, so each inch is coated, and then pour out any excess.

2. Fill the glass three-quarters full with ice cubes. Add the remaining ingredients and stir.

A NOTE: Distiller's Gin No. 6 is crafted with care by the North Shore Distillery. It's available throughout the Midwest and in some other spots (check online if you can't easily find it). If you can't manage to get a bottle, you can sub in another dry gin, but it might make Anna a smidge less lovely.

"Saturday night at the Canterbury was about to take its toll. He had not planned his night of gin and song. A visit to the Canterbury was not indelibly inspired in his social diary, like evenings at the dome and the Theatre Royal."

—PETER LOVESEY, *MAD HATTER'S HOLIDAY*, 1973

Chambord

Not only a favorite in festive cocktails such as the Rebecca (page 106) for all occasions, from retirements to birthdays to coronations, Chambord's rich, luxurious raspberry-ness is also a key ingredient in desserts and as a dessert itself when sipped without accompaniment. Instantly noticeable on the liqueur shelf thanks to its round, regal, and crown-adorned bottle, Chambord (or, to say it fully, Chambord Liqueur Royale de France) has very regal connections. As legend says, it's a descendant of a liqueur that was crafted in the late seventeenth century in France's Loire Valley, a liqueur that was toasted for its good taste by Louis XIV while he was visiting the Château de Chambord (a famous spot of French Renaissance architecture he helped restore). He had good reason for his admiration of that pre-Chambord, judging by its descendant, as it's made from a delicious combination of black raspberries and blackberries infused in a spirit; then a second layer of spirits is added; and then after the proper amount of time the spirits are drawn off, at which time the fruit is carefully crushed (hey, being regal takes this once in a while), with the juices saved to be combined with Cognac and an assortment of citrus peels, herbs, spices, vanilla, and honey.

APRÈS COUP

This is a public service announcement: The Après Coup is not for the middle of a party. It's a drink for you and your other party-thrower (or throwers, if you live with many) to have after the gamboling guests have gone back to their own houses and the music has been dialed down to a more manageable volume. This one's for the post-party calm, where it's demanded that one sit on the couch for a solo drink before starting to either clean up or call it quits and hit the sack. For those moments, the Après Coup is the best possible liquid companion.

CRACKED ICE

1½ OUNCES GIN

1 OUNCE CHAMBORD

¼ OUNCE MARASCHINO LIQUEUR

DASH OF PEYCHAUD'S BITTERS

1. Fill a cocktail shaker or mixing glass three-quarters full with cracked ice. Add the gin, Chambord, maraschino liqueur, and bitters. Stir well.

2. Strain into a cocktail glass (or, if there aren't any clean ones left, grab any old glass that isn't tattooed with lipstick or halfway full with an old drink).

" 'You could,' retorted the old lady, 'if you looked after your stomach and your morals. Here comes Frank Bellingham—looking for a drink, no doubt. Young people today seem to be positively pickled in gin.' "

—DOROTHY L. SAYERS, *THE QUEEN'S SQUARE*, 1932

APRICOT SOUR

The "sour" is one of the basic cocktails—I've even read that all cocktails are either, at root, a "sour" or a "bitter." As David Embury put it in his classic tome *The Fine Art of Mixing Drinks* (Doubleday, 1948), "a Sour is simply a combination of citrus juice (lemon or lime or both), sugar or other sweetening, and liquor." Of course, various combinations and percentages come into play, as well as flourishes, and garnishes, and this, and the other, and then it's fruit salad time.

In the Apricot Sour, you could use apricot brandy and a have a fine drink. But I enjoy making it with apricot liqueur, with one caveat: Get real apricot liqueur, not apricot schnapps or some other overly sweet concoction. Like maraschino liqueur, real apricot liqueur is dry and flavorful but not super-sweet. You may find that you'll want to drop the smooch of simple syrup here—you may also find you want to add a cherry. I won't warn you against either, because I'm unfussy that way.

ICE CUBES

2 OUNCES APRICOT LIQUEUR

½ OUNCE FRESHLY SQUEEZED LEMON JUICE

¼ OUNCE SIMPLE SYRUP (PAGE 12), OPTIONAL

1. Fill a cocktail shaker halfway full with ice cubes. Add the apricot liqueur, lemon juice, and simple syrup, if using. Shake well.

2. Strain into a cocktail glass.

BALLETS RUSSES

The Ballets Russes was a Russian ballet troupe in the early part of the twentieth century that was a phenomenon, altering the course of performance dancing. Does this mean that you, when drinking the mixture of the same name, will want to begin dancing in balletic style, swooping across the room while wearing a tutu and/or tight pants and perhaps shoes with long laces? Well, sure. But isn't that what a good drink is supposed to make you want to do?

ICE CUBES

2 OUNCES VODKA

1 OUNCE CRÈME DE CASSIS

½ OUNCE FRESHLY SQUEEZED LIME JUICE

1. Fill a cocktail shaker halfway full with ice cubes. Add the vodka, crème de cassis, and lime juice. Shake well.

2. Strain into a cocktail glass. Garnish with a small piece of tulle.

Cherry Heering

One of the world's most famous cherry liqueurs—or cherry brandies, as it's based on brandy, though not as dry as other cherry brandies like kirsch (page 101)—Heering cherry liqueur started its trail of world conquest in Denmark in 1818. The road at first was slow, until British travelers got hooked on it in the early nineteenth century. As these intrepid English went from globe-corner to globe-corner, they brought along the Heering to ensure that no matter where their travels (or conquests) took them, they'd have a reliable tipple to sip as the sun went down—either on its own or in an increasing number of cocktails (the Singapore Sling, on page 112, may be the most well known). The taste that encouraged this bottle-carrying comes specifically from Danish Stevns cherries, which are full-bodied and dark. They're crushed (and when I say "they" I mean the whole cherry kit and kaboodle: fruit, pits, and pulp), placed in oak casks along with a neutral base spirit, and left to age with a few secret spices (as memorable liqueurs are known to have) for three years or more. After which time it's whisked around the world. It could be this globalizing that leads to Heering cherry liqueur being known by a number of names (some things get changed in translation), including cherry Heering and Peter Heering.

◄BLACK FOG

I n the beginning, it's only a shadow of a shadow on the evening's horizon. Then it creeps closer and closer, and now it's a dark mass, like a swarm of bees wearing murky purple-tinted outfits, and now it's closer still, just down at the bar, and it's rolling toward you, closer, approaching like night . . . but with bubbles. This Black Fog may not be on a horror movie marquee, but it sure goes down more smoothly than many horror movies. Don't let the conceivably odd pairing scare you.

ONE 14.9-OUNCE CAN GUINNESS STOUT

1 OUNCE FRAMBOISE

1 OR 2 MINT LEAVES, FOR GARNISH

1. Fill a pint glass almost to the top with the Guinness.

2. Slowly pour the framboise into the glass, swirling it as you pour. Garnish with a mint leaf (or two, if you're feeling it).

A VARIATION: Sometimes this is mixed using the French black raspberry liqueur Chambord, but I like the slightly stronger framboise (which is usually made from regular red raspberries and has a bit more kick).

BLOOD AND SAND

N ot only a ferocious choice for the signature mix at a Halloween wing-ding, a terrific pick for the headlining combo at a horror film marathon, or an awfully swell selection for a bloody (fake blood, that is) beach party, the Blood and Sand is also a pretty peppy option for a Sunday brunch. Maybe mumbling the name when asked is safest, but the fresh orange juice mingling with the cherry brandy, rich vermouth, and Scotch will dispel any questions once the sips start.

ICE CUBES

¾ OUNCE SCOTCH

¾ OUNCE CHERRY HEERING

¾ OUNCE SWEET VERMOUTH

¾ OUNCE FRESHLY SQUEEZED ORANGE JUICE

ORANGE SLICE, FOR GARNISH

1. Fill a cocktail shaker halfway full with ice cubes. Add the Scotch, cherry Heering, vermouth, and orange juice. Shake well.

2. Strain into a cocktail glass. Garnish with the orange slice.

BOURBON BELLE

A classically minded waltzer that takes advantage of our modern ability to use a wider range of more readily available ingredients (in this case, Mathilde Pêches liqueur, which is concocted from vine-ripened peaches according to a hundred-year-old recipe), the Bourbon Belle is also a reflection of its creator, who carries the same name in her role as a member of Boston's chapter of LUPEC (Ladies United for the Preservation of the Endangered Cocktail). You can find more out about LUPEC Boston at their lovely, well-written, and charming blog (www.lupecboston.com), and if you enjoy the spirits and the dancing, I suggest you visit them without waiting any longer than it takes you to make this drink.

CRACKED ICE

2 OUNCES BOURBON

½ OUNCE SWEET VERMOUTH

½ OUNCE MATHILDE PÊCHES

3 DASHES ANGOSTURA BITTERS

BRANDIED CHERRY, FOR GARNISH

1. Fill a cocktail shaker or mixing glass halfway full with cracked ice. Add the bourbon, sweet vermouth, Mathilde Pêches, and bitters. Stir well.

2. Strain into a cocktail glass and garnish with the cherry.

A NOTE: Can't find a brandied cherry? Find some fresh sweet cherries, and soak them in brandy for at least 1 week before using (be sure to warn your guests if you don't pit them first).

A SECOND NOTE: Bourbon Belle herself suggests using Buffalo Trace for the bourbon and Cinzano for the vermouth. If it were me, I'd sure follow her advice.

CASSISCO

I would never willingly encourage a person to drink and fence. (How about to drink while putting up a fence? Sure. Indeed, I would say never build a fence without a drink to cool off. This drink would work well, now that I dwell on it a minute, in this barrier-building situation. But let's get back to the main event.) With a sharp foil, saber, or épée in hand, a drink isn't the safest choice. Once the weapons are set aside, as well as the mask, jacket, and glove, and not to mention the aggressive tendencies, then by all means, take up a Cassisco and toast the match. It'll help you cool off and refocus on mellower pursuits.

. . . .

ICE CUBES

1½ OUNCES CRÈME DE CASSIS

1½ OUNCES TRIPLE SEC

CHILLED CLUB SODA

1. Fill a highball glass three-quarters full with ice cubes. Add the crème de cassis and triple sec. Stir once westerly and once easterly.

2. Fill the glass almost to the brim with the club soda. Stir again, four times each way. *En garde!*

CORKSCREW

A s a corkscrew is the opening device for a bottle of wine, this light charmer can be "a good gateway cocktail for those who find some of the more aromatic cocktails a bit much." At least that's what's said by happy cocktail scribe Jay Hepburn on his delightful (and delightfully boozy) website Oh Gosh! (which you'll find at perhaps the best URL of all: www.ohgo.sh). Oh Gosh! covers Jay discovering both classics and newer mixes, as well as talking about techniques he picks up along the way, with an international flair (he's in London). When making this recipe, Jay uses Havana Club Añejo Especial, a slightly more aged rum, and he suggests straining the drink through a fine-mesh strainer—I'd follow his lead.

. . . .

ICE CUBES

1½ OUNCES WHITE RUM

½ OUNCE DRY VERMOUTH

½ OUNCE CRÈME DE PÊCHE

¼ OUNCE FRESHLY SQUEEZED LIME JUICE

LIME SLICE, FOR GARNISH

1. Fill a cocktail shaker halfway full with ice cubes. Add the rum, dry vermouth, crème de pêche, and lime juice. Shake well.

2. Strain the mixture into a cocktail glass. Garnish with the lime slice.

DESERT HEALER

I t might be the laying on of hands and it might be a long hot bath and it might be a more serious healing, but even everyday folks like us (not to mention pop stars, politicians, and powerful industrialists) need a little healing now and again. For those days when just a glass or two of medicinal aid is all that's needed, and you're not actually traveling past the front door, I'd like to prescribe (note: I'm not an actual medical professional) a Desert Healer. Or two. It's much cheaper (mentally and financially) than searching the red hills for a therapeutic guru, and more enjoyable too. And after that second one, you'll feel much better (especially if you combine this with one of the above remedies—taking a bath, that is—and a close personal friend). Maybe I should become a medical professional after all.

ICE CUBES

2 OUNCES GIN

1 OUNCE CHERRY HEERING

1½ OUNCES FRESHLY SQUEEZED ORANGE JUICE

CHILLED GINGER BEER

1. Fill a cocktail shaker halfway full with ice cubes. Add the gin, cherry Heering, and orange juice. Shake well.

2. Fill a goblet halfway full with ice cubes. Strain the mixture over the ice. Top with ginger beer, and stir briefly.

A NOTE: I've also seen this called a Desert Cooler, but I don't think it'll deliver any miracle cures with that name. I've also seen it made with less gin and more OJ, but how would that heal anyone?

A SECOND NOTE: You could, if you're goblet-less, serve this in a highball glass.

FLASH

Even though this drink contains only four ingredients, the potentially disparate style of their personalities puts it into the kitchen-sink category. The name may say "scarlet speedster," but the omnivorous nature of this imbibable means that more than four may actually slow you down. With that in mind, keep the rounds to equal or less than the number of the powerhouses that make the sum total here: Cointreau, kirsch, Bénédictine, and maraschino. And have that red tracksuit on hand when starting to stir this up.

. . . .

CRACKED ICE

¾ OUNCE COINTREAU

¾ OUNCE KIRSCH

¾ OUNCE BÉNÉDICTINE

¾ OUNCE MARASCHINO LIQUEUR

FRESHLY GRATED NUTMEG, FOR GARNISH (OPTIONAL)

1. Fill a cocktail shaker or mixing glass halfway full with cracked ice. Add the Cointreau, kirsch, Bénédictine, and maraschino liqueur. Stir well.

2. Strain into a cocktail glass. Garnish with a little grated nutmeg if you feel it will color the flames.

GEORGE'S SPECIAL

Here's something I learned from George's Special, a fact about the world (at least the world of boozes) that never fails, a little insight that at first might not seem like much in significance when set up alongside larger, more important facts. But I like it, and you might too. Here it is: gin, apricot brandy, and lemon juice are a darn yummy trio. And hey, while the knowledge of that trio's power isn't the kind of fact that changes the course of history, it sure might change the course of your next hip hoedown, and that matters too.

. . . .

ICE CUBES

2 OUNCES GIN

1 OUNCE APRICOT BRANDY

1 OUNCE FRESHLY SQUEEZED LEMON JUICE

MARASCHINO CHERRY, FOR GARNISH

1. Fill a cocktail shaker halfway full with ice cubes. Add the gin, brandy, and lemon juice. Shake well.

2. Strain into a cocktail glass. Garnish with the cherry.

A NOTE: This is straight out of *The Speakeasies of 1932*, a worthy volume packed with spotlights on 36 Prohibition-era favorites in New York City, with descriptions by Al Hirschfeld and screenwriter Gordon Kahn.

GONG

Whether you go in for tiger gongs, wind gongs, opera gongs, nipple gongs, or more esoteric members of the gong family, I insist that before ringing the gong to start a ceremony, concert, meditation, railway journey, or film (or to summon the butler), that you take a step back in order to shake up, strain, and stir this Asian-influenced highball, drink deep, and then start swinging. That way, you'll be drinking the Gong and playing the gong all at once. Then the universe will be back in order. (Who knew a drink could have such influence?)

....

ICE CUBES

2½ OUNCES SAKE

1½ OUNCES POMEGRANATE LIQUEUR

CHILLED GINGER ALE

ORANGE SLICE, FOR GARNISH

1. Fill a cocktail shaker halfway full with ice cubes. Add the sake and pomegranate liqueur. Shake well.

2. Fill a highball or comparable glass with ice cubes. Strain the sake-pomegranate mixture over the ice in the glass.

3. Top off the highball glass with ginger ale, filling it nearly to the top. Stir briefly, and garnish with the orange slice.

A NOTE: I think PAMA pomegranate liqueur makes a beautiful harmony with the other ingredients in this drink. It's made with pomegranate juice, vodka, and a smidge of tequila, and it has a deep ruby coloring backed by a rich berry taste.

GRADUATE

Ever get up really early because you have to rush to the airport to barely catch a flight (missing breakfast on the way), then be crammed in like tightly packed sardines on a plane that manages to fly through four hours of turbulence to stop in Philadelphia when you thought you were flying straight through to Boston, and then you're not allowed off the plane to actually browse the City of Brotherly Love, but only ensnared on the tarmac while rain keeps the wings at ground level for two hours, and then, *then*, when you finally do get back up in the air and make that flight to Boston, somehow your luggage gets lost even though you didn't switch planes, and then your B&B is closed and the gentleman you ring to get in has no idea what you're talking about, and it takes another hour while you sit on the porch at midnight waiting to see a bed or a bar . . . ? Ever had one of those days? Want to know how to make it all better? Once you've finally gotten to the fair Athens of America, find your way across the river into Cambridge, to Upstairs on the Square (www.upstairsonthesquare.com) and ask to see Augusto Lino, the amiable and knowledgeable bar manager. He'll make you the following drink, which he designed, and you'll be able to leave the madness behind—you could say you'll graduate from it.

. . . .

ICE CUBES

1 OUNCE CRÈME DE CASSIS

1 OUNCE CAMPARI

½ OUNCE FRESHLY SQUEEZED LEMON JUICE

CHILLED BRUT CHAMPAGNE OR SPARKLING WINE

1. Fill a cocktail shaker halfway full with ice cubes. Add the crème de cassis, Campari, and lemon juice. Shake well.

2. Strain into a flute glass, and top with the Champagne.

A NOTE: For history's sake, Lino says this drink is "a variation on a cocktail called the Theresa, which calls for equal parts lemon juice, Campari, and crème de cassis. We serve hundreds of these every spring during the week of Harvard Commencement. This cocktail gently introduces bitterness, a flavor that fits the description 'acquired taste'—hence the name, because if you like the drink, you've graduated from sweet cocktails."

INTERNATIONAL RELATIONS

H ere's a globally grand hypothesis for a glorious gala. Invite the gals and guys over for a costume party with a hitch: They have to show up dressed as someone famous from the area where each of the main ingredients of this intercontinental cocktail originates. The options are nearly endless, but for starters, how about Sherlock Holmes (played by either Jeremy Brett or Robert Downey, Jr.) for the British gin; Milwaukee Bucks basketball player Andrew Bogut (born in Australia of Croatian parents) for the slivovitz, of which Croatian Maraska is a nice variety; and armor-wearing Joan of Arc in honor of bitter French apéritif Amer Picon? As the fourth ingredient is orange juice, dressing as an orange would be okay as well. That would be quite a United Nations, all sipping the same drink. For a night, at least, we might even see one party's worth of world peace.

ICE CUBES

1½ OUNCES GIN (A DRY BRITISH VARIETY IS BEST)

½ OUNCE SLIVOVITZ

½ OUNCE AMER PICON

½ OUNCE FRESHLY SQUEEZED ORANGE JUICE

LEMON SLICE, FOR GARNISH

1. Fill a cocktail shaker halfway full with ice cubes. Add the gin, slivovitz, Amer Picon, and orange juice. Shake well.

2. Strain the mixture into a cocktail glass and garnish with the lemon slice. Toast in many languages.

A NOTE: Mostly produced in Eastern Europe and often called plum brandy (which makes sense, as the name is derived either from the Serbo-Croatian *šljiva* or the Czech *slíva*, both of which mean plum), slivovitz is a spirit distilled from plums and plum pits. Often consumed solo, it also adds a nice flavor and backbone to cocktails. It is usually a clear drink, but sometimes you may come across colored varieties, which are best avoided, as they likely contain an additive.

"I was going to mix the cocktails and have them ready, just before any of you turned up, when it struck me that I might invent a new one with a strain of slivovitz in it."

—G.B. STERN, "GEMINI," *THE POCKET BOOK OF MYSTERY STORIES*, 1941

KIRSCH RICKEY

The Rickey is one of the old families that have propped up bars and barflies for many a high time, and due to that pedigree and popularity (which has, to speak straight, waxed and waned over time), the recipe has gone through some permutations and has had many variations. But at its beautifully most basic, the Rickey is a spirit or liqueur, some freshly squeezed lime juice (always lime, unless your town is destitute of limes, in which case lemon could be used, but maybe call it an Ah-Rickey), and some awfully bubbly club soda. The most well known is the Gin Rickey, which, being dry, usually comes with a splash (¼ to ½ ounce) of simple syrup. But I enjoy a good liqueur-based Rickey, like this Kirsch Rickey, whose cherry-almond accents blend well with the lime and soda; perhaps especially on a June afternoon when summer is just starting to come on strong (if it's a little dry, add a touch of simple syrup as needed).

½ OUNCE FRESHLY SQUEEZED LIME JUICE

2 OUNCES KIRSCH

¼ TO ½ OUNCE SIMPLE SYRUP (PAGE 12), OPTIONAL

ICE CUBES

CHILLED CLUB SODA

1. Add the lime juice and kirsch (and simple syrup, if using) to a highball glass or comparably sized glass. Stir.

2. Add 2 or 3 large ice cubes or a few smaller cubes to the glass. Top it off with club soda. Stir again. Serve with a stirrer or straw.

VARIATIONS: There are other liqueurs that make mighty Rickeys, including apricot liqueur, maraschino liqueur, and sloe gin, and other base spirits that are also dandy, such as applejack and rum—though both the latter will benefit from that sweet touch mentioned above. See a modern take on the Rickey and a little more history on page 70 with the Rive Gauche Rickey.

"Here is another drink as to which confusion reigns among both authors and dispensers."

—DAVID A. EMBURY, *THE FINE ART OF MIXING DRINKS*, 1948

LADY GODZILLA

T he cocktail revolution, thankfully, is an international one, and through that internationalism it's possible to learn about ingredients that we might consider exotic but that in other cultures are revered and used daily. Of course, without people bringing us together, these ingredients and drinks would not make the trip around the world to be introduced to every lover of creative cocktails. Which is why we're lucky to have cocktail chroniclers like Yuri Kato (who is the publisher of www.cocktailtimes.com as well as a crackerjack cocktailer), whose *Japanese Cocktails: Mixed Drinks with Sake, Shochu, Whisky, and More* (Chronicle Books, 2010) opens up the world of enticing, aromatic, and creative Japanese drinks, techniques, styles, and ingredients. One such ingredient is umeshu, a Japanese liqueur made from ume fruit, a base spirit, and sugar, which is used in this very recipe from Yuri's indispensable book. Look for umeshu online if you can't find it in a nearby liquor store or Asian market.

4 OR 5 FRESH MINT LEAVES

¼ OUNCE UMESHU

ICE CUBES

1½ OUNCES WHITE TEQUILA

1 OUNCE MIDORI MELON LIQUEUR

¼ OUNCE FRESHLY SQUEEZED LEMON JUICE

FRESH MINT SPRIG, FOR GARNISH

1. Add the mint leaves and the umeshu to a cocktail shaker. Using a muddler or long wooden spoon, muddle well.

2. Fill the cocktail shaker halfway full with ice cubes. Add the tequila, Midori, and lemon juice. Shake well.

3. Strain into a cocktail glass (chilled if possible). Garnish with the mint sprig.

LA JOLIA

B ra-na-na-fo-nandy, made from grapes so handy, brandy, meets up with banana-fana-fo-fo-nana, cuddling with spirit and sugar it's dandy, banana, and then comes together with ci-trus-mo-mus, orange and lemon squeezed freshly, citrus. Sha-sha-sha-shake, shake, so shaky, and stra-ain-a-ainy, through your shaker so speedy, strain-it, into a co-co-co-cocktail, gla-has-bo-bass, cocktail glass. And believe me, it's just as jolly to drink as it is to sing.

CRUSHED ICE

1½ OUNCES BRANDY

1 OUNCE CRÈME DE BANANA

¾ OUNCE FRESHLY SQUEEZED ORANGE JUICE

¼ OUNCE FRESHLY SQUEEZED LEMON JUICE

1. Fill a cocktail shaker halfway full with crushed ice. Add the brandy, banana liqueur, and orange and lemon juices. Shake rapidly.

2. Strain into a cocktail glass.

A NOTE: I think crushed ice makes this nice and frothy, but if you can't get it, then substitute cracked ice.

A SECOND NOTE: Crème de banana is a basic banana liqueur made by combining a neutral spirit or brandy with banana essence or flavoring; it's available under a number of different brand names.

LORRAINE COCKTAIL

I 've said it before and I'll say it again: Having a posse of pals to pal around with makes any day pretty pleasant, every night like a Saturday night, and every morning as much fun as Sunday brunch. Sometimes though, members of said posse have to move along to Brooklyn, Belize, Brescia, and other locales for family obligations or musical careers, to be nearer their favorite bars, because they met that special someone on a plane, and even, on odd occasions, for work. When these sad days occur, be sure to send them along their happy trails with a generous toast of the Lorraine Cocktail. Its bittersweet and tangy composition is one that will show these friends you care enough to serve a swell sipper, while still honoring the singe of sadness the occasion warrants.

ICE CUBES

2 OUNCES KIRSCH

¾ OUNCE BÉNÉDICTINE

½ OUNCE FRESHLY SQUEEZED LIME JUICE

1. Fill a cocktail shaker halfway full with ice cubes. Add the kirsch, Bénédictine, and lime juice. Shake well.

2. Strain into a cocktail glass.

Kirsch

The first (but not the only) thing to learn about kirsch is that sometimes it's called by the more mellifluous Kirschwasser (which is a kick to say in a somewhat rolling R's accent after a few drinks, too). This translates to "cherry water," and kirsch is actually a type of fruit brandy created using (at least in the traditional manner) Morello sour cherries. As the story goes, originally these cherries were found only in Germany's Black Forest, and so kirsch can trace its history back to the forest (you can picture the Brothers Grimm sipping it when writing their famous fairy tales). Much in the manner of cousin maraschino liqueur (page 104), kirsch is distilled—usually double-distilled—with the whole cherry, pits and fruit alike, for a result that's not sweet, but clear, dry, and slightly nutty (the pits instill a bit of almond flavoring). The clearness comes from the fact that it's not stored in oak casks (unlike other fruit liqueurs and brandies), which tend to impart flavor and coloring, but instead is usually kept in some sort of lined wooden cask or barrel. Beyond being drunk chilled by itself before and after meals—depending on whom you're with—it's also a hit in cocktails like the Justine (page 175) and is used as a filling for chocolates and in other dessert treats.

LUNACY

This fruity freshener is from Paul Abercrombie's entertaining and healthy volume *Organic, Shaken and Stirred* (Harvard Common Press, 2009). I'm not saying this drink will rid you of the possibility of catching the common cold, but it will surely make you feel better than sitting around sipping chicken soup and sniffling. As Paul tells us, "Despite its name, this is a drink that's wonderfully well balanced." That quote not only describes the drink, but also the book itself, and the author—well, except he may be a bit of a loon. In the best way, though, the way that translates into encouraging you to jump on the organic cocktail bandwagon after reading his book, because you've realized that if someone as fantastic as Paul is shaking organic style, then you should be, too.

8 ORGANIC BLACKBERRIES

¼ OUNCE FRESHLY SQUEEZED LEMON JUICE (BETTER MAKE IT ORGANIC)

½ OUNCE SIMPLE SYRUP (PAGE 12)

1½ OUNCES REPOSADO TEQUILA

¾ OUNCE LILLET BLANC

¾ OUNCE VEEV AÇAÍ

ICE CUBES

1. Place 5 of the blackberries in a cocktail shaker. Add the lemon juice and simple syrup, and muddle well with a muddler or slightly crazy wooden spoon.

2. Add the tequila, Lillet, and açaí spirit, and fill the shaker halfway full with ice cubes. Shake well.

3. Fill an old-fashioned glass three-quarters full with ice cubes. Strain the mixture into the glass, and garnish with the remaining 3 blackberries.

MORNING CALL

Yodel-ay-eee-ooo, yodel-ay-eee-ooo! Combine that high-pitched yelp with a quick dip in a mountain stream at 7 a.m., or even the echoing buzz from an alarm clock, and you'll have only half (at most) of the waking power that this cocktail brings. This spring-in-your-daybreak state of mind is the reason you should consider serving this eye-opener instead of, or at least alongside, eggs the next time you share a cabin with a number of pals, or the next Saturday you decide to host a huge breakfast for friends who are about to have a full-day badminton tourney—or, if no one's feeling quite so enthusiastic, a full day of watching one of those seldom-spotlighted Olympic events such as badminton.

CRACKED ICE

1½ OUNCES ABSINTHE

¾ OUNCE MARASCHINO LIQUEUR

¾ OUNCE FRESHLY SQUEEZED LEMON JUICE

1. Fill a cocktail shaker or mixing glass halfway full with cracked ice. Add the absinthe, maraschino, and lemon juice. Stir well, and wake up.

2. Strain into a cocktail glass.

PANTALUS

Here's a variation on the Tantalus, which is made with Forbidden Fruit liqueur instead of pomegranate. As Forbidden Fruit liqueur isn't readily available anymore (at least not in new bottles—if you have a half-full older bottle still on a shelf, give me a holler), I brought in PAMA pomegranate liqueur instead and altered the ratios just a smidge on the brandy side, with results that may not be quite as forbidden, but are still luscious enough that you can flirt with it.

ICE CUBES

1½ OUNCES BRANDY

1 OUNCE PAMA POMEGRANATE LIQUEUR

½ OUNCE FRESHLY SQUEEZED LEMON JUICE

1. Fill a cocktail shaker halfway full with ice cubes. Add the brandy, PAMA, and lemon juice. Shake well.

2. Strain into a cocktail glass. If possible, garnish with a small pair of purple pants.

A NOTE: According to Harry McElhone and Wynn Holcomb's convivial book *Barflies and Cocktails*, the Tantalus came from Jack Bushby of the Cecil Bar in Paris. Thanks, Jack.

Maraschino

A number of maraschino liqueurs are available under different names, but perhaps the best known (and my favorite) is Luxardo, which has been made by the same family for many years, following the same recipe. It has a clear appearance and a dry, flavorsome bouquet—crisp and delectable over ice cubes all on its own, or used within classic and current cocktails, where its taste and aroma blend well with other ingredients. Beyond the flavor, Luxardo is known for its large patented green glass bottle, which nestles in a hand-fitted straw holder. First it's distilled, then aged for two years in Finnish ash vats, after which it's diluted some and mixed with pure cane sugar.

Though a standout, Luxardo does share one thing with all true maraschino liqueurs: It's made from the fruit and pits of the Marasca cherry, and it's more dry than sweet. This leads to the term *maraschino liqueur* being somewhat confusing, due to the fact that most maraschino cherries one buys in the grocery store today are overly saccharine numbers created with dyes and sweetening agents. This sometimes (shudder) leads to people subbing in the syrupy juice from these jars of cherries for true maraschino liqueur. Friends, stay away from making this mistake. True maraschino liqueur is more of a fruit brandy, distilled and crafted over time, with a dry result—a touch of cherry flavor and a hint of almond and nuttiness (thanks to the cherry pits)—that is not syrupy in the least and that shines in drinks such as the Frothy Dawn and the Aviation (pages 34 and 55, respectively). So always be sure to get true maraschino liqueur—double-check the label if need be. And, for that matter, if you want real maraschino cherries, here's another hint: Get a reliable brand (Luxardo makes great cherries, too), or make your own by soaking sweet cherries in actual maraschino liqueur for at least two weeks.

PERSEPHONE'S EXILIAR

I created this mythological miscellany for a contest judged and arranged by none other than Gary Regan himself and put out to the world in his Ardent Spirits newsletter (Gary being one half of Ardent Spirits, and Mardee Haldin Regan the other), which if you're at all interested in cocktails or spirits you should be signed up for (if you aren't signed up, get yourself to www.ardentspirits.com immediately). The contest had to do with making up drinks for specific brands of spirits and liqueurs, and ended with Gary making the drinks at the 2010 Manhattan Cocktail Classic (for more on that, visit www.manhattancocktailclassic.com, and yes, I'm almost like a Web browser all by myself).

The name comes from the Persephone of Greek mythology, who is stuck in the Underworld half the year, thanks to some bad choices involving pomegranate seeds. *Exiliar* is Spanish for "exile" and gives a shout-out both to the tequila and to the time Persephone has to spend in the Underworld—and also *exiliar* sounds a lot like *elixir*, which is what we call poetic niceness here at my house.

. . . .

ICE CUBES

2 OUNCES WHITE TEQUILA (I SUGGEST LUNAZUL BLANCO FOR MAXIMUM ESCAPE.)

1 OUNCE PAMA POMEGRANATE LIQUEUR

½ OUNCE FRESHLY SQUEEZED ORANGE JUICE

2 DASHES REGAN'S ORANGE BITTERS NO. 6

1. Fill a cocktail shaker halfway full with ice cubes. Add the tequila, PAMA, orange juice, and orange bitters. Shake well.

2. Strain into a cocktail glass (chilled, if possible).

A NOTE: Not to toot my own cocktail shaker, but yep, this won the Lunazul Blanco part of the above-mentioned contest. In case you wondered how that part of the story turned out.

REBECCA

A celebratory combination that comes together with very little chichi (which at one time meant "fuss" and which I'm trying to bring back into circulation), the Rebecca is a charming sparkling cocktail highlighted by Chambord, a French liqueur made from black raspberries. Serve it up anytime one of your favorite people is commemorating a special occasion such as college graduation, a new home purchase, the birth of a girl, or the end of a particularly arduous week. One caveat: I created this for a pal to celebrate her leaving a mundane corporate job, and now she is the Chief Tasting Officer for Deluxe Foods (www.deluxe-foods.com). Which means that after drinking this, delightfully unexpected things can happen.

ICE CUBES

2 OUNCES VODKA

1 OUNCE CHAMBORD

4 OR 5 FROZEN RASPBERRIES

CHILLED BRUT CHAMPAGNE OR SPARKLING WINE

1. Fill a cocktail shaker halfway full with ice cubes. Add the vodka and Chambord. Shake well.

2. Add the frozen raspberries to a cocktail glass. Strain the vodka-Chambord combo into the glass.

3. Fill nearly to the top with Champagne.

A NOTE: Use raspberries that have been freshly picked, gently washed, carefully dried, and quickly frozen for maximum Rebecca-ness.

"Darling, would you run out and buy a bottle of Champagne? I can't entertain as shabbily as this and I've spent everything I have buying vulgar things like Scotch and gin. I daren't even cash another check."

—VIRGINIA ROWANS, *HOUSE PARTY*, 1954

THE REEF

A cross the undulating waves, behind the very path that your ship is navigating, the Jolly Roger flies loosely atop a ghostly ship, with boards that seemingly flake off in the breeze . . . and is that a skeletal hand draped over the ship's wheel? Turn your leaking dinghy, and what's in the other direction? Are those eight long tentacles, with hand-size suckers dotting each one, and beady eyes peering out of the depths? And that noise, did your boat just hit something out of eyesight in the deeps? Have no fear, mate, because it was in this same situation that I uncovered this treasured drink in a copy of *Beachbum Berry's Grog Log (SLG, 1998)*, a thin volume by rum royalty Jeff Berry that is essential for any tropical drink lover. May your watery adventure turn out as lucky.

ICE CUBES

½ OUNCE FRESHLY SQUEEZED LIME JUICE

½ OUNCE TRIPLE SEC

½ OUNCE PASSION FRUIT LIQUEUR

1 OUNCE WHITE RUM

1. Fill a cocktail shaker halfway full with ice cubes. Add the lime juice, triple sec, passion fruit liqueur, and rum. Shake well.

2. Add 1 ice cube to a coupe-style champagne glass or a cocktail glass. Strain the mix over the ice cube.

A NOTE: If possible, make sure your rum is from Puerto Rico.

A SECOND NOTE: There are a few passion fruit liqueurs on the market, some of which taste tropical and fresh and some of which are overly saccharine and, well, gross. If you can find it, try Passoã, which has a fruity, fresh, island-hopping taste.

"Like a reef, there is a dangerous element lying under the cooling surface of this one."

—THE MANAGEMENT, *REEF RESTAURANT*, LONG BEACH, CALIFORNIA, CIRCA 1962, AS QUOTED IN *BEACHBUM BERRY'S GROG LOG*, 1998

RHETT BUTLER

D o you need to don a stunning patterned or bright white cravat, a dark and lengthy coat and tails, gray formal vest, tall boots, coiffed hair and dreamy mustache, and lush southern accent and charm while leaning back to quaff the drink named after one very famous movie gentleman? Heck, yeah. And if you don't agree, well, frankly my dear reader, I guess I'll probably be okay with that, too (maybe I'm not as tough as Mr. Gable, now that I think about it).

ICE CUBES

2 OUNCES SOUTHERN COMFORT

½ OUNCE ORANGE CURAÇAO

½ OUNCE FRESHLY SQUEEZED LIME JUICE

½ OUNCE FRESHLY SQUEEZED LEMON JUICE

LEMON TWIST, FOR GARNISH (OPTIONAL)

1. Fill a cocktail shaker halfway full with ice cubes. Add the Southern Comfort, orange curaçao, and lime and lemon juices. Shake well.

2. Strain the mix into a cocktail glass. Squeeze the lemon twist over the drink and then curl it around the edge of the glass.

A NOTE: Although Rhett did say that he shan't be lonely, if you think he is, then fill a cocktail shaker halfway full with ice cubes. Then add 2 ounces Southern Comfort, 1 ounce cranberry juice, and ½ ounce freshly squeezed lime juice. Shake well and strain into a cocktail glass, and serve a Scarlett O'Hara alongside the Rhett, and don't give a damn.

4

for

Fishing

GINGER BLISS & THE VIOLET FIZZ

Take a bucket of ice along with the bucket of bait next time you round up the pals and the poles to head to the fishing hole, along with the ingredients for the following drinks, and turn your day of fishing into a day of fantastic-ness. Don't feel like dealing with the killing of actual fish? These drinks also go well with a Go Fish marathon.

1. Old Trout
(page 143)

2. The Reef
(page 107)

3. Blood and Sand
(page 89)

4. Loch Lomond
(page 271)

4

SHOOTING STAR

With a strong dose of the Italian strawberry liqueur Fragolino, it's possible to at first believe that sweetness overpowers this particular celestial cocktail. Step back, though, and you'll see that there are also lemon juice and peach bitters along for the ride (I suggest Fee Brothers for the latter, by the by). Which means there's an underlying tang and hint of bitterness here, too. The result? Not quite bittersweet, but rather sweetbitter, sort of mirroring the career of the Kansas City band of the same name as this drink (and of so many bands that follow the same path), which has been playing since the late 1970s, recording plenty of tunes and playing loads of live shows to energetic fans, but never quite breaking through to that superstar level. Hey, maybe if you know any bands like this, make them a Shooting Star, to let them know you appreciate what they do.

ICE CUBES

1½ OUNCES GIN

1 OUNCE FRAGOLINO

½ OUNCE FRESHLY
SQUEEZED LEMON JUICE

DASH OF PEACH BITTERS

STRAWBERRY SLICE,
FOR GARNISH

1. Fill a cocktail shaker halfway full with ice cubes. Add the gin, Fragolino, lemon juice, and bitters. Shake well.

2. Strain into a cocktail glass. Garnish with the strawberry slice.

A NOTE: Fragolino is a sweetish liqueur made from wild strawberries that grow around Lake Nemi, a volcanic lake not far south of Rome. If you can't find it readily, try online spots like Internet Wines and Spirits (www.internetwines.com).

SILVER JUBILEE

P ip-pip, old chap, it's not as though we get to celebrate a Silver Jubilee
each day (as it's for a monarch's twenty-fifth year of monarching), so we'd
better have a cracking tipple, and Bob's your uncle. The classic gin keeps
the consumers from being cheesed off, and the heavy cream takes it to blooming
heights. But, the luvvly-jubbly crème de banana is what'll cause all partygoers to
take a fancy to it—even if your jubilee isn't actually for a monarch but is merely
an excuse to wear tiaras and crowns and carry scepters.

ICE CUBES

2 OUNCES GIN

1 OUNCE CRÈME DE BANANA

½ OUNCE HEAVY CREAM

1. Fill a cocktail shaker halfway full with ice cubes. Add the gin, crème de banana, and heavy cream. Shake well.

2. Strain into a cocktail glass.

A NOTE: Think this Jubilee is just off of jovial because of its garnishlessness? Add a thin piece of chocolate or a thick round of banana, or both.

SINGAPORE SLING

hen thaumaturgic troubadour Tom Waits sings the opening track on the album *Rain Dogs* about sailing to Singapore where we're all as mad as hatters, he doesn't specifically mean (I'm guessing here, admittedly, until I get to ask him about it, which may well be the happiest day of my life if it does happen) that we're going to get that way by consuming several Singapore Slings apiece. But he does point to how the town this drink is named after could lend itself easily to the naming of a drink containing a wild assortment of ingredients, including English gin, Dutch Cherry Heering liqueur, French Bénédictine, and multiple fruit juices, all brought to bubbling by club soda.

While this classic has traveled far and has had a number of iterations, permutations, and generations, the most legendary legend is that it was first assembled by bartender Ngiam Tong Boon in 1915 at the Raffles Hotel. Don't forget to toast him when serving the opening round of Singapore Slings, or it's truly possible to end up going mad as a hatter.

ICE CUBES

1½ OUNCES GIN

½ OUNCE CHERRY HEERING

¼ OUNCE BÉNÉDICTINE

¾ OUNCE FRESHLY SQUEEZED LIME JUICE

1½ OUNCES FRESH PINEAPPLE JUICE

CHILLED CLUB SODA

LIME TWIST, FOR GARNISH

1. Fill a cocktail shaker halfway full with ice cubes. Add the gin, cherry Heering, Bénédictine, lime juice, and pineapple juice. Shake in Singapore fashion (which is very well).

2. Fill a highball glass three-quarters full with ice cubes. Strain the mixture into the glass. Top with chilled club soda, filling it almost to the top. Squeeze the lime over the glass, and then drop it in.

A VARIATION: The original Raffles Hotel version has ½ ounce Cointreau added, and this is probably not a bad idea. But I've grown to like the drink without it.

A NOTE: I used to make this with less lime juice and no pineapple juice. But as I've gotten older, I've adjusted my ways.

SPRINGTIME FIZZ

T he frolicking Fizz family of drinks crested in popularity in the 1910s, '20s, and '30s, when its consortium of a citrus fruit juice (usually lime or lemon), carbonated water, and a spirit, along with other ingredients (often a sweetener) in certain variations and measured out often in roundabout manners, kept folks cool under their various layers of clothing. This extended family member recognizes its legacy with lime juice, club soda, and gin, but modernizes too with the addition of dried hibiscus flower (bringing a tart tang and some color) and PAMA pomegranate liqueur for a hint of sweet and a second layer of tang. It keeps folks cool like other Fizzes, even if hemlines have been raised or lowered quite a bit in the last century.

. . . .

1 DRIED HIBISCUS FLOWER

½ OUNCE FRESHLY SQUEEZED LIME JUICE

ICE CUBES

1½ OUNCES GIN

1 OUNCE PAMA POMEGRANATE LIQUEUR

CHILLED CLUB SODA

1. Add the hibiscus flower and lime juice to a cocktail shaker. Using a muddler or wooden spoon, muddle well.

2. Fill the cocktail shaker halfway full with ice cubes. Add the gin and PAMA. Shake with springtime fervor.

3. Fill a highball glass three-quarters full with ice cubes. Strain the mixture through a fine-mesh strainer into the glass.

4. Fill the glass almost to the top with club soda. Stir briefly.

A NOTE: Even with the strainer, a few hibiscus bits might just make it into the drink—this is okay. If you lack a fine-mesh strainer, there might be more than a few bits; just be ready for your teeth to get a little messy. Look for dried hibiscus flower in gourmet food stores, specialty shops, and at Dandelion Botanical (www.dandelionbotanical.com).

A SECOND NOTE: If you own a soda siphon, this is a great place to use it, as the Fizz should really fizz.

. . . .

"Bear in mind that all drinks called Fizz's must be drank as soon as handed out, or the natural taste of the same is lost to the customer."

—HARRY JOHNSON, *BARTENDERS' MANUAL*, 1882

SUMMER IN MADAGASCAR

C rafted by the Grand Marnier company (or the House of Grand Marnier, to be formal), Navan liqueur is made from 100 percent natural Madagascan vanilla that's aged for at least 6 months with Cognac that's at least 10 years old. Add in bourbon (and here, I suggest a nice mellow bourbon such as Maker's Mark), which is aged as well, and black tea, which has to be steeped a bit, and there's a lot of depth and years behind this drink. Peculiar, when dwelling on it, as summer itself tends to go by far, far too fast.

3 FRESH STRAWBERRIES

3 FRESH BLACKBERRIES

ICE CUBES

1 OUNCE NAVAN VANILLA LIQUEUR

¾ OUNCE BOURBON

1 OUNCE BREWED BLACK TEA, COOLED

¾ OUNCE POMEGRANATE JUICE

1. Add 2 strawberries and 2 blackberries to a cocktail shaker. Using a muddler or long wooden spoon, muddle well.

2. Fill the shaker halfway full with ice cubes. Add the Navan, bourbon, tea, and pomegranate juice. Shake well.

3. Fill an old-fashioned glass three-quarters full with ice cubes. Strain the mixture into the glass (I think straining through a fine-mesh strainer is a good idea here, if you have one).

4. Garnish with the remaining strawberry and blackberry, attaching them together on a toothpick if you aren't worried about guests impaling their cheeks.

A NOTE: This cocktail could just as easily have landed in the Spice of the Drinking Life chapter, but since the overall flavor impression is fruity, it found a happy home here.

SUNSHINE COCKTAIL #2

Hold on there, hot stuff, don't wrinkle your forehead at me. I'm not dissing you (like the kids say these days) by skipping up to Sunshine Cocktail #2 without first going over #1. Sunshine #1 is fine as frog hair (as the saying goes), with its 2 ounces gin, ¾ ounce sweet vermouth, a dash of orange bitters, and an orange twist. However, for you, on this delightful day, I'm delivering Sunshine #2 not as a backup, but as the front-runner, because I know you'll appreciate its singular signature taste. See, that's not a dis in the least.

ICE CUBES

1½ OUNCES WHITE RUM

1 OUNCE DRY VERMOUTH

½ OUNCE CRÈME DE CASSIS

¼ OUNCE FRESHLY SQUEEZED LEMON JUICE

1. Fill a cocktail shaker halfway full with ice cubes. Add the rum, vermouth, crème de cassis, and lemon juice. Shake well.

2. Strain into a cocktail glass. Garnish with sunshine.

XANTHIA

Let us go now, you and I, let us go to Xanthia. A kingdom built by butterflies, who carry vials of cherry brandy on their wings, and floral, herbal liqueurs in tiny little airplane bottles, held tightly in their butterfly hands. Let us go there, you and I, and I will bring a wineskin full of juniper and spirit clear, and you will come on thirsty feet, and gather round a frozen stream, and pick the frozen bubble off, to add to all the bounty here. And we will shake the world in our hands, and drink deep of all it offers, and frolic in the meadowlands, and sleep once we've had our fill of Xanthia, this enchanted land, and then rise again, to go now to Xanthia once more, again and again we can go, at least until our liquor store shelves of Chartreuse and Heering run low.

ICE CUBES

1 OUNCE CHERRY HEERING

1 OUNCE GREEN CHARTREUSE

1 OUNCE GIN

1. Fill a cocktail shaker halfway full with ice cubes. Add the cherry Heering, Chartreuse, and gin, in a fantasy-inspired manner, or at least dreamily.

2. Strain into a cocktail glass. Drink, and frolic.

A NOTE: You could also stir this together over cracked ice. But something about cherry Heering makes me want to shake it.

NOW, I DON'T WANT TO SAY THESE ARE PARTY "RULES," BECAUSE LAYING DOWN A HARD AND FAST LINE CONTROLLING WINGDINGS DAMPENS THE FUN. AND THIS ISN'T SOMETHING ANYONE WANTS. BUT THE FOLLOWING, LET'S CALL THEM SUGGESTIONS, WILL HELP TO ENSURE PARTY SUCCESS.

1. Plan on serving warmers in winter and coolers in summer, and follow along the same lines during spring soirées and fall fêtes, too. What I'm really getting at is that, if possible, you should serve drinks that match up seasonally with the time of year and the temperature of the time when you're having the affair. Giving guests a hot mug of cheer when it's snowing outside makes them merry from the get-go.

2. Pick one or two specific signature drinks for the party, and have them match up to your party's personality (or the one you'd like it to have). Then, start touting these signature drinks on invites and e-vites. It'll start generating buzz and excitement and make your party stand out from the rest (which is what everyone wants, of course). It'll also make it easier for you to prepare, because you won't have to worry about covering every single boozy base—you can just stock up on the ingredients for the signature drinks.

3. I once received a fortune cookie along with some Chinese takeout that said "Proper prior planning prevents poor performance." Very good advice, especially when relating to being a good host or hostess. Think about it like this: First, be sure to stock up on the crucial ingredients for your signature cocktails (decided on in step 2), and even get a little more than you

think you'll need, because there are always a few extra guests (hey, someone's cousin is going to be in town, right?). If you end up having too much, then you just stock your bar a bit. Also, cut and chop and do whatever garnishing you can beforehand. You don't want to go this route a week before, but a couple of hours before is great, as it gives you more time to hang out with guests.

4. Now, I'm not saying that your friends and family members have a tendency to have one drink too many, but even without the last drink, you should always have a good taxicab number (or maybe two) on hand. This keeps people from even worrying about driving under the influence. Also, don't forget to have a yummy nonalcoholic drink on hand for the designated drivers at the party.

5. This final suggestion I'm going to bring up to "rule" status, because it is something you should never forget: As the one throwing the party, you should still have fun. It's amazingly sad to me to watch a host or hostess stressing, instead of laughing, at his or her own frolicking and rollicking evening (or brunch). So follow the steps above, and you can focus on having fun too, instead of being bogged down by the details of throwing a party.

ZENZERO TROPICALE

I (along with my wife, Nat) got the nicest batch of gingersnaps once from pal Jill (her husband, pal Ed, contributed the Ellipse on page 196). The snaps were a bit more cookie-y than many gingersnaps, but with goodly ginger flavor and a little bit of chewiness. I ate lots of them. And I also used a few of them as garnishes for this exotically named cocktail, which contains VeeV Açaí, a spirit with tropical leanings and a little oomph, and Domaine de Canton ginger liqueur, which is truly gingerrific, and sweet vermouth to round out the edges and add an herbal voice. The combo, with the gingersnap garnish, is a delight around the winter holidays, both because this tends to be gingersnap season and because giving a glimpse of the tropics during the colder months reminds us that summer isn't ever that far away.

ICE CUBES

1½ OUNCES VEEV AÇAÍ

1 OUNCE DOMAINE DE CANTON GINGER LIQUEUR

½ OUNCE SWEET VERMOUTH

GINGERSNAP OR GINGER COOKIE, FOR GARNISH

1. Fill a cocktail shaker halfway full with ice cubes. Add the Veev Açaí, ginger liqueur, and vermouth. Shake well.

2. Strain into a cocktail glass. Garnish with that cookie. (Notch it just a bit for proper rim balancing. But after that, you can do a lot of dunking with it.)

LAST WORD, PAGE 137

CHAPTER 5

TAKE YOUR

HERBAL

MEDICINE

A s an honorable herbal-liqueur drink distributor (which, once the following pages are turned, you will be), doling out these healthy but incredibly delectable mixtures in a manner designed to heal revelers of any party ailments, whether it be doldrums or malaise or the inability to shake their groove thing, you need to take the following oath:

I swear by Garibaldi, Negroni, and Portofino, and I take to witness all the bitter liqueurs and all the sweeter herbal liqueurs, to keep, according to my cocktail-shaking ability and my good taste, this oath of home entertainers. To consider dear to me, as my parents, the lush liqueurs that serve as the bedrock of my herbal concoctions; to live in common with them and, if necessary, which is always, to share my Red Moon with everyone; to look upon my Atomula as though it be made for my own siblings, and to teach partygoers about the herbal drinks as they demand it.

I will prescribe Bossa Nova Specials for the good of my patients (which I take to mean those I've invited over for frolicking) according to my ability and my judgment and will never deliver a poorly constructed Bitter Handshake to anyone. I will preserve the purity of my Shanghai Gins and my Hanky Pankys. I will not shirk on serving a well-balanced Monte Carlo even to those who may believe they do not enjoy rye and Bénédictine mixed with bitters, and I will deliver even for attendees to whom the idea of an artichoke-based liqueur is scary the Cynartown, and I will leave no herbal liqueur bottle unopened when called upon to revive dull evenings at any time of the year.

Into every house where I come I will enter only for the good of the party, bringing necessary herbal liqueurs to make Cornells, Pimm's Cups, and Super-sonics, depending on the season and the situations that need remedying. All that may come to my knowledge in this chapter, from Alaska Cocktail to Widow's Kiss, which ought to be spread from wingding to wingding, I will not keep secret and will reveal.

If I keep this herbal oath faithfully, may I enjoy my life and practice my art, respected by all those who enjoy a good drink at all times of day and night; but if I swerve from it or violate it, may the reverse be my lot.

ALASKA COCKTAIL

I'm not 100 percent positive that this drink was created to celebrate the purchase of the great state of Alaska (only the territory of Alaska at the time) from the Russian Empire on March 30, 1867, for $7.2 million. I am positive that I saw it first in Jacques Straub's book *Drinks* (Hotel Monthly Press, 1914). It may be (this would get the dates closer) that it was created to honor Alaska be-coming a recognized territory in 1912 (before becoming a state in 1959). Beyond being fun dates to toss around when making this cocktail for chums, what does all this history give us? A darn fine reason for toasting not once, not twice, but three times—and I always suggest multiple toasts.

ICE CUBES

2 OUNCES OLD TOM GIN

1 OUNCE YELLOW CHARTREUSE

DASH OF ORANGE BITTERS

1. Fill a cocktail shaker halfway full with ice cubes. Add the whole state (okay, just the gin, Chartreuse, and bitters). Shake well.

2. Strain into a cocktail glass.

A NOTE: Old Tom gin is a slightly sweeter version of regular London (or dry) gin. It has recently become available again after a long lull (say, 100 years), and it is perhaps best known for being the name ingredient in the Tom Collins—first mentioned, as far as I know, in A. William Schmidt's book *The Flowing Bowl*. If your local place doesn't carry it, try finding it online.

A SECOND NOTE: I like Regan's Orange Bitters No. 6 here, but feel free to experiment with others if you must.

AMER PICON HIGHBALL

A mer Picon is a French apéritif that was once (here I'm referring to that golden era at the end of the 1800s and the early 1900s) very popular in cocktail dens and in cocktails. It had a slightly bitter presence and a touch of orange flavor that fit nicely into simple tall treasures like this recipe, as well as more complex mixtures and tinctures. It can be hard to track down today, though you can find it online. One warning, intrepid one: Like other somewhat esoteric ingredients (and some not so esoteric, too) the formula has been changed over time. The current version, while not bad, has a bit less character and heft than the original. You can find (and maybe find more easily, which is an extra bonus) a substitute called Torani Amer that is a smidge stronger, and well worth a try in drinks calling for Amer Picon.

CRACKED ICE

2½ OUNCES AMER PICON

½ OUNCE GRENADINE
(PAGE 14)

ICE CUBES

CHILLED CLUB SODA

1. Fill a mixing glass or cocktail shaker halfway full with cracked ice. Add the Amer Picon and grenadine. Stir well.

2. Fill a highball glass halfway full with ice cubes. Strain the mixture over the ice. Top with club soda until the glass is just about full. Stir again, briefly.

AMERICANO

Brilliant when consumed on a late spring day at 4 p.m. at an outdoor café near the Arno in Florence, the Americano is refreshment sung with a bitter-herbal chorus. It's been consumed as a warm-weather aperitivo for well over a hundred years, tracing its history back to 1860, when Gaspare Campari served it at his bar. At that time it was called the Milano-Torino in honor of Campari (the bitter red liqueur from Milan) and Cinzano vermouth (from Turin). The name was changed when it was noticed that a large number of visiting Americans had fallen in love with the drink. This falling in love thing is something that still happens (I'm a perfect example).

ICE CUBES

2 OUNCES CAMPARI

2 OUNCES SWEET VERMOUTH

CHILLED CLUB SODA

ORANGE SLICE, FOR GARNISH

1. Fill a highball glass three-quarters full with ice cubes. Add the Campari and vermouth. Stir gently.

2. Add club soda to the glass until the glass is almost full. Garnish with an orange slice.

Campari

Ah, love. To say that love is wonderful and makes the world worthwhile is almost so obvious as to be silly—I mean, how many songs say the same? How many poems? How many novels turn whole plots on love? But you know what really underlines how important love is? The fact that it was a driving force in the bitter Italian liqueur Campari becoming not only available worldwide, but also crucial to the drinking experience of the many people who adore everything about it, from the signature taste to the red glow.

Our love story starts in the 1800s in Cassolnovo, Italy, where Gaspare Campari was born. At the age of 14, after moving to Turin, Gaspare became an apprentice *maître licoriste* (a combination bartender, liquor maker, and problem solver) at the Bass Bar. There Gaspare started testing a liquor of his own, trying a little of this herb mixed with a little of that root, a little spice mixed with a little spirit, and a little fruit with a little sweet, and then a little of all of the above in various proportions and preparations, until he came to a recipe he knew would change the liqueur landscape. It took him until 1860, and he titled it after his family name: Campari.

At first it was available only in Italy, where it became very popular. Then, Gaspare's son Davide was born, grew up, grew to love the liqueur named after his family, and starting working at their Caffé Campari in Milan, where he spread the legend of the liqueur. Then, one day, when the stars were shining through the bottles filled with red in the shop, Lina Cavalieri walked through the doors. Lina was a popular opera singer, and she and Davide got along smashingly, and they started to become more than friends, if you know what I mean. Then—tragedy!—Lina had to move to Nice, France, for an opera part. Davide was crushed, but a lightbulb went off: Why not begin exporting Campari, starting in Nice? Then he would be able to bring the liqueur to those in need around the world and also be able to visit his lady love. When you retell this story, I suggest having Campari, either on its own with a twist, with soda and a twist, or in a cocktail such as the classic Negroni (page 142), with someone you love.

ATOMULA

B ut, Professor, if you flip that switch, and rotate the knobs on the ginormous clicking computer, and swirl the dial around to the red zone, and start cackling gleefully (and why does your hair all of a sudden stand on end like a thicket?), and open the sky during a lightning storm, and plug your cocktail shaker into a massive generator, and tip those bottles of rum and Becherovka and syrup into the system, Professor, won't that unleash the Atomula on the unknowing world? Bwwwahahahaha, my little sidekick! That's my exact ingenious idea.

ICE CUBES

1½ OUNCES DARK RUM

1 OUNCE BECHEROVKA

½ OUNCE ROSEMARY SIMPLE SYRUP (SEE A SECOND NOTE)

ROSEMARY SPRIG, FOR GARNISH

1. Fill a cocktail shaker halfway full with ice cubes. Add the rum, Becherovka, and rosemary simple syrup. Shake well.

2. Strain the mixture into a cocktail glass. Garnish with the rosemary sprig.

A NOTE: Becherovka is an herbally bitter digestif made with 32 herbs and spices, including anise and cinnamon, though only two people at one time ever know exactly how much of each herb is used (like most liqueurs and their ilk, it's a secret recipe). It's been made since 1807 in the Czech Republic.

A SECOND NOTE: Making rosemary simple syrup is simple. Just add 1 cup fresh rosemary leaves, 2½ cups water, and 3 cups sugar to a medium-size saucepan. Stirring occasionally, slowly bring the mixture to a simmer over medium-low to medium heat. Then lower the heat a bit, keeping the mixture at a simmer for 5 minutes. Turn off the heat, and let the syrup completely cool in the pan. Strain through cheesecloth or a very fine strainer, and then store in an airtight container in the refrigerator.

BIJOU

Wow, do you ever have those moments when you come across a drink (or a book, a movie, a song, a theory) and are so struck by it that you have to say out loud, "Why haven't I tried (or read, seen, heard, considered) that already?" That's how the Bijou was for me, when I first really took note of it while re-perusing *The Stork Club Bar Book* by writerly gadabout Lucius Beebe (originally published in 1946 by Rinehart but handily reissued in 2003 by New Day) and had to take it for a spin. It was (and is) delicious. The lighter flowery notes of green Chartreuse on top, the back-end herbal notes of the sweet vermouth on the bottom, and the glorious burst of gin in the middle make for a complex and creative cocktail. And to think, the definition of *bijou* is "a small, exquisitely wrought trinket." I can get behind "exquisitely wrought"—and think you will agree—but this is no mere trinket. It's a treasure.

CRACKED ICE

1½ OUNCES GIN

¾ OUNCE GREEN CHARTREUSE

¾ OUNCE SWEET VERMOUTH

MARASCHINO CHERRY, FOR GARNISH

LEMON TWIST, FOR GARNISH

1. Fill a cocktail shaker or mixing glass halfway full with cracked ice. Add the gin, Chartreuse, and vermouth. Stir well.

2. Add the cherry to a cocktail glass. Strain the mixture into the glass. Twist the twist over the glass and drop it in.

A VARIATION: In a few books, this recipe has the addition of a dash of orange bitters. It's not a bad adornment.

A SECOND VARIATION: I've seen this made with orange curaçao instead of Chartreuse. You can try it that way if you want, but don't expect me to give the drink the same amount of praise.

A NOTE: Feel the double garnish is too much? Let the cherry go free and just use the twist.

BITTER HANDSHAKE

F rom fertile minds come delicious drinks. I read that in the bathroom of a bar. It wasn't a bar that Andrew Bohrer (who tends the blog at www.caskstrength.wordpress.com) works at, but it could have been, as he's known throughout Seattle (check his blog to see where he's currently slinging drinks) and more and more in other spots, for his classical leanings and avant-garde ways. About this Fernet-Branca sure-to-be classic, Andrew says, "The name, Bitter Handshake, refers to Fernet-Branca being the 'bartender's shot,' or as I call it, 'the bartender's handshake,' a blessing and/or a curse that another bartender may send you at any point—a greeting, a good-bye, a handshake. All that being said, the Bitter Handshake is not quite as bitter as it sounds, and people that have never had Fernet-Branca find it enjoyable and upon tasting a sample alone, have no idea how they've come to like the drink." It's best when served over a single large ice ball, but can also be served over ice cubes or straight up.

ICE CUBES

1 OUNCE FERNET-BRANCA

1 OUNCE BLOOD ORANGE
REDUCTION (SEE A NOTE)

1 OUNCE RYE SIMPLE SYRUP
(SEE A SECOND NOTE)

WIDE ORANGE TWIST,
FOR GARNISH

1. Fill a cocktail shaker or mixing glass halfway full with ice cubes. Add the Fernet-Branca, blood orange reduction, and rye simple syrup. Stir well.

2. Strain into a cocktail glass, or strain into an old-fashioned glass that is three-quarters full with ice cubes or contains one large ice ball. Twist the twist over the glass and drop it in or drape it around the ice.

A NOTE: To make blood orange reduction, reduce 1 cup fresh blood orange juice in a saucepan over medium heat by one-third. Add a touch of sugar (a teaspoon is nice), which will give it a fuller mouth feel, and then add one last splash of fresh juice, which will add a little brightness.

A SECOND NOTE: To make rye simple syrup, add 1 cup of rye whiskey and 1 cup of sugar to a saucepan and heat over medium-high heat. Stirring regularly, bring just to a boil, and then turn the heat down to medium-low. Let it simmer for 5 minutes, and then take it off the heat and let it cool completely in the pan. Store in the fridge. If you don't want to take the trouble to make this, you can instead sub in ½ ounce rye and ½ ounce Simple Syrup (page 12).

BOSSA NOVA SPECIAL

Though this upbeat number features an ensemble of different players, including white rum, Galliano (see page 200), apricot brandy (not to be confused with apricot liqueur, which is sweeter though not overly sweet), pineapple juice, lemon juice, an egg white for frothiness, and a pineapple chunk for snacking, the reason the melody is so delish is how well these players play together. It's truly "bossa," which in Brazil means doing something with panache and charisma, and which also means you need to shake it in an out-of-the-ordinary manner, swinging hips and giving your shaking extra pizzazz and wiggle. If you're shy, don't fret. After one of these, you'll be dancing in everything you do.

ICE CUBES

1 OUNCE WHITE RUM

1½ OUNCES GALLIANO

¼ OUNCE APRICOT BRANDY

2 OUNCES FRESH PINEAPPLE JUICE

¼ OUNCE FRESHLY SQUEEZED LEMON JUICE

1 EGG WHITE, PREFERABLY ORGANIC

PINEAPPLE CHUNK, FOR GARNISH

1. Fill a cocktail shaker halfway full with ice cubes. Add the rum, Galliano, apricot brandy, pineapple and lemon juices, and egg white. Shake exceptionally well.

2. Fill an old-fashioned glass three-quarters full with ice cubes. Strain the mixture over the ice. Garnish with the pineapple chunk, spearing it on a toothpick if you're not scared of spearing a cheek when drinking.

A NOTE: This is a variation on a drink originally created, I'm told, by Cecil E. Roberts for a competition at the Nassau Beach Hotel. It won the competition.

A WARNING: As this drink contains raw egg, it shouldn't be served to the elderly or to those with compromised immune systems.

CORNELL

While there are a number of "perhapses" and "could be's" when wondering which Cornell this cocktail was named after, I like to believe it was for writer Cornell Woolrich. For one, his pulp, mystery, suspense, and noir novels and stories flow with graceful despair and tend to have characters who are tragically flawed and end up smack in front of a cinematic steamroller of fate that's going to flatten them. So he deserves a smooth drink with the dry flavor of maraschino and the kick of gin. For two, one of his stories, "It Had to Be Murder," was turned into the film *Rear Window*—Woolrich had many works adapted for movies and television—so this is the ideal assimilation for a noir movie night. For three, after the second Cornell, you'll feel much more comfortable in your trench coat and fedora.

ICE CUBES

2 OUNCES GIN

1 OUNCE MARASCHINO LIQUEUR

1 EGG WHITE, PREFERABLY ORGANIC

1. Fill a cocktail shaker halfway full with ice cubes. Add the gin, maraschino liqueur, and egg white. Shake sneakingly well.

2. Strain into a cocktail glass, while always watching your back.

A VARIATION: There's another Cornell, which is equal parts gin and dry vermouth. Not bad, either, and probably won't get you shot for serving it.

A NOTE: I think a strongly flavored London-style gin, such as Voyager, works well here.

A WARNING: As this drink contains raw egg, it shouldn't be served to the elderly or to those with compromised immune systems.

CYNARTOWN

The modern cocktail world is wonderful. 'Nuff said. Well, almost. Where does that wonderfulness spring out of? From the availability of fantabulous liqueurs from all over the globe? Surely. Well, almost. Without the modern masters shaking up fresh creations with these liqueurs, it wouldn't be so wonderful, right? Modern masters like Phil Ward, who is currently the mastermind behind the drinks at Mayahuel (www.mayahuelny.com) and renowned for creating drinks like this one, drinks that not only use those newly available ingredients from near and far, but also use them in a way that takes you exactly where you want to go.

. . . .

CRACKED ICE

2 OUNCES GIN

¾ OUNCE CARPANO ANTICA

½ OUNCE CYNAR

1 SOUR CHERRY, FOR GARNISH

1. Fill a cocktail shaker or mixing glass halfway full with cracked ice. Add the gin, Carpano Antica, and Cynar. Stir well.

2. Strain into a cocktail glass (preferably chilled). Garnish with the cherry.

FRIAR MINOR

The Friars Minor, known more commonly as the Franciscans, were formally established when St. Francis of Assisi went to see Pope Innocent III, who gave him and his disciples verbal sanction after St. Francis made him one of these refreshing highballs. Okay, it probably had more to do with St. Francis's saintly nature, charity, and goodness, but he was from Assisi, one of the most beautiful towns in Umbria, Italy, and this drink's defining personality comes from Ramazzotti, an Italian amaro that a has a rich, complex, herby flavor, underlined by the barest stitch of sweet intertwining with a balanced smidge of bitterness (see page 148 for more on amaros). Which means that though it's by no means monk-like, this drink is well worthy of toasting with, especially on April 16 (which is that date in 1209 when St. Francis met the Pope).

. . . .

ICE CUBES

2 OUNCES BOURBON

1½ OUNCES RAMAZZOTTI

1 OUNCE FRESHLY SQUEEZED ORANGE JUICE

CHILLED CLUB SODA

1. Fill a highball glass three-quarters full with ice cubes. Add the bourbon, Ramazzotti, and orange juice. Stir monastically.

2. Fill the glass almost to the top with club soda. Stir again (a little less monastically, and a little more party-astically).

Cynar

A liqueur made from, of all things, artichokes, Cynar was unleashed on the world in 1952. Don't let its main ingredient put you off, though, because it tastes much, much better than you might guess. I think of it as a member of the amaro family of Italian liqueurs (even though it doesn't have "amaro" in the title), due to its tiny touch of bitterness balanced by a healthy, smooth underlying herbal-ness and a sweet touch that makes it a pleasure both on its own and in cocktails like the modern classic Cynartown (page 133). This tastiness isn't developed only through the artichoke, but also in combination with 13 herbs and spices. It is used in Italy as a digestivo.

When originally introduced, Cynar almost instantly drew folks into its fan base, mostly because they thought it had mystical herbal health benefits. However, in the 1960s, Cynar produced a number of TV commercials starring Ernesto Calindri, an Italian movie and television star and a perfect Italian gentleman. The spots featured Ernesto in the middle of some chaos (an energetic family, a busy street) sipping Cynar, or Cynar and soda, without a care in the world as the Cynar took him to a more peaceful place. So even if you aren't usually an artichoke fan, or if you think that an artichoke liqueur might be taking the vegetable too far, take my advice and try a sip of Cynar (pronounced CHEE-nar). Your worries will melt away in its good taste.

GARIBALDI

Not feeling like a routine Mimosa for a breakfast beverage on a sleepy Saturday? Deciding that you'd rather give yourself a bitter pick-you-up instead of a Bloody Mary for a liquid side dish during Sunday brunch? Want to imagine that you're an Italian patriot marching across the morning in hopes of national unification? Then listen up, because I have the very drink for you: the Garibaldi, named after the French-born Italian patriot Giuseppe Garibaldi, whose red-shirted army (mirrored in the red color of this drink's defining ingredient, Campari) helped unify Italy in 1860.

ICE CUBES

2 OUNCES CAMPARI

5 OUNCES FRESHLY SQUEEZED ORANGE JUICE

1. Fill a highball glass three-quarters full with ice cubes. Add the Campari and the orange juice.

2. Stir well.

HANKY PANKY

Isn't this a playful name for a drink? One that amorous girls and guys can use to flirt at the bar, without coming off as crass or just annoying? For example, isn't saying "How'd you like a little Hanky Panky?" much sillier and therefore more genuine than saying "Are you lost? Because Heaven is a long way from here?" The fact that you can follow it up with a good cocktail makes meeting that desired someone almost too easy. The Hanky Panky comes from the 1920s, when it was created by Ada Coleman, the top bartender at the American Bar in London's Savoy Hotel (Ada was the predecessor of the more famous Harry Craddock, who penned the revered *Savoy Cocktail Book*). Coquettish name, history, and an herbal bit of kapow? Maybe you should just be flirting with this drink.

CRACKED ICE

1½ OUNCES GIN

1½ OUNCES SWEET VERMOUTH

¼ OUNCE FERNET-BRANCA

WIDE ORANGE TWIST, FOR GARNISH

1. Fill a cocktail shaker or mixing glass halfway full with cracked ice. Add the gin, sweet vermouth, and Fernet-Branca. Stir well.

2. Strain into a cocktail glass. Twist that twist over the glass, and then either drop it in or drape it on the rim of the glass.

A NOTE: Want to make your Hanky Panky even more desirable? Use Carpano Antica instead of any old sweet vermouth. Its flavor enhances the taste, and the fact that it was the first sweet vermouth, created in 1786, enhances the story.

IBF PICK-ME-UP

I sn't it swell to have friends? Especially when you're jolly naturally and want some folks to go jumping around with from house to house trying recipes from this very book. However, it's at least as important to have friends around to pick you up when you're not as jolly, after spending a day with a junky boss who takes credit for your work and keeps bringing you down, or after a day when you've bet your bubble money on the wrong pony, or even after a day when you just woke up feeling blue. Those days, good friends come in more than handy. And if their friendship involves both kind words and a glass brimming with this ebullient elixir, the day turns finer even faster. Since this recipe is from *Barflies and Cocktails* (published in 1927 and reprinted in 2008 by Mud Puddle Books) by Harry McElhone, proprietor of Harry's New York Bar in Paris, and caricaturist Wynn Holcomb, you'll know it's not the first time this concoction was used to reorient a bad day, and that knowledge connects you to past drinkers, expanding your circle of friends even more. That's pretty darn swell, indeed.

ICE CUBES

1½ OUNCES BRANDY

½ OUNCE ORANGE CURAÇAO

½ OUNCE FERNET-BRANCA

CHILLED BRUT SPARKLING WINE

1. Fill a cocktail shaker halfway full with ice cubes. Add the brandy, orange curaçao, and Fernet-Branca. Shake well.

2. Strain into a white wine glass. Fill nearly to the top with sparkling wine.

A NOTE: Wondering about the curious IBF in the title? It stands for International Bar Fly—a title worth aspiring toward.

LAST WORD

T his drink, according to legend, was created by Frank Fogarty during Prohibition. Not a bartender, Mr. Fogarty was "the Dublin Mistral," one of the tip-top monologists in vaudeville. According to Brett Page's *Writing for Vaudeville* (re-released by General Books, 2010), in his act Mr. Fogarty "often opens with a song and usually ends his offering with a serious heart-throb recitation." This setup matches the drink itself (if you can stretch the stage a bit), with the drink starting with the gin's song, moving through the maraschino and Chartreuse acts, and ending with the heart-throbbing tang of fresh lime. The most recent last word on this delightfully balanced cocktail, though, is its large rise in popularity, as it's showing up on stages (or bars) from east to west to north to south. This new reciting of the word is due to legendary bartender Murray Stenson of Seattle's Zig Zag Café, who rediscovered the Last Word and put it on the Zig Zag menu, to much applause.

ICE CUBES

¾ OUNCE GIN

¾ OUNCE MARASCHINO LIQUEUR

¾ OUNCE GREEN CHARTREUSE

¾ OUNCE FRESHLY SQUEEZED LIME JUICE

1. Fill a cocktail shaker halfway full with ice cubes. Add the gin, maraschino, Chartreuse, and lime juice. Shake well.

2. Strain into a cocktail glass and drink without another syllable spoken.

A NOTE: Fogarty was also elected president of the White Rats, the vaudeville union, in 1914. Which sounds like a much more dubious pleasure than being president of the Last Word drinking club.

MINT COOLER

H oly moley, I do declare that it's getting so hot that I can feel the temperature rising from minute to minute, and no matter how much I fan myself, no matter what I'm wearing, no matter if I search out the shadiest portion of the backyard, that heat is finding me as quick as a dog finds a biscuit that's been dropped on the floor. I fear I'm going to melt like Frosty the Snowman did in the greenhouse.

If you've ever felt this way, or felt like a party was going south due to the heat, let me tell you, there's only one way out (and no, it's not by buying an air conditioner), and that's by pouring out a round of Mint Coolers. It might seem that a Scotch drink couldn't be a cooldown because of the spirit's warming nature. However, the addition of crème de menthe and its cooling minty powers that appear when it's combined with ice and club soda, balances out the big boy Scotch, and reroutes it from winter warmer to summer solution. Heck, I think this one would keep Frosty from turning to drips even in Miami.

ICE CUBES

2 OUNCES SCOTCH

½ OUNCE WHITE CRÈME DE MENTHE

CHILLED CLUB SODA

1. Fill a highball glass three-quarters full with ice cubes. Add the Scotch and crème de menthe. Stir briefly.

2. Fill the glass with chilled club soda. Stir again. Sit back and watch the sun set.

MOLLY PICON COCKTAIL

little sister to the better-known and more straightforwardly named Amer Picon Highball (page 123), Molly also uses the hard-to-find Amer Picon. And, as with big brother, you might substitute Torani Amer here, as the current incarnation of Amer Picon is lighter than when this drink was first made. Whichever bottle you invest in, I suggest you employ it in a family evening during which you serve both brother and sister drinks, as they complement each other nicely. Following along the theme, maybe you should serve them at a family reunion or other family occasion so that both families, yours and the Picon family, can get to know each other.

CRACKED ICE

1½ OUNCES GIN

1½ OUNCES AMER PICON

¾ OUNCE SWEET VERMOUTH

¼ OUNCE ORANGE CURAÇAO

1. Fill a cocktail shaker or mixing glass halfway full with cracked ice. Add the gin, Amer Picon, sweet vermouth, and orange curaçao. Stir well.

2. Strain the mixture into a cocktail glass.

A VARIATION: I've seen this made sans orange curaçao, but I do enjoy that slight sweet hint. Feel free to drop it if you wish.

---

5 Drinks for Conquering the World

GINGER BLISS & THE VIOLET FIZZ

5 Drinks for Conquering

Attempting to actually conquer the world (even if you're as genius—mad genius, that is—as Gene Hackman playing Lex Luthor) is probably going to end up being quite a bit more hassle than it's worth. All those legions of bumbling sidekicks and stacks of discarded plans everywhere, and having to deal with talking in a really scary accent, just drag out the day. Instead, bring over some friends to play Risk or Monopoly (to conquer the world of New Jersey property), and serve up these world-conquering cocktails.

1. Napoleon
(page 141)

2. Alexander
(page 256)

3. Brave Bull
(page 168)

4. They Shall Inherit the Earth
(page 48)

5. The Whip of the Conqueror
(page 160)

MONTE CARLO

The impulse, on first spying the Mediterranean moniker of this mixture, might be to have it as the signature cocktail for a night of baccarat and tuxes or as an intriguing accompaniment to an evening of James Bondian board games where you're trying to take over—or prevent a takeover of—the world. While these sound like winning wingdings, and while this drink could probably take its place handily among those proceedings, I'd like to propose a different venue to serve it at: a toga party. Why, you might ask? Because a leisurely Saturday toga party could be seen as happening in honor of Julius Caesar. Who, if you didn't know, packed his fleet into a particular port when craftily waiting for a rival to arrive in 48 BC. That post was the port of Monaco, which just so happens to lie adjacent to the *quartier* now called Monte Carlo.

CRACKED ICE

2 OUNCES RYE

¾ OUNCE BÉNÉDICTINE

DASH OF ANGOSTURA BITTERS

1. Fill a cocktail shaker or mixing glass halfway full with cracked ice. Add the rye, Bénédictine, and bitters. Stir well.

2. Strain into a cocktail glass and bet high.

A VARIATION: Feeling a need to double down in a completely different style? There's also a Monte Carlo Imperial cocktail that contains 1½ ounces gin, ¾ ounce crème de menthe, and ¾ ounce freshly squeezed lemon juice, shaken with ice cubes, strained into a flute glass, and topped with chilled sparkling wine.

NAPOLEON

This border-busting wallop is, interestingly, driven in taste by two ingredients that are found in lesser amounts than you'd expect: the forceful and awe-inspiring Italian digestivo Fernet-Branca and the inspirational and subtle French apéritif Dubonnet (in its Rouge form). Though, now that I mull over the geographical and historical implications of the drink's name and the emperor it comes from (let's take it for granted that a drink of this much international oomph comes from him and not the pastry), it does make sense. Of course, I might expect it'd be served in a smaller glass (ba-dump-bump).

CRACKED ICE

1½ OUNCES GIN

¼ OUNCE FERNET-BRANCA

¼ OUNCE DUBONNET ROUGE

¼ OUNCE ORANGE CURAÇAO

LEMON TWIST, FOR GARNISH

1. Fill a cocktail shaker or mixing glass halfway full with cracked ice. Add the gin, Fernet-Branca, Dubonnet, and curaçao. Stir well.

2. Strain into a cocktail glass and garnish with that empire-building twist.

"A marble-eyed waiter with a pushed-in face and a malevolent twist to his mouth came over, snapped a napkin, nodded. I ordered bourbon for myself, Dubonnet for Dulcy, and Bob ordered a bottle of Napoleon for himself."

—HAROLD Q. MASUR, *BURY ME DEEP*, 1948

NEGRONI

A true classic in my mind (a mind I'll admit is addled a bit here and there on some nights), the Negroni when made right is the liquid definition of the Hopi word *suyanisqatsi*, which means "life of harmony." See, not to get up in your philosophical grill during happy hour, but I'm positing that you have to have balance in order to have harmony in life. Or, to put it another way, "All work and no play makes Jack a dull boy." In the same manner, the Negroni has to be balanced perfectly among its ingredients: gin, Campari, and sweet vermouth. Without this precise balance, the drink falls out of harmony. It can still be a solid cocktail if there isn't enough vermouth, I suppose, but it will never find its way to cocktail nirvana. Remember this, and always raise your Negroni-ing to the higher level.

ICE CUBES

1½ OUNCES GIN

1½ OUNCES CAMPARI

1½ OUNCES SWEET VERMOUTH

ORANGE TWIST, FOR GARNISH

1. Fill a cocktail shaker halfway full with ice cubes. Add the gin, Campari, and sweet vermouth, giving each the same amount of attention. Shake well.

2. Strain into a cocktail glass, and garnish with the orange twist.

A NOTE: The Negroni is sometimes made on the rocks, in an old-fashioned glass—I've made it that way myself and don't frown on the practice—and sometimes it is stirred instead of shaken. But as I've aged (like a fine cocktail, one hopes), I've grown to like the extra chill of the shake and the amalgamating of the shaken result.

A VARIATION: Since we're pals (hopefully even after the above lecture), I'll let you in on a secret: If you sub rye for gin and dry vermouth for sweet, you'll be happily greeting an Old Pal.

OLD TROUT

I believe, Bessie, that Old Trout is pickin' and grinnin' at the ol'-timey musi-calium hoedown upon this-here Saturday. They'll be carryin' their fixin's in a poke, with a heapin' helpin' of Campari to get it started (And did you know Campari is Italian? Don't that just crack ya yallar?) and a full part of that orange juice in there fresh from the fruit or it ain't worth a hoot and holler. To keep the folks from getting katty-wonkered or overheated, they also slop bubbles in there, which makes that Old Trout just hum and honk from sunrise to sunset. You sure shouldn't miss it no how, no way, cause it's the yee-hawingest time you'll have this year.

ICE CUBES

1½ OUNCES CAMPARI

1½ OUNCES FRESHLY SQUEEZED ORANGE JUICE

CHILLED CLUB SODA

ORANGE SLICE, FOR GARNISH

1. Fill a cocktail shaker halfway full with ice cubes. Add the Campari and orange juice. Shake well.

2. Fill a highball glass three-quarters full with ice cubes. Strain the mixture over the ice.

3. Fill the glass almost full with club soda. Stir briefly. Garnish with the orange slice.

A NOTE: Feeling too old for shaking? Feel free to build this over ice in a highball glass. But you'll still need to stir well, or that trout'll be sour.

A VARIATION: Want a drink akin to this but without bubbles? Check out the Garibaldi on page 135.

PIMM'S CUP

Not just for cooling you off after a serious match of lawn tennis played in a backyard garden on an estate outside of Ramsgill in the UK, the Pimm's Cup is now poured whenever and wherever folks desire an enlivening beverage. You might see it made with 7UP or with fresh lemonade, and both can be delightful (though I like the ginger ale version best-est), but all versions use Pimm's No. 1, which is made according to James Pimm's secret original recipe, reportedly known to only six people. The Pimm's reliability in this drink is due partially to the plain fact that Pimm's No. 1, made with gin, herbs, and a touch of fruitiness, is enchanting in spring and summer. Also, the other Pimm's varieties (at one time there were six, made on bases of gin, Scotch, brandy, rum, rye, and vodka) are not as readily available, though if you are in the UK during the colder months, I suggest you try Pimm's Winter Cup, based on brandy, spices, and orange peel.

ICE CUBES

2 OUNCES PIMM'S NO. 1

CHILLED GINGER ALE

CUCUMBER SLICE,
FOR GARNISH

1. Fill a large Collins glass three-quarters full with ice cubes. Add the Pimm's.

2. Top off the glass with ginger ale. Garnish with the cucumber slice.

Aperol

A luminous dream of a liqueur—delicate with a feather's touch of
orange and the barest trace of bitter buried beneath a soft sweetness—
Aperol is an Italian staple, famous for being a part of the Italian Spritz
(Aperol, Prosecco, and either an orange slice or an olive as garnish—or
sometimes both), which is a favorite at the five o'clock hour when
sipped at a café after the workday is done. Aperol's lightness, in flavor
and in alcohol content (11 percent), makes it ideal in this situation.
Thanks are due to the Barbieri Brothers, who presented Aperol—their
combination of bitter and sweet oranges, gentian, rhubarb, and more
than 30 herbs and spices—to the world at the 1919 Padua Expedition
in Italy. Their idea was that it would be a fantastic alternative to some
of the heavier Italian aperitivos and digestivos on the market, and it was
a good idea, because starting around World War II it became hugely
popular in Italy and in many other places. For a long time, sadly, the
United States wasn't one of those other places, as Aperol wasn't available
stateside for many years, until 2005. Luckily for us, we don't have to
smuggle bottles into the country anymore, and we can slip into the
Aperol dream with a trip to the local liquor store, using it in cocktails
such as the Portofino (page 146) and Ti Penso Sempre (page 281).

PORTOFINO

A cosmopolitan affair, the Portofino comes from *un bel libro* called *Cocktail: Classici & Esotici* (Demetra, 2002) that I found in a wonderful Florence (Italy, that is) bookstore. Using English liqueur Pimm's No. 1 (for more on Pimm's, see page 144) and Italian favorite Aperol (which is light, orange, and barely bitter), the Portofino is the very liquid definition of captivating, in the "takes your breath away" way and not the "holds you hostage" way. Which is probably why it was named after one of the most beautiful port cities. Located on the Italian Riviera in the Genoa province (I just had a lightning bolt of an idea: Serve this at a party with the Genoese on page 196 and have everyone dress as Italian beachgoers), the town of Portofino has a history almost as wonderful as this drink. According to reports that go all the way back to Pliny the Elder (and why would he lie?), the town was settled by the Romans and named Portus Delphini, which means Port of the Dolphin, in honor of the dolphins that frolicked in the gulf around it.

ICE CUBES

2 OUNCES PIMM'S NO. 1

1 OUNCE APEROL

CHILLED GINGER ALE

ORANGE SLICE,
FOR GARNISH

MARASCHINO CHERRY,
FOR GARNISH

1. Fill a highball glass three-quarters full with ice cubes. Add the Pimm's and Aperol and stir briefly.

2. Fill the glass almost to the top with ginger ale. Stir again and garnish with the orange slice and the cherry, attaching them together with a toothpick if needed (and if you think it's safe).

PRAIRIE HIGH

Y ou can take this drink four ways. You can use it to toast those pioneering spirits who explored the prairie from mountain high to valley low. You can sip it sentimentally, thinking back to when you were finishing high school, even if you weren't on the prairie. You can consume it while you also consume the finely wrought words and photos on the blog Prairy Nation (www.prairynation.wordpress.com), written by my pal Jen Dreiling, the very blog I was reading when consuming this enlivening highball for the first time. (Sadly, as of this writing, the blog is in hibernation—but still worth reading for back posts until new ones arrive.) You can make it for friends from all corners of the globe in a nod to its international nature, as it contains American rye and bitters, the Italian amaro Averna, and ginger ale, which brings in Eastern flavors and bubbly goodness. Come to think of it, you can also take it a fifth way, which is to combine all the above, having as many Prairie Highs as necessary to get through the list.

ICE CUBES

1½ OUNCES RYE

½ OUNCE AVERNA

1 DASH FEE BROTHERS
WHISKEY BARREL AGED
BITTERS

CHILLED GINGER ALE

LEMON SLICE, FOR GARNISH

1. Fill a cocktail shaker halfway full with ice cubes. Add the rye, Averna, and bitters. Shake well.

2. Fill a highball glass halfway full with ice cubes. Strain the mix over the ice cubes and into the glass.

3. Fill the glass nearly to the top with ginger ale. Stir briefly. Squeeze the lemon slice over the glass and drop it in like a tumbleweed tumbling.

Amaros

Amaro, in Italian, means "bitter." As a type of drink, amaro refers to a whole family of Italian after-dinner digestivos, and while all of them contain at least a hint of a bittering agent, don't be confused into thinking that all of them are going to lean heavily onto the bitter side of the taste scale. On the contrary, there is a whole range of bitterness and sweetness contained within the family.

And it's somewhat of a contentious family—or at least trying to draw any borders around it makes some folks contentious. For me, if it's Italian, herbal, brown, and usually consumed after the meal, I consider it part of the family, even if the word *amaro* isn't directly in the name (though many brands do have it there). This may push the boundaries a bit, but it also makes for one heck of a family reunion.

Though anyone would be hard pressed to pin down the first amaro, the family started with someone combining herbs and liquor for medicinal purposes. Outside of the relief they give when you've eaten too much, I'm not sure how many are used medicinally today, but they certainly make me feel better after drinking them. For years, these liqueurs were almost always sipped solo, but more and more you're seeing them used as flavoring agents within a mixed drink, due to the individual personalities of each and the awe-inspiring layers of flavors they tend to impart. For proof, mix up cocktails such as the Friar Minor (page 133), which uses Ramazzotti amaro, or the Prairie High (page 147), which calls for Averna.

With all that said, what brands actually fall into the family? The list is long, but some outstanding (and readily available—there are many, many more you'll find in Italy but not here) members include Nonino, Cynar (made from artichokes, but still a part of the family), Averna, Ramazzotti, Zucca (made with rhubarb), CioCiaro, S. Maria al Monte, and Fernet-Branca. The levels of bitterness are somewhat subjective, though for me, the list above goes from least to most bitter.

Much like bitters themselves (and here I'm talking about those bitters detailed on page 27), amaros have specific flavor profiles. This means that you shouldn't switch one for another in a recipe. Not that the resulting recipe might not be amazing, but it won't be the same drink—which might just mean you'll need to exercise your drink-naming skills.

RED MOON

L et's go over them now: There's the blue moon, which of course means feeling down in the mouth, but also can signal (in some psychic paths) being relaxed, making it ideal for more solitary pursuits, and also means a rare event. Then there's the orange moon, which usually goes along with the harvest, and is orange-ish; let's call it the moon of hayrides and jolliness. There's the yellow moon, or banana moon, which denotes a very frolicsome outlook—the moon of blender drinks, one might say. And then there's the Red Moon, an herbal moon, a moon made to be consumed on a late spring night when the rabbits are just beginning to howl and the air is charged with excitement and energy and the need for a drink that matches the color of the big philosopher in the sky. This drink, that is.

1½ OUNCES BECHEROVKA

5 OUNCES BLACK CURRANT JUICE

CHILLED CLUB SODA

1. Fill a highball glass three-quarters full with ice cubes. Add the Becherovka and black currant juice. Stir briefly.

2. Top the glass off with club soda. Stir again, briefly. Gaze at the moon.

A NOTE: For more information on the Czech digestif Becherovka, see page 127.

RED-NOSED REHBOCK

T he wave of bartenders shaking and singing and slinging more mixes using the many liqueurs and spirits out there doesn't stop at the end of a lounge door, or a restaurant exit, or a drive-in theater's bar. There are many home bartenders coming up with drinks that'll make your special occasions even more special. This particular glass of bubbliciousness, for example, comes from Matt Bohlmann, Seattle-area bon vivant (and husband of seasoned party thrower Maile, whose maiden name lent itself to this title). As Matt says, this is a "great (and bracing) Christmas morning eye-opener. With dry Champagne, use a little bit less Campari."

½ OUNCE CAMPARI

1 OUNCE CRANBERRY JUICE

CHILLED BRUT CHAMPAGNE

DASH OF ORANGE BITTERS

1. Add the Campari and cranberry juice to a flute glass. Stir once.

2. Fill the flute with Champagne almost to the top. Stir calmly and briefly. Top with the dash of orange bitters.

REVELATION

And though I did walk through the valley of poorly stocked bars, I did fear no badly made cocktail, because as this very desiccated desert did swarm around me, with annoying bar patrons who talked loudly and angrily of reality TV, I heard a voice that said, "Hold out your hand and preach the word of Revelation, and your evening is going to turn from sour to herbal with the touch of Bénédictine, from blah to ba-ba-bam with kümmel's caraway and a whisper of mint." And my evening (and yours, if you play your bottles right) passed the pabulum and turned into taste, and my drinks, and my drinking companions, were made whole again.

CRACKED ICE

1½ OUNCES BÉNÉDICTINE

1 OUNCE KÜMMEL

½ OUNCE WHITE CRÈME DE MENTHE

MINT SPRIG, FOR GARNISH

1. Fill a cocktail shaker or mixing glass halfway full with cracked ice. Add the Bénédictine, kümmel, and crème de menthe. Stir well.

2. Strain into a cocktail glass. Garnish with the mint sprig and a little prayer.

4

Criminal Cocktails

GINGER BLISS & THE VIOLET FIZZ

Some drinks scream out for inclusion in a hard-boiled pulp story, consumed in rapid fashion by either a gentleman in a long dark trench coat, a curvy blond in stiletto heels, or a person about to make a really bad choice. These are those drinks (making them the mixes to make when reading Hammett, Chandler, Williford, or their crime-writing contemporaries).

1. Dutch Charlie's
(page 233)

2. Widow's Kiss
(page 163)

3. Black Fog
(page 89)

4. Touchless Automatic
(page 215)

SHANGHAI GIN

The modern world of marvelous cocktails and cocktailians stretches, some might say, to Shanghai from every other port of call imaginable, making this drinking world a large and sometimes daunting place to dive into. This is a shame. Drinking, we can agree, is supposed to be the opposite: joyful, enjoyable, and an activity done in comfortable company. Luckily, the big ol' cocktail universe once in a while reminds us that it is, after all, not so big, and is full of friends both known and yet to meet. Take this very drink as Exhibit A. I picked up this recipe from San Francisco bartender Thad Vogler, who once made me a drink at the wonderful Heaven's Dog (www.heavensdog.com) and who now slings 'em up right at Bar Agricole (www.baragricole.com). I didn't realize it at the time, but Thad is the cousin of one of my closest pals, Rebecca Staffel, the inspiration for the Rebecca (page 106). Now, if that isn't a small world, then I'm seeing things backward.

ICE CUBES

¾ OUNCE GIN

¾ OUNCE FRESHLY SQUEEZED LEMON JUICE

¾ OUNCE YELLOW CHARTREUSE

¾ OUNCE BÉNÉDICTINE

1. Fill a cocktail shaker halfway full with ice cubes. Add the gin, lemon juice, Chartreuse, and Bénédictine. Shake well.

2. Strain into a cocktail glass and give someone a hug.

"Shorty recovered himself, no mean feat after the MacKelvie-provided shot of green Chartreuse, and the Fishwicke-provided shot of Bénédictine he had thrown down on top of everything else."

—KINGSLEY AMIS, *ENDING UP*, 1974

THE SICILIAN SLING

Doesn't the moniker this rollicking refresher carries bring up images of gangsters talking about a particular arm-breaking move? Well, step back from preconceived notions (and any movie or TV stereotypes), and step up to the bar to receive a glass full of exuberant herbalizing, with Italian amaro Averna (which is about in the middle of the bitter scale when looking over the amaro family) mingling with Bénédictine's deeper voices and cherry brandy's cheerful and strong sweetness. When adding lemon juice's tang and club soda's bubbles to the plentiful palate, the result will break any hold a dusty, hot summer's day has on you. But that's the only violence involved. Which makes sense, as this was created by Jeremy Sidener (who also brought us the Tourist, page 159), one of the Midwest's finest bartenders and gentlemen, and a fella who's much more likely to give out hugs than any sort of arm-bustings.

· ·

ICE CUBES

1½ OUNCES AVERNA

½ OUNCE CHERRY BRANDY

½ OUNCE BÉNÉDICTINE

½ OUNCE FRESHLY SQUEEZED LEMON JUICE

CHILLED CLUB SODA

1 OR 2 FRESH BASIL LEAVES, FOR GARNISH

1. Fill a cocktail shaker halfway full with ice cubes. Add the Averna, cherry brandy, Bénédictine, and lemon juice. Shake well.

2. Fill a highball glass three-quarters full with ice cubes. Strain the mixture into the glass. Top with chilled club soda, filling it almost to the top. Gently smack the basil leaf or leaves and let them rest on the drink's top.

A NOTE: Jeremy suggests Hiram Walker cherry brandy, which is of the sweeter variety (in the same realm as cherry Heering). And do you really wanna go against him and possibly miss out on the hugs?

SOLERA CLUB

et me yell this up front: I'm not looking to start any sort of East Coast/ West Coast bartenders' war (where the flying ice might keep you and me from getting cocktails delivered regularly). So don't expect me to quote Tupac in "California Love," where he rolls out rhymes about the West being best. But if I was going to start rhyming about bartenders on the West Coast (which is the coast I live on most of the time, so I should be sticking up for it somewhat, right?) in rap style, multiple lines would be devoted to the wizard of the West Coast, Jeffrey Morgenthaler, who writes about bartending and mixology in charismatic and helpful style (www.jeffreymorgenthaler.com), who is bar manager and drink menu designer at Portland's Clyde Common (www.clydecommon.com), and who has been at the forefront of scrumptious advancements in modern bartending, such as barrel-aged cocktails, homemade tonic, and more. He's also the creator of the Solera Club, which is a hub of superior ingredients that together make drinking smarts worth singing about. And then some.

CRACKED ICE

2 OUNCES MEDIUM-DRY SHERRY

1 OUNCE CYNAR

½ OUNCE CRÈME DE PÊCHE

1 TEASPOON ABSINTHE

WIDE ORANGE PEEL, FOR GARNISH

1. Fill a cocktail shaker or mixing glass halfway full with cracked ice. Add the sherry, Cynar, crème de pêche, and absinthe. Stir well.

2. Strain into a cocktail glass (chilled if possible). Garnish with the orange peel.

Fernet-Branca

Fernet-Branca may be the most renowned and honored of the Italian amaros (learn more about amaros on page 148) and a drink beloved by many worldwide. Created in 1845 by pharmacist Bernardino Branca, working with a Dr. Fernet from Sweden, Fernet-Branca was originally painstakingly put together as a medicinal remedy to aid cholera and malaria patients and was then tested and used in hospitals. The drink is still made following the original recipe, and still by the Fratelli Branca company, run today by Count Niccolò Branca (isn't it nice when the liqueurs stay in the family?). It combines a wide assortment of herbs, spices, roots, and other all-natural ingredients from the far corners of the world—gentian root, rhubarb, myrrh, cinchona bark, galanga, saffron, and more. The Count and select family members are the only ones with the secret to how the herbs are treated in production, which means he is intricately involved in making Fernet-Branca. Fernet-Branca has a uniquely rich, bitter, and layered taste that has led to many imitations, so watch for the eagle-over-the-world logo to ensure you have the real thing.

It's the taste that sometimes has folks blanching after they take their first sip of Fernet-Branca. Bracing, with backbone and a bit of bite, the flavor is, I think, one most will enjoy, if they give it a chance—either solo or when mixed in cocktails like the IBF Pick-Me-Up (page 136) and the Napoleon (page 141). It's an institution in Italy (where its powers as an after-dinner—especially after a big dinner—drink are legendary), a favorite when mixed with Coke in Argentina, a legendary hangover helper, and, as Andrew Bohrer tells us on page 130, is often used as a "handshake" between bartenders.

Fratelli Branca also makes other delish drinks in its distillery near the center of bustling Milan, Italy, including Branca Menta, which adds sugar and peppermint oil to Fernet-Branca (making it a lighter option and ideal over ice in summer); Stravecchio brandy, which spends time in Europe's biggest cask before bottling; coffee liqueur Borghetti, which can be hard to find in the States but is worth tracking down for its pure coffee flavor created by combining only coffee, sugar, and alcohol; and the Carpano family of vermouths, a family that includes both Carpano Antica and Punt e Mes, two sweet vermouths whose flavors make them integral ingredients in many drinks.

SUPERSONIC

I 'm not a preacher (though I am the son of a preacher man, as the song says), so I don't want to begin preaching. I'm also not someone who ever thinks it's a smart idea to drink when angry—I'm firmly in the camp that thinks drinking should be merry and done with mates. And, finally, I don't want to be seen as having anything against the people of Oklahoma, who are okay by me.

But, but, but, the buts dribble out against the above three statements each time I shake up a Supersonic, a cheering cocktail made in honor of my one-time NBA home team, the Seattle Supersonics. Who were stolen (well, I'm a bit bitter, but that's how I see it) by some businessmen and moved to Oklahoma. Here though, is a thought that might balance out the scales and make it better: If, whenever you make a Supersonic, you think of Gary Payton, Shawn Kemp, Nate MacMillan (in his playing days), and all the ex-Sonic ballers, well, it'll help things go down smoother.

ICE CUBES

1½ OUNCES GIN

1 OUNCE GREEN CHARTREUSE

½ OUNCE FRESHLY SQUEEZED LIME JUICE

¼ OUNCE SIMPLE SYRUP (PAGE 12)

LEMON TWIST, FOR GARNISH

1. Fill a cocktail shaker halfway full with ice cubes. Add the gin, Chartreuse, lime juice, and simple syrup. Shake as if you were dribbling the ball extra hard.

2. Strain into a cocktail glass. Squeeze the twist over the drink, and then swish it into the glass.

THREE BITTERS

I f you have a couple weeks of vacation time and a small part of your savings you can spare, and you enjoy good food, relaxation, art, and incredibly diverse liqueurs, then what are you doing here, reading this book? You should be in Italy right now! Staying at one of the remarkably inexpensive (while still having all the amenities of home) villas, apartments, and homes offered by the folks at Amici Villas (www.amicivillas.com), folks who will take such good care of you that you'll think you're staying with your parents (as long as you get along well with said parents—if not, with close friends), if your parents lived in the rolling harmonious hills and valleys on the Tuscany/Umbria border. If you can't take off right now for Italy (and feel free to cry right away if this is the case; I sure will understand), then I suggest pouring this drink, which is adapted from one by drink writer Derek M. Brown, printed first at www.theatlantic.com, to drown your sorrow. Since it contains three captains of Italian liqueur, it'll take away a tiny sliver of the sting.

ICE CUBES

½ OUNCE CAMPARI

½ OUNCE CYNAR

¼ OUNCE FERNET-BRANCA

1 OUNCE FRESHLY SQUEEZED ORANGE JUICE

½ OUNCE SIMPLE SYRUP (PAGE 12)

¼ OUNCE FRESHLY SQUEEZED LEMON JUICE

ORANGE SLICE, FOR GARNISH

SPRIG OF CHOCOLATE MINT, FOR GARNISH (OPTIONAL)

1. Fill a cocktail shaker halfway full with ice cubes. Add the Campari, Cynar, Fernet-Branca, orange juice, simple syrup, and lemon juice. Shake well.

2. Strain into a chilled cocktail glass. Garnish with the orange slice and, if you want to fancy it up, the sprig of chocolate mint.

TOURIST

Sometimes being a tourist, wide-eyed and weighed down with maps, is a thrill. After a few days, though, the feeling of wanting to belong tends to seep in, and also the desire to have a good watering hole to visit where you'll feel at home. Now, I can't help with this desire to get away from the tourist designation at every place you might visit. If you're ever visiting Kansas, though, and want to discover that welcoming bar, then head to Lawrence and get yourself to the Eighth Street Taproom (www.eighthstreettaproom.com). Jeremy Sidener, convivial bar manager and creative cocktail creator (who always keeps a view toward the classics), is not only going to exude that welcoming vibe through his own person, but he can also make you a Tourist (this drink, that is), which is one of his own creations. And drinking a Tourist is much better than feeling like one.

ICE CUBES

1¼ OUNCES PIMM'S NO. 1

½ OUNCE CAMPARI

½ OUNCE CRÈME DE NOYAUX

1¼ OUNCES FRESHLY SQUEEZED RED GRAPEFRUIT JUICE

2 OUNCES CHILLED CLUB SODA

1 PEELED LYCHEE *OR* ORANGE OR LEMON TWIST, FOR GARNISH (OPTIONAL)

1. Fill a cocktail shaker halfway full with ice cubes. Add the Pimm's, Campari, crème de noyaux, and grapefruit juice. Shake like a native.

2. Fill a Collins or comparably sized glass three-quarters full with ice cubes. Strain the mixture over the ice and into the glass. Top with the club soda. Stir briefly.

3. If you have a peeled lychee, add it to the drink for a garnish. If not, twist either an orange or lemon twist over the glass, and then add it.

THE WHIP OF THE CONQUEROR

F eaturing the bracing and bountiful *bam!* of Italian digestivo Fernet-Branca over a layer of rumbling dark rum and a lovely lash of apricot liqueur and a tiny tang of lime, the Whip should be unveiled only when attempting world conquest (in the board game Risk, that is) or having a marathon video game session when the games are medieval or oriented earlier (such as Prince of Persia, say) or having a double elimination ('cause every player needs a second chance) shuffleboard tournament where the winner triumphs thanks to the singular method of ricocheting the puck off the sidewalls to hang gracefully on the board's edge—without falling over. A conqueror indeed.

ICE CUBES

1½ OUNCES DARK RUM

1 OUNCE FERNET-BRANCA

½ OUNCE APRICOT LIQUEUR

¼ OUNCE FRESHLY SQUEEZED LIME JUICE

LIME TWIST, FOR GARNISH

1. Fill a cocktail shaker halfway full with ice cubes. Add the rum, Fernet-Branca, apricot liqueur, and lime juice. Shake in a whip-cracking motion.

2. Strain into a cocktail glass, and garnish with the lime whip. Oh, I mean twist.

Bénédictine

An herbal miracle elixir, Bénédictine is spiritual (well, I feel it has at least a healing aura about it, and as it was used as a medicinal brew for years, I don't think I'm the only one) and a bit mysterious. Bénédictine has a dramatic history—we're lucky it's even around today. The recipe for this revered liquid revelation goes back all the way (as legend tells it) to the Renaissance. During this time, Dom Bernardo Vincelli, a monk at the Abbey of Fécamp, mixed together an assortment of 27 spices, plants, and herbs to combine all of their medicinal powers, with a little spirituous liquid and sweetening added for even more healing. Soon, this—the original recipe for Bénédictine—was being used by many for aches and pains, and simply because it tasted so darn good. But then (and this comes with a large intake of breath at the travesty), the French Revolution kicked off, and a French nobleman purchased the recipe and hid it in his library for safekeeping—and then lost it.

The world may have forever been deprived of this lovely liqueur, and been the sadder (and the less healthy) for it, if heroic Alexandre Le Grand hadn't come on the scene (really, this story should be transported to the big screen). In 1863, he unearthed an ancient book of spells, within which he found an intriguing recipe for a magical mixture. After translating and rewriting the recipe and tracking down the 27 crucial ingredients (including angelica, hyssop, juniper, myrrh, saffron, aloe, arnica, and cinnamon), Le Grand brought Bénédictine back (with a touch of updating). While the recipe remains a closely guarded secret, at least we can rest assured that it probably won't be lost again, because the clamor from the crowds who enjoy Bénédictine by itself, mixed with brandy to become the popular B&B, and as a key cocktail component in mixes such as the Monte Carlo (page 140) and the Revelation (page 150), would be so large as to start another revolution.

WIDOW'S KISS

This should be a cocktail constructed in honor of an all-female metal band of the same name, a cocktail that would then be served at the merch tables at every show of said band on their world tour. Though, thinking it through, this is a complex, poised, think-y bit of an adult beverage, with its usage of the Normandy apple brandy Calvados, French lighter and darker herbal liqueurs Chartreuse and Bénédictine, respectively, and reliable Angostura bitters, one that might be less wild in the streets than our hypothetical ladies-in-leather band. However, the ingredients list is world-spanning, which matches up with the world tour angle. How about a compromise: This can be the signature drink on a tour for a female band called Widow's Kiss, but they play metal on orchestra instruments.

ICE CUBES

1½ OUNCES CALVADOS

¾ OUNCE GREEN CHARTREUSE

¾ OUNCE BÉNÉDICTINE

DASH OF ANGOSTURA BITTERS

1. Fill a cocktail shaker halfway full with ice cubes. Add the Calvados, Chartreuse, Bénédictine, and bitters. Shake well.

2. Strain into a cocktail glass.

A VARIATION: In some select tomes of lore, this is made slightly differently, with equal parts Chartreuse, Bénédictine, and maraschino liqueur, and the yolk of an egg. Sounds like a dangerously delicious morning drink. Be sure to shake it well if going this route and not to serve it to any elderly widows (or anyone with a compromised immune system).

A NOTE: I feel a drink this dangerous should be shaken. But if you want to stir your widow over cracked ice, I'll bet you'll still get kissed.

ALL-AMERICAN MONGREL, PAGE 167

CHAPTER 6

IT'S A NUTTY,

NUTTY

WORLD

. . . .

To completely connect to the current chapter, we must first brush up a bit on our dictionary savvy, which is (when accompanied by drink) always amusing and informative. The word *nutty* has four definitions. (Well, four that are in regular usage, that is. Perhaps after a few Brave Bulls, different definitions may occur. Which is right and proper, because drinks shared with companions should lead at least somewhat to both linguistic philosophies and newly created shared languages.) In order of usage rates, we start with the first, which does refer to something that contains or has a lot of nuts in it, such as the drink in this chapter called From the Terrace, which features nocino, an Italian liqueur made from walnuts.

The second definition we have for *nutty* is correlated to the first, but takes itself less literally, in that it is attached to something that resembles nuts (but may not in fact contain nuts), and this definition usually, if not in point of fact, refers to the taste or flavor of a dish or drink. Following along the logical path of our first definition's example, we'd look toward such cocktails as the Blenheim, which pulls a nuttiness from the Tia Maria liqueur, which isn't based on nuts but has a nutty flavor; and the Class Division, whose main player, advocaat, is also nutty while not being built with nuts.

After our first two definitions, we get a smidge more abstract—slangy, even—as the third definition has *nutty* as a reference to insanity or madness. You might believe this would have nothing to do with drinks, though a soupçon of madcap-ness does follow along many memorable evenings sharing some of these beverages with friends, such as the fantastic Flying Carpet, or the noggin-stretching Zeno's Paradoxical. These drinks may fit into one of our first two definitions as well, but also (along with most of the others in this nutty chapter) match up like socks with the third definition.

Finally, a more archaic definition, wherein *nutty* defines the feeling when one is incredibly fond of a person, a dog, a type of cheese, a specific issue of the comic book *Action Philosophers* (put out by Evil Twin Comics), or one of the drinks in this chapter. For example, it's acceptable even today in most modern prose to make the statement "I'm nutty about the Mrs. Dr. Jones" or "My golly, I'm just nutty for Sweet Harmonics." This final definition could perhaps be used by consumers for every drink in this nutty chapter. But to find out whether that's accurate, stop the defining, and start drinking.

ALL-AMERICAN MONGREL

G awd, I love mongrels. In this case, I am referring to mixed-breed dogs (of which I have two, named Sookie and Rory) as well as this particular drink, which uses not only boon companion Scotch, Italian lass Aperol, and happily-easier-to-find-today-than-yesterday bianco vermouth, but also Nux Alpina, a brandy-based walnut liqueur. Its nuttiness really drives this cocktail for me in the way that a tiny bit of Shih Tzu can drive the personality of an 80-pound mongrel. Isn't it wonderful how things sometimes become more than what you might expect at first? I first had this at one of my top Seattle tippling spots, Vessel (www.vesselseattle.com). Bar champ Jim Romdall, who manages Vessel, created this cocktail, showing that he, too, knows what makes a good mongrel.

. . . .

CRACKED ICE

1½ OUNCES BLENDED SCOTCH

½ OUNCE APEROL

½ OUNCE BIANCO VERMOUTH

¼ OUNCE NUX ALPINA WALNUT LIQUEUR

FLAMED ORANGE PEEL, FOR GARNISH (SEE A SECOND NOTE)

1. Fill a cocktail shaker or mixing glass half-way full with cracked ice. Add the Scotch, Aperol, vermouth, and Nux Alpina. Stir well.

2. Strain into a cocktail glass, and garnish with the flamed orange peel.

A NOTE: Jim suggests the Famous Grouse for Scotch (which is one of my favorites, too), and Dolin for the vermouth. As he's a, well, genius, I sure wouldn't trust anyone else's suggestions.

A SECOND NOTE: For flaming a twist, you'll want to be sure you have an oval-shaped twist about 1½ inches long. First, light a match, holding it in one hand about 4 inches above the drink. With the other hand, hold the twist, peel side facing the drink, above the match. Twist the twist quickly, so that the oils shoot out, flaming as they pass through the flame into the drink.

. . . .

" 'Fine,' I said, 'nothing like keeping up to schedule.' I swallowed my fifth? sixth? seventh? Scotch. 'Pretty good clock, isn't it? Dependable.' 'Sure,' said the barman."

—PATRICK QUENTIN, *PUZZLE FOR PLAYERS*, 1938

BLENHEIM

Though the name brings to mind Germanic fortresses, my guess (and I admit it's a guess, because I haven't researched a definitive source, but if you have one, please send it to me, and I'll buy you a round next time) is that it's named after a town nestled in the Jamaican hills, where one Sir Alexander Bustamante was born. Sir Alexander was given the Order of National Hero for his work toward liberating the island. I don't think that the connection to this drink means it'll cause you to liberate anything (unless it's liberating yourself and your friends another cocktail), but rather that the drink's flavor is driven by Jamaican-born Tia Maria, a liqueur that combines coffee, vanilla, and sugar.

ICE CUBES

2 OUNCES VODKA

1 OUNCE TIA MARIA

½ OUNCE FRESHLY
SQUEEZED ORANGE JUICE

1. Fill a cocktail shaker halfway full with ice cubes. Add the vodka, Tia Maria, and orange juice. Shake well.

2. Strain into a cocktail glass.

BRAVE BULL

Hola, torero—there's no need to kill any four-legged living creature, even one with large horns, to prove yourself this sun-speckled afternoon. Today, my friend, you only have to drink the bull (and that not to prove yourself, but just because it is *delicioso*). There is, though, a very definite need to wear a *montera* or similarly extravagant headpiece, as well as a shimmery outfit that matches a matador's *traje de luces*, the suit of lights. Decked out and sparkling provides more enjoyable machismo anyway.

ICE CUBES

2 OUNCES WHITE TEQUILA

1 OUNCE TIA MARIA

LEMON TWIST,
FOR GARNISH (OPTIONAL)

1. Fill a cocktail shaker three-quarters full with ice cubes. Add the tequila and Tia Maria. Stir briefly.

2. If you're feeling the wind in your hair, twist the twist over the glass and let it join the rodeo.

A VARIATION: Often, you'll see this made with Kahlúa instead of Tia Maria. I think the latter is a bit more bullish, but feel free to ride with Kahlúa.

CLASS DIVISION

D own with class division! Up with Class Divisions! No, I'm not confused; I'm just trying to emphatically underline that this bit-of-the-beachside drink is a chilled slogan you should get behind. Maybe it doesn't demand marching in the streets, but marching with slogans on poles ("More Class Divisions! Less class warfare!") around the backyard might be entertaining.

ICE CUBES

1½ OUNCES WHITE RUM

1 OUNCE ADVOCAAT

½ OUNCE FRESH PINEAPPLE JUICE

1. Fill a cocktail shaker halfway full with ice cubes. Add the rum, advocaat, and pineapple juice. Shake well.

2. Strain into a cocktail glass. Serve with a straw, as the advocaat may settle a bit.

A NOTE: Advocaat is a creamy, rich liqueur made from eggs, sugar, a base spirit (usually brandy), and spices and such that tends toward nuttiness (in flavor, that is).

LIQUEUR SPOTLIGHT

Tia Maria

Come close, ladies and gentleman, and listen to the luscious and inspiring legend of Tia Maria. We have to travel back to the unrestful seventeenth century to begin the story, landing in Jamaica, a country that like much of the Caribbean was in the midst of colonial revolution. In the middle of the struggles, a lady had to flee her plantation home with only her maid. But what a maid, as she managed to grab two incredibly important things before leaving: the lady's best black pearl earrings and (even more important) the family liqueur recipe, which was, as you might expect, a secret. Handed down from generation to generation and called "Tia Maria" after that smart and responsible maid, the recipe was kept secret and served only to close friends for many years. Until around 1950, when it was tasted by a Dr. Kenneth Leigh Evans in Jamaica. He was so struck by the liqueur's coffee-vanilla-nut personality that he went home and worked to re-create it in his lab (one hopes he okayed this with the family), tinkering until he came up with the modern version.

THE FLYING CARPET

ather round, my young friends (and by "young" I mean at least 21 and definitely young at heart). Pull your mats up close to the fire as the light dims, and let me unfurl a fantastic story for you. It involves a seemingly plain carpet, one that could be overlooked by many, but not by the observant and the believers, those who peer past the mundane and into the extraordinary right around the corner (or right into the liquor cabinet). A carpet that's related to the famous floor covering of Tangu, but a level above, a level that doesn't have you squatting on the floor, but transports you and your comrades via a single sip—or maybe two.

ICE CUBES

1½ OUNCES FRANGELICO

1 OUNCE GIN

½ OUNCE CRÈME DE CACAO

½ OUNCE DRY SHERRY

FRESHLY GRATED NUTMEG, FOR GARNISH

1. Fill a cocktail shaker halfway full with ice cubes. Add the Frangelico, gin, crème de cacao, and sherry. Shake well.

2. Strain into a cocktail glass. Garnish with a mist of grated nutmeg, and prepare to travel.

A NOTE: Frangelico is an Italian hazelnut liqueur with a rich layered flavor and a very distinctive bottle in the shape of a Franciscan monk. It supposedly traces a history back 300 years, to a religious hermit named Fra Angelico, who was famous for both his piety and his homemade liqueurs.

FRENCH CONNECTION

I think this goes without saying, but let me remind you: Never drink and drive. Especially in a high-speed car chase like the one in the movie. But, if you want to have a sturdy glassful while playing Mario Cart or another driving video game, or while you're playing the driving card game Mille Bornes ("a thousand mile markers" in French), then this wheel-spinning amaretto-brandy drink might be the perfect choice. A slim warning though: If Gene Hackman bursts through your door during the middle of your racing evening and says, "All right, Popeye's here! Get your hands on your heads, get off the bar, and get on the wall!" I'd be darn sure you have enough of the necessary ingredients to make him a drink.

. . . .

CRACKED ICE

2 OUNCES AMARETTO

2 OUNCES BRANDY

ICE CUBES

LEMON TWIST, FOR GARNISH

1. Fill a mixing glass or cocktail shaker halfway full with cracked ice. Add the amaretto and brandy. Stir well.

2. Fill an old-fashioned glass with ice cubes. Strain the mixture into the glass and garnish with the lemon twist.

A VARIATION: In his excellent book *The Joy of Mixology*, cocktailian Gary Regan makes this with Grand Marnier instead of amaretto and Cognac instead of just brandy. Which seems like a tasty connection to try.

. . . .

"A discussion of wine and their vintages followed; and it was but a few moments before Vance had launched into one of his favorite topics—namely, the rare cognacs of the west-central Charente Departement in France—the Grande Champagne and Petite Champagne districts and the vineyards around Mainxe and Archiac."

—S.S. VAN DINE, *THE SMELL OF MURDER*, 1938

FRIDAY KALOHE

When the immortal Loverboy sang "Everybody's working for the weekend," they may not have realized that there are, oddly, a number of people out there who would rather be at work than anywhere else. And you know what? This isn't a bad thing, except when it's taken too far, and they start to forget that work doesn't always (and shouldn't) equal life. There are vistas beyond the cubicle walls, people. And your friends and family miss you.

There are many of us who may dig our jobs but also love Fridays and every jolt that they stand for, but who have to deal with those who may not want the workweek to ever end. So, on Friday afternoon, suggest kicking off early for a cocktail. If they don't step up, then maybe start playing a few secret tricks: Misplace their mouse, put a cupcake on their chair, schedule them for a meeting and then serve this drink at the meeting. Insist that they have it to preserve the sanctity of meetings, and then after they have that first one, my guess is they'll be ready for a second. Let the weekend begin.

. . . .

ICE CUBES

1½ OUNCES BOURBON

1 OUNCE KAHANA ROYALE MACADAMIA NUT LIQUEUR

½ OUNCE AMARO CIOCIARO

DASH OF FEE BROTHERS WHISKEY BARREL AGED BITTERS

1. Fill a cocktail shaker halfway full with ice cubes. Add the bourbon, macadamia nut liqueur, CioCiaro, and bitters. Shake well— it's Friday, so show you appreciate it.

2. Strain into a cocktail glass.

FROM THE TERRACE

Though this is a drink with heaps of personality (and, between us, a tiny kick) and is the kind of drink that won't be taken for granted, one that doesn't wallflower within a crowd, I still think it's ideal for late-spring affairs. You know the events I'm talking of, where attendees are wearing lightweight white dresses, or slightly nicer shorts and short-sleeve shirts, nothing overly exciting, comfortable but classy, the right stuff to watch the sun go down from just outside the house, with flowers in bloom in the cherry tree and green shades everywhere. This drink fits those relaxed, not rowdy times, with its layers of flavors driven by nocino, bitters, and gin, but with edges smoothed by simple syrup.

ICE CUBES

2 OUNCES GIN

1 OUNCE NOCINO WALNUT LIQUEUR

½ OUNCE SIMPLE SYRUP (PAGE 12)

1 DASH FEE BROTHERS WHISKEY BARREL AGED BITTERS

WIDE ORANGE TWIST, FOR GARNISH

1. Fill a cocktail shaker halfway full with ice cubes. Add the gin, nocino, simple syrup, and bitters. Shake well.

2. Strain into a cocktail glass. Garnish with the orange twist.

A NOTE: Don't shirk on the twist or you may get tipped off the terrace—you want a triumphantly wide twist here, not one that's tiny.

A SECOND NOTE: Nocino is a dark brown Italian walnut liqueur, traditionally made in the Emilia-Romagna region of Italy from unripe green walnuts. There is a group, Ordine del Nocino Modenese, from this northern region that exists to promote this traditional liqueur, and an annual festival in July celebrating it.

JUSTINE

W hile you might be tempted to dwell on the mysterious name of this well-mannered mixer (Is it from an all-girl prog-rock band that dresses medievally? A paean to an erotic French novel? Or a shout-out to a long-ago saint?), instead I think the focus here should be on two intriguing ingredients, crème de noyaux and kirsch. The first is an almondy pink-tinged charmer named after the French word for "core," referring here to the kernels of the apricots used to make it—kernels that have an essence of almonds. The second, kirsch—or Kirschwasser to really impress—is a fruit brandy made from cherries, including the pits, which bring a slight almond character as well. It's the combination of these two that lessen the need to weigh out the name issue. It would take too much time, and who wants to wait?

ICE CUBES

2 OUNCES VODKA

1 OUNCE CRÈME DE NOYAUX

1 OUNCE KIRSCH

¼ OUNCE ORGEAT SYRUP

1 OUNCE HEAVY CREAM

1. Fill a cocktail shaker halfway full with ice cubes. Add the vodka, crème de noyaux, kirsch, orgeat, and cream. Shake well.

2. Strain the mixture into a cocktail glass.

A NOTE: Feel this is too foolish without a garnish? Add a strawberry slice.

A SECOND NOTE: Orgeat is an almondy syrup that you can find in gourmet stores as well as good liquor stores. It is perhaps most famous for being used in the Mai Tai.

MRS. DR. JONES

A curvy combination of brandy, Castries Peanut Rum Crème, cream, and Navan vanilla liqueur (which is a Madagascan vanilla smoother jolted by its Cognac base), Mrs. Dr. Jones is the kind of lady you'll want to invite over for chocolate by the fire, when the lights have been turned down low and the kids (or dogs) have been put to bed and the band Hot Chocolate's sexy rumblings rumble out from the stereo system to a room where the electric lights have been turned off in favor of candles but the electricity is still on high (if you know what I mean). Make sure you make two Mrs. Dr. Jones, though, because nothing ruins romance like a battle over a single glass. • SERVES 2

ICE CUBES

3 OUNCES BRANDY

1½ OUNCES CASTRIES PEANUT RUM CRÈME

1 OUNCE HEAVY CREAM

1 OUNCE NAVAN VANILLA LIQUEUR

1. Fill a cocktail shaker halfway full with ice cubes. Add the brandy, Castries peanut liqueur, cream, and Navan. Shake well.

2. Strain equally into two cocktail glasses and slip into something more comfortable.

A NOTE: If you want to add a garnish, try floating a couple of honey-roasted peanuts on top.

MY PISTACHIO DAYS

You've naturally heard the old saying, "As exuberant as if I were still in my pistachio days," right? Referring to when a person takes a sip of something delicious that instantly induces a jolly nostalgia that has the drinker up and dancing a jig in no time? I think it may have been Shakespeare who said it first, in one of the lesser-known plays? Wait, are you really telling me you don't know the saying? Well, take a sip of this mix and you'll soon understand it, as this nutty number will have you dancing in no time.

ICE CUBES

1½ OUNCES DARK RUM

1 OUNCE DUMANTE VERDENOCE PISTACHIO LIQUEUR

½ OUNCE FRESHLY SQUEEZED ORANGE JUICE

1 DASH FEE BROTHERS PEACH BITTERS

1. Fill a cocktail shaker halfway full with ice cubes. Add the dark rum, Dumante, orange juice, and bitters. Shake well.

2. Strain into a cocktail glass.

A NOTE: Dumante Verdenoce pistachio liqueur is made in Sicily, on the slopes of Mount Etna, using all-natural ingredients and a lot of love. (In case you didn't know, the story goes that if young lovers meet under the moonlight in a pistachio grove right as the pistachio nuts are turning ripe, they'll be blessed with happiness and good fortune.)

5

Drinks for Hot Days and Nights

GINGER BLISS & THE VIOLET FIZZ

Hey, cool off. There's not one good reason to let that thermometer shake its mercury at you in a commanding manner. Show it that you know how to take control of your environment by cooling things down via a few fast gulps or some slow sips of these chillers.

1. Springtime Fizz
(page 113)

2. Tropicaliana
(page 217)

3. Roman Cooler
(page 245)

4. Baltimore Bracer
(page 191)

5. Prairie High
(page 147)

THE RIVER OF STARS

This is less a carouser's cocktail choice and more of a meditative tipple for two who have a big blanket out on a hillside or backyard during a clear summer night, a night that's right for soft talking, slow sipping, and staring up at the big sky above, thinking not only about how large it is, but also about how lucky you are to be where you are at this one moment. The contemplative but companionable nature of this drink comes from vital ingredient Frangelico, a hazelnut liqueur made in the Piedmont region of Italy and known not only for its plentiful flavor, but also for its monk-shaped bottle and name, which comes from the revered hermetic monk Fra Angelico, who lived in the Piedmont hills.

ICE CUBES

1½ OUNCES GIN

1 OUNCE FRANGELICO

½ OUNCE BÉNÉDICTINE

1 EGG WHITE, PREFERABLY ORGANIC

1. Fill a cocktail shaker halfway full with ice cubes. Add the gin, Frangelico, Bénédictine, and the egg white. Shake very well, while staring skyward.

2. Strain into a cocktail glass.

A WARNING: As this drink contains raw egg, it shouldn't be served to the elderly or to those with compromised immune systems.

SHINE ALONG THE SHORE

Whether strolling along the Seine, ambling beside the Adriatic, or rambling next to Rewalsar Lake, there's no need to be dry on the inside, next to all that water outside. Now, the first reach, or first imaginative reach, in this situation might be toward a tall, tropical thirst-quencher. Remember, though, before making this real or dreamed drink, that not every body of water lends itself to bikinis and short shorts—some are best appreciated when you're wearing a parka. For a non-hot-weather water assembly, you'll want a cocktail that manages to warm you up and match your riverboat persona. The Shine Along the Shore is ready for the ride.

. . . .

CRACKED ICE

1½ OUNCES DARK RUM

1 OUNCE AMARETTO

½ OUNCE SWEET VERMOUTH

WIDE ORANGE TWIST, FOR GARNISH

1. Fill a cocktail shaker or mixing glass halfway full with cracked ice. Add the rum, amaretto, and vermouth. Stir well.

2. Strain into a cocktail glass. Twist the twist over the glass and drop it in.

A NOTE: I like a pretty wide twist here, so don't fear following the same route.

A SECOND NOTE: Though many consider it something consumed most often by college students on a bender, good amaretto is a true Italian treat and something worth tracking down (or trying again, if you gave up on it because of its mass-market associations). Brands such as Gozio, Luxardo, and Disaronno craft amarettos with care and good ingredients, with results that deliver rich almond flavor (which comes from apricot or peach pits, usually) without too much sweetness.

. . . .

"He banged two pint mugs on the table, poured in steaming coffee until they were two-thirds full. Then he brought down one of those bottles of rum, black as tar, popped the cork, and filled the mugs to the brim. He filled the plates and we ate. The rum was like a hot rasp running across the tongue."

—GIL BREWER, *THE THREE-WAY SPLIT*, 1960

SWEET HARMONICS

Say you're finishing up dinner with that platinum gal or guy pal who makes your heart palpitate, or that you've gotten the last candle lit before an evening consisting solely of dessert and drinks with said shining star, and you're trying to decide: Should I burst out in a loud love lyric at the top of my lungs? Should I improvise a scintillating song to be sung at side-splitting levels to share my feelings with everyone within shouting distance? Is that echoing-off-the-walls hymn to my night's hero or heroine the way to a perfect rest of the evening? Or should I resist the rocking refrain and bring the harmonics via this melodic liquid glee club instead? Unless you're in the singing class of Lionel Ritchie, I suggest sticking to the latter idea.

. . . .

ICE CUBES

1½ OUNCES COGNAC

1½ OUNCES NOCINO WALNUT LIQUEUR

½ OUNCE GALLIANO

½ OUNCE HEAVY CREAM

FRESH PEPPERMINT LEAF, FOR GARNISH

1. Fill a cocktail shaker halfway full with ice cubes. Add the Cognac, nocino, Galliano, and cream. Shake extra-well.

2. Add the peppermint leaf to a cocktail glass. Strain the mix over the peppermint (singing—softly—while straining, if needed).

6 Fresh Cocktail Books for You
. . . .

We live in a fantastic time not only for finding new liqueurs and new brands of base spirits as well as mighty intriguing mixes and garnishes, but also for finding cocktails made by bright and creative bartenders. Add to that the fact that we're able to read about new cocktails and new takes on classic cocktails and also to get heaps of insight, history, and party advice in a host of fun new books. The following are by no means the only ones out there, but they are a great place to start.

1. *The Essential Bartender's Guide: How to Make Truly Great Cocktails*, by Robert Hess (Mud Puddle Books, 2008)

2. *The Bartender's Gin Compendium*, by Gaz Regan (Xlibris, 2009)

3. *Spice & Ice: 60 Tongue-Tingling Cocktails*, by Kara Newman (Chronicle Books, 2009)

4. *Organic, Shaken and Stirred: Hip Highballs, Modern Martinis, and Other Totally Green Cocktails*, by Paul Abercrombie (Harvard Common Press, 2009)

5. *Japanese Cocktails*, by Yuri Kato (Chronicle Books, 2009)

6. *The Modern Mixologist: Contemporary Classic Cocktails,* by Tony Abou-Ganim (Agate Surrey, 2010)

ZENO'S PARADOXICAL

 ay your chum calibrates a drink for you that consists of Kentucky bourbon, Italian walnut liqueur, Italian sweet vermouth, and cardamom bitters. If you take a good-size gulp (not that I'm usually a fan of gulping, but this is science—sacrifice is necessary), let's postulate that you've drunk half of the drink. Now, to finish the drink, you first have to drink half of the remaining half. Then, you're halfway to being done, but before you can be done, you have to drink half of that half. Then half of that half. As everything goes and goes, you can never actually be done, because you always have to drink half first. And now you know why philosophers drink so much.

....

CRACKED ICE

1¾ OUNCES BOURBON

1 OUNCE NOCINO WALNUT LIQUEUR

½ OUNCE PUNT E MES VERMOUTH

2 DASHES SCRAPPY'S CARDAMOM BITTERS

1. Fill a mixing glass or cocktail shaker with cracked ice. Add the bourbon, nocino, Punt e Mes, and bitters. Stir well.

2. Strain the mixture into a cocktail glass.

A NOTE: Scrappy's is a Seattle company that makes bitters and cocktail flavorings and syrups in an artisanal manner. If your liquor or gourmet grocery or philosopher's store doesn't carry their products, try online at spots like cocktailkingdom.com.

....

"I gave him some whiskey. He held it as some-body else might hold a rare flower. He drank it slowly. In between sips, I could hear the breath in his throat."

—JOHN FARRIS, *BABY MOLL*, 1958

CHAPTER 7

THE SPICE

OF THE

DRINKING LIFE

· ·

Having a chapter of cocktails and highballs and their ilk revolving around "spices" is quite a challenge, as (A) there are lots of quibbles over what constitutes a "spice," and (B) so many liqueurs have at least one "spice" in them, and then (C) because of A and B it's somewhat hard to narrow the field in a way that helps the hopeful hoedown planner pick a properly spiced cocktail to go along with a hayrack ride. However, by applying a little method to the boozy madness, I believe that this chapter has been scaled back enough to be helpful, without scaling back so far as to seem limited.

With that in mind, the following drinks develop their personalities with the help of a particular overriding spice slant or a spice combo, brought to the fray by one or more liqueurs. Still confused? Well, let's break it down into examples. Starting at the beginning, the Absinthe Cocktail of course hinges on absinthe (which is really a spirit but pals on shelves with liqueurs), bringing its sharp anise profile to the drink.

From there, the spices come fast and furious, as if they were being milled straight into your mouth (well, we are talking about drinks here, people). For a couple more examples, take the Baltimore Bracer, which gets its anise taste from the sweetish liqueur anisette, or the Kingston Heights, bringing its caraway and cumin spices to the fore via the liqueur kümmel.

There are also more esoteric spices on display in these drinks, spices from faraway corners of the globe, including the Ginger Bliss's namesake, a spice found in the Caribbean favorite Domaine de Canton; and spices showing off in drinks such as the Tuscan Mule, which travels from Renaissance Florence through the emotive vanilla contained in Italian liqueur Tuaca; and the Touchless Automatic, which sings to any partaking of the allspice in its key ingredient, St. Elizabeth Allspice Dram.

Once you begin diving into these drinks and their various spices, it becomes less confusing (and if someone has a problem with how we're defining "spice," then cut that person off). The spices here aren't bothered by fitting into a pre-approved shelving system, but instead are happy to be grouped together under a single phrase: They taste first-rate. That's what matters, right? Serving up interesting and delicious drinks that feature the most flavorful ingredients one can find. That's the spice of life.

ABSINTHE COCKTAIL

I f you haven't already gone skipping through the streets to celebrate the fact that absinthe is not only available again in the United States, but is also being distilled in a fine manner in the United States again, then I suggest quickly making a few of the below in the classic manner (rapidly and lovingly) and starting the celebration.

Not a psychotropic hallucinogenic, or at least not any more than any other potent spirit, absinthe is an anise-flavored kick in the pants made with a variety of herbs and spices, with different brands using different concoctions but almost always boasting the flowers and leaves of the herb *Artemisia absinthium*, also known as "grand wormwood." The traditional method of slowly dripping water through a sugar cube into a glass of absinthe is a rather pretty way to consume absinthe, and it does let you watch the milky opaqueness, or *louche,* blossom. Absinthe is also dandy when combined with other liqueurs and spirits and mixers in cocktails, but I most often have it in this preparation, because of its chilly simplicity and my lack of patience (hey, I can admit this). However you decide to have your absinthe, let's just agree that we're happy that we're able to, finally, have it legally again.

ICE CUBES

2 OUNCES ABSINTHE

1 OUNCE SIMPLE SYRUP (PAGE 12)

LEMON TWIST, FOR GARNISH

1. Fill a cocktail shaker halfway full with ice cubes. Add the absinthe and simple syrup. Shake well.

2. Strain into a cocktail glass. Twist the twist over the glass and let it find its way into the glass.

A NOTE: Want to learn more about absinthe and interact with other absinthe devotees? Check out the Wormwood Society (www.wormwoodsociety.org) and see the Liqueur Spotlight on page 225.

"*One's emotions in Rome were one's private affair, like one's glass of absinthe before dinner in the Palais Royal.*"

—HENRY ADAMS, *THE EDUCATION OF HENRY ADAMS*, 1918

ASAP

Hurry, hurry, don't wait around, get to it, make haste, step on it, hit the gas, shake a leg, strike like lightning, put a little quick in it, burn rubber, hightail it, fly like a bat outta hell, strike a match to the hotfoot, move it, move it, move it. Now wait just a cotton-picking minute! This tall, tropical flourish may have a rapid-sounding name, but it's made to be savored when reclining poolside, or yardside if nothing else. Maybe hurry to make it, but don't hurry to finish it off. Life's meant to be enjoyed, not rushed through.

ICE CUBES

1½ OUNCES DARK RUM

½ OUNCE FALERNUM

½ OUNCE TUACA

½ OUNCE FRESH PINEAPPLE JUICE

CHILLED GINGER ALE

LIME SLICE, FOR GARNISH

1. Fill a highball glass three-quarters full with ice cubes. Add the rum, falernum, Tuaca, and pineapple juice. Stir, but only twice.

2. Top the glass off with ginger ale. Stir again. Garnish with the lime slice.

A NOTE: Falernum is a liqueur spiced usually with lime and ginger and other flavors, with a rum and sugar base. It's also available in a nonalcoholic version, but guess which one I like better?

Tuaca

Ah, Florence. The breathtaking Duomo and Brunelleschi's dome and tower, Botticelli's *Birth of Venus* and the Uffizi galleries, Michelangelo's *David* (in original and copy), the white truffle panini at Procacci, and every other corner filled with art, culture, food, and lovely liqueurs. The heart of the Italian Renaissance, Florence was inspired and shepherded by many people, but one of the most influential was Lorenzo de' Medici, or Lorenzo the Magnificent, who supported many artists, was the city's main leader for most of his time, and, the legend says, created a vanilla-inspired liqueur that was the model for Tuaca. Two brothers-in-law (of each other, not of Lorenzo), Gaetano Tuoni and Giorgio Canepa, were fans not only of Lorenzo but also of his liqueur, and they used it as their goal when crafting their own liqueur in 1938, naming it by combining their own last names into Tuoca, which eventually changed to Tuaca. Today, it's made in Livorno, Italy, which is where many American servicemen first tasted it during World War II, enjoying it enough that they brought it back to the States. And who can blame them? It has layers of vanilla, lemon, orange, and spice, backed by a base of brandy, and it's dandy when artistically taken over ice or when combined in cocktails and highballs such as the Tuscan Mule (page 219).

BALTIMORE BRACER

oesn't this toughie seem to be something a minor criminal has a pull of before going to take part in a bank job or before giving a local roustabout the bum's rush? I love Baltimore, but when paired with "Bracer" it oozes muscles and gunplay. Which is a lark, in a way. Not that this drink doesn't have a serious brandy undertone (it does), but that's balanced by anisette's lighter spice and an egg white's foaminess. (For more on anisette, see page 275.) It all adds up to make this particular bracer more of a morning drink, something to fortify one for breakfast and not for bank-robbing.

CRACKED ICE

1½ OUNCES BRANDY

1½ OUNCES ANISETTE

1 EGG WHITE, PREFERABLY ORGANIC

1. Fill a cocktail shaker halfway full with cracked ice. Add the brandy, anisette, and egg white. Shake well.

2. Strain into a cocktail glass.

A NOTE: In *The Old Waldorf-Astoria Bar Book* by Albert Stevens Crockett, the final instruction here is "fizz with carbonic." I think this is best un-fizzed, but if you want to add a little brightly sparkling soda at the end, I won't phone the fuzz.

A WARNING: As this drink contains raw egg, it shouldn't be served to the elderly or to those with compromised immune systems.

BARBADOS

I f ever there were a cocktail that demanded—in an islandy laid-back manner, not really demanding so much as cajoling in a friendly way, persuading, one might say—through the combined sublime efforts of sultry dark rum, bouncy and tangy lime juice, and sweet and spicy falernum (a rum-based liqueur with lime and spices that's sometimes referred to as a syrup when it's rum-less) swaying folks to relax in shorts and T-shirts or even less while curling toes in warm sand, this is that cocktail.

CRUSHED ICE

1 OUNCE FALERNUM

1½ OUNCES DARK RUM

½ OUNCE FRESHLY SQUEEZED LIME JUICE

1. Fill a cocktail shaker halfway full with crushed ice. Add the falernum, rum, and lime juice. Shake well.

2. Strain into a cocktail glass.

A VARIATION: According to island legend, if you bury the falernum in sand and add Cointreau instead, it's a Barbaresque.

A NOTE: The crushed ice gets this one good and slushy (which is how you want it). If you can't get crushed ice, go with cracked ice and shake well.

A SECOND NOTE: To really get your Barbados going, use a dark rum made in the country of the same name, such as Mount Gay.

BLANCHE

I 'd like to believe this cocktail was concocted in the 1930s or thereabout as a way to honor a particular Blanche who really needed a splash of sweetness in her life or who delivered sweetness to others—someone like Blanche Devereaux, the Rue McClanahan character from television's show of sweetness, *The Golden Girls*. Do you know anyone sweeter? This drink is candy-ish enough that you might want to stick with just one, unless you've had a really bad day and the doughnut store is closed.

ICE CUBES

1 OUNCE ANISETTE

1 OUNCE COINTREAU

1 OUNCE ORANGE CURAÇAO

1. Fill a cocktail shaker halfway full with ice cubes. Add the anisette, Cointreau, and orange curaçao. Shake well.

2. Strain into a cocktail glass, sweetly.

I HAVE TO ADMIT, I HAVE A LOT OF LOVE FOR CLASSIC READS. IT COULD ALMOST BE SEEN AS A PROBLEM, SINCE I TEND TO PICK UP ANY OLD BAR BOOK I CAN GET MY HANDS ON, WHICH MEANS MY BOOKSHELVES ARE ALWAYS OVERFLOWING.

Partially, I like tracking down when and where the best drinks came from, but I also just like listening, in a manner of speaking, to the old cocktailians speak. The following quotes let you listen in to the conversation as well:

1. "Shake the shaker as hard as you can: don't just rock it: you are trying to wake it up, not send it to sleep!"
—Harry Craddock, *The Savoy Cocktail Book* (Constable, 1930)

2. "The well-made cocktail is one of the most gracious of drinks. It pleases the senses. The shared delight of those who partake in common of this refreshing nectar breaks the ice of formal reserve. Taut nerves relax; taut muscles relax; tired eyes brighten; tongues loosen; friendships deepen; the whole world becomes a better place in which to live."
—David A. Embury, *The Fine Art of Mixing Drinks* (Doubleday, 1948)

3. "In the collection of this volume's data we gradually came to realize that the great drinks around the world, like the ethics of draw poker, the length of ladies' skirts and width of men's pantaloons—the accepted, the proven, thing is the right thing; the best thing, and all of these proven experiences march here."
—Charles H. Baker, *The Gentleman's Companion, Volume II: Being an Exotic Drinking Book, or Around the World with Beaker, Jigger, and Flask* (Crown, 1946)

4. "All drinking is divided into three parts: The first part is the preface to a meal; the second part is the companionate to a meal; and the third part—perhaps inhabited by the Belchii—goes on for hours and hours after you have dined."
—Crosby Gaige, *Cocktail Guide and Ladies' Companion* (M. Barrows, 1941)

5. "First of all, you can't make chicken whiskey (three drinks and you lay) taste like Gran-dad or Old Taylor, and that goes for gin, Scotch, brandy, or any liqueur. If you're going to serve drinks, make them out of the best ingredients you can find—and you won't find them at chiseling, cut-rate liquor stores."
—Trader Vic, *Trader Vic's Book of Food and Drink* (Doubleday, 1946)

THE BRUJA SMASH

I f only Marvel Comics' Incredible Hulk had been a gamma-irradiated southern European magician instead of an American scientist, he might well have
gone around growling "Bruja Smash!" instead of walloping out his common
catchphrase "Hulk smash!" It would have been a more mystical and international
series and would have (in its general fruitiness) mirrored this take-the-sweat-off
chiller from snazzily dressed bar superhero Andrew Bohrer (a Seattle superstar
bartender and a cocktail writer who blogs at Cask Strength, www.caskstrength.
wordpress.com). Happily, Andrew himself is a well-spoken hero and, instead of
grunting when talking about this drink, says, "It is very rustic looking, but subtle
and fresh."

CRUSHED ICE

7 FRESH MINT LEAVES

7 FRESH RASPBERRIES

1½ OUNCES WHITE TEQUILA

1 OUNCE STREGA

½ OUNCE FRESHLY
SQUEEZED LEMON JUICE

1 MINT SPRIG, FOR GARNISH

1. Fill a cocktail shaker halfway full with
crushed ice. Add the mint leaves, raspberries, tequila, Strega, and lemon juice. Shake
really well.

2. Dump the contents of the shaker (no
straining here) into a large tulip-style beer
glass or other good-sized pretty vessel.

3. Fill the glass with crushed ice, garnish
with the mint sprig, and serve with a straw.

ELLIPSE

Adrink this thoughtful (in the sense that it's both well thought up and that it'll make you gaze into the horizon while weighing hefty matters, such as where the next drink will come from) had to spring fully formed from the mind of one of today's great poets, like Athena springing from the head of Zeus. But even poets must weigh ingredients before getting it right, and so Ed Skoog—one of today's finest poets, whose latest collection is *Mister Skylight*—tinkered and labored until balancing the fresh, the wicked, and the bubbly. The result leads to singing Greek lyrics in the backyard in no time.

1 TEASPOON FRESH MARJORAM LEAVES

ICE CUBES

2 OUNCES STREGA

CHILLED PROSECCO

FRESH MARJORAM SPRIG, FOR GARNISH

1. Add the marjoram to a cocktail shaker. Using a muddler or wooden spoon, muddle gently.

2. Fill the cocktail shaker halfway full with ice cubes. Add the Strega. Shake well.

3. Strain (with a fine-mesh strainer) into a flute glass. Top with Prosecco, almost to the rim, and garnish with the marjoram.

GENOESE

Music, art, culinary delights, architecture, and a famous port—the Italian city of Genoa deserves a drink named after its inhabitants, an admirable drink. This one fits perfectly, as its first-rate taste flows from two essential Italian beverages, the hearty wine derivative grappa and the after-dinner anise liqueur Sambuca, and it also has two more ingredients that may just have been brought into the city via the port: dry vermouth (from France) and vodka (from Russia).

ICE CUBES

1 OUNCE VODKA

1 OUNCE GRAPPA

½ OUNCE SAMBUCA

½ OUNCE DRY VERMOUTH

1. Fill a cocktail shaker halfway full with ice cubes. Add the vodka, grappa, Sambuca, and vermouth. Shake well.

2. Strain into a cocktail glass.

A NOTE: Grappa is a type of pomace brandy, made from grape seeds, skins, and pits—the leftovers from making wine. There's grappa that's good, there's grappa that tastes of gasoline, and there's grappa that's transcendent.

Sambuca

It's appropriate that Sambuca, a liqueur that has wisps of flavor slipping on and off the tongue surrounded by the dominant anise (from the oils of the star anise, combined with a clear grain spirit, sugar, and spices), has a history that's more than a little hard to pin down definitively. There are so many good legends that you could tell multiple stories in one evening when serving a drink with Sambuca—such as the Genoese (page 196). Start with the fact that the name might come from the Arabic *zammut*, which is the name of an ancient anise-infused beverage brought to the port city Civitavecchia (this is what the Molinari company says, and they do make a fine Sambuca). Or go with the *Oxford English Dictionary*, which declares that it comes from the Latin *sambucus,* defined as "elderberry." Of course, it could also come from the Indian word *sondf* (sometimes seen as *soambu*), meaning "fennel," or a second Arabic word, *sambuq*, a type of sailing vessel that the *zammut* may have been carried on to Italy. One thing that is (mostly) agreed upon is that near the tail of the 1800s, one Luigi Manzi began making his Sambuca Manzi available to the public in Civitavecchia. Then, in 1945, expanding the reach of Sambuca to all of Italy—and eventually the world—Angelo Molinari began producing and exporting his Sambuca. With these various stories, it's no wonder that besides being consumed in cocktails, Sambuca is enjoyed on its own with or without ice, traditionally with three espresso beans (as representatives of health, happiness, and prosperity, some believe) floated on top (to order, ask for *Sambuca con la mosca*, or "Sambuca with the fly").

GINGER BLISS

H ere's one for serving alongside candles, the Commodores' greatest hits, and caviar before a dinner between only you and your beau or belle, or that person who in your daydreams becomes your beau or belle in the near future. The bubbly nature of this liquid bliss demonstrates a classy side, while the homemade basil simple syrup shows off dedication. The gingerific Domaine de Canton just shows you're in the booze-know (which is pretty powerful as a flirting tool, I think). And who to thank for this sure-to-be-memorable evening? Me, sure, but even more so wine and spirits writer and wine educator Kelly Magyarics, who came up with the Ginger Bliss (and whom you can read more from and about at www.kellymagyarics.com). As Kelly says, "Sparkling wine is perfect to use in a cocktail, as the bubbles deliver the aromatics of other included ingredients every time you take a sip. Be sure to select a high-quality sparkling wine—either Champagne, *Crémant*, or a traditional method California bottle."

. . . .

¾ OUNCE DOMAINE DE CANTON GINGER LIQUEUR

½ OUNCE FRESHLY SQUEEZED LEMON JUICE

¾ OUNCE BASIL-INFUSED SIMPLE SYRUP (SEE A SECOND NOTE)

3 DASHES FEE BROTHERS ORANGE BITTERS

4 OUNCES CHILLED CHAMPAGNE OR BRUT SPARKLING WINE

LEMON TWIST, FOR GARNISH

FRESH BASIL LEAF, FOR GARNISH

1. Add the Domaine de Canton, lemon juice, basil syrup, and orange bitters to a chilled flute glass.

2. Top with Champagne, and stir gently while looking slightly sultry.

3. Garnish with the lemon twist and basil leaf. (Kelly suggests smacking the leaf first to release the oils. And you'll look so cool doing it.)

A NOTE: Domaine de Canton is a Cognac-based liqueur that's flavored with Vietnamese ginger, vanilla, ginseng, and other spices.

A SECOND NOTE: To make the basil-infused simple syrup, add ½ cup each water and sugar to a medium-size saucepan set over medium-high heat. Bring it to a simmer, and reduce the heat to medium. Simmer until the sugar is completely dissolved. Remove from the heat and add ½ cup fresh basil leaves. Let sit for 1 hour, and then strain. Store in the refrigerator for up to 1 month.

GOLDEN FROG

When the west wind blows and the prairie dogs howl and the electric fire fades to embers, everyone within hearing range comes close together so that they can listen to the fable of the Golden Frog. It's a saga involving a host of herbal witches dancing around walnut trees waving strands of mint and wearing saffron strands behind their ears, a military commander defending a fort against all odds under the anise and vanilla stars, the juice squeezed fresh from a yellow jewel, and the underlying strength pulled clear out of snow and ice. As you lean in to hear the final lines, listen closely: You can find yourself within this froggy fable, if only you pick up that shaker and start to shake.

ICE CUBES

1½ OUNCES VODKA

1½ OUNCES GALLIANO

½ OUNCE STREGA

¼ OUNCE FRESHLY SQUEEZED LEMON JUICE

1. Fill a cocktail shaker halfway full with ice cubes. Add the vodka, Galliano, Strega, and lemon juice. Shake well.

2. Strain into a cocktail glass. Drink, ribbit, and drink again.

A NOTE: The first time I saw this amphibious amalgamation, it was blended with the ice and not shaken. I think a frog in a blender is somewhat icky, so I avoid that preparation.

Galliano

Perhaps best known for its association with the Harvey Wallbanger (page 38), Galliano is also a hit in other cocktails (such as the melodic Sweet Harmonics on page 182) and when sipped all on its own, with ice or without, before or after a meal, or alongside a plate of pecorino Romano and bread during a lazy afternoon. With this ability to get along, it's somewhat hard to imagine that Galliano was named after a famous military hero, but it could be that Major Giuseppe Galliano wasn't just a successful military man, but also amazingly fun at parties. Even so, he is mostly known for defending a fort packed with 2,300 Italian soldiers against an army of 80,000 during the Abyssinian war. This heroic behavior is what led to Arturo Vaccari naming his new creation, a golden-hued liqueur, after our famous *maggiore*. In the late 1800s, Arturo thought that southern Italian pioneers going to California to try their hand at mining gold might need a little reminder of home on their travels, as well as a lush drink for when the days were hard. With all this in mind, he combined Italian herbs, roots, barks, spices, and flower seeds with those from other countries (30 in all), including anise, Iris Florentina, coriander, lavender, mint, yarrow musk, vanilla, and more, and contained them in a tall, elegant bottle modeled after Roman columns. The result is a spiced mixture that has floral and herbal hints, and one that looks and tastes amazing, no matter where you're drinking it. Even Pope Leone XIII's doctor approved of Galliano, saying (many years ago), "I hereby declare that I find Liqueur Galliano good for the health and of excellent taste."

HOPE'S FARM SPECIAL

N ot sure who Hope is, or what she (or he) grows on the farm (limes, perhaps?), but here's a huge "Thank you!" to that optimistic person for this drink, which I found in the pocket-sized *Holiday Drink Book* (Peter Pauper Press, 1951). Featuring a double dose of rums, the heady rum-and-lime-and-secret-spices-and-herbs liqueur falernum, and lemon juice, it might seem that this should be served near a beach bonfire, or around a pool when everyone is excited to blow up their floaties. Following the above-mentioned book's idea, though, takes us along a different, snowier, path, serving this when people need to remember that the sun is shining somewhere, that the snow and ice (which are pretty but cold) won't last forever, and that winter holidays are just as jubilant as summer, especially when serving up sunshine-y fancies like this at holiday hoedowns.

ICE CUBES

1 OUNCE WHITE RUM

1 OUNCE DARK RUM

¾ OUNCE FALERNUM

½ OUNCE FRESHLY SQUEEZED LEMON JUICE

DASH OF PEYCHAUD'S BITTERS

1. Fill a cocktail shaker halfway full with ice cubes. Add the white and dark rums, the falernum, the lemon juice, and the Peychaud's. Shake well (it'll keep you warm).

2. Strain into a cocktail glass.

"Saint Nick himself is depicted with red cheeks and cherry nose that somehow are more suggestive of the warmth within than of the cold without."

—*THE HOLIDAY DRINK BOOK*, 1951

HOT NIGHT IN HIDALGO

Here, the cocktail shaker isn't dwelling (imaginatively, as it may be) within the town of the same name in either Illinois or Texas, but rather in the many towns and villages in Mexico called Hidalgo or a variation thereof. This localized location traces back to the drink's signature ingredient, Damiana liqueur, which is made from the leaves of the damiana shrub. Damiana is also fabled to be an aphrodisiac, which is why making a plan to wear your rebozo or serape for too long isn't well thought-out—this is a drink to be shared with one other person and little clothing (it is a hot night indeed).

ICE CUBES

2 OUNCES DARK RUM

1½ OUNCES DAMIANA

¾ OUNCE FRESH PINEAPPLE JUICE

PINEAPPLE CHUNK, FOR GARNISH

1. Fill a cocktail shaker halfway full with ice cubes. Add the rum, Damiana, and pineapple juice. Shake well.

2. Strain into a cocktail glass. Garnish with the pineapple chunk, in a smooth manner.

A NOTE: Damiana is a spiced and herbed liqueur made in Mexico. It has a very distinctive feminine-shaped bottle (based on an Incan goddess), and it is said (sometimes in whispers) to contain mystical powers relating to that most feverish of emotions: love.

THE HOUNDS THEY START TO ROAR

I created this for a particular Mixology Monday, or MxMo as it's called, a Monday tradition in which a bunch of cocktail, drink, and liquor bloggers create or present a drink under a particular theme. A different blog hosts every week, and they round up links to the themed posts on their site and send readers out and about and around the interweb to see all the posts on that theme (they're also posted at www.mixologymonday.com). The themes tend to be a particular spirit, liquor, or ingredient, but for the one that inspired this drink, Andrew Bohrer (who blogs at Cask Strength, www.caskstrength.wordpress.com) chose Tom Waits as the theme. Which was dandy with me, 'cause I dig me the Waits. And my favorite Waits CD is *Rain Dogs*. The title for this recipe is from a line within the song "Tango Till They're Sore."

Rain Dogs also has a dandy song called "Jockey Full of Bourbon," so I wanted my drink to have a bourbon base, and bourbon is also mentioned multiple times within the record. The only other spirit dropped in the album is brandy (in "Union Square"), so I decided to double up on base spirits a bit, and then I wanted to bring in some bitters, in honor of the line in "9th & Hennepin" that mentions bitters. I wanted to add another ingredient to the drink that isn't mentioned in one of his songs but that has at least a tangential connection, so I chose St. Elizabeth Allspice Dram. It's based on an older ingredient called pimento dram, which I could see Waits-style sailors drinking on a leaking dinghy.

ICE CUBES

2 OUNCES BOURBON

¾ OUNCE ST. ELIZABETH ALLSPICE DRAM

½ OUNCE BRANDY

2 DASHES PEYCHAUD'S BITTERS

1. Fill a cocktail shaker, mixing glass, dented top hat, or lady's leather boot halfway full with cracked ice. Add the whole bunch of ingredients. Stir well.

2. Strain into a cocktail glass or goblet while growling a sad song.

A NOTE: Feel this needs a garnish? I suggest an ice pick, a dented fender from a '54 Ford, or a tattooed tear.

A SECOND NOTE: I used Gran Duque d'Alba brandy here, cause I'm walking Spanish down the hall.

JASPER'S JAMAICAN

T ake Jasper along to beachside balls, where his true tropical nature can be fully appreciated by the bevy of shorts-and-swimwear-attired revelers. Featuring St. Elizabeth's Allspice Dram, a modern marvel in the manner of a traditional pimento dram, this drink was adapted from another beachside essential, *Beachbum Berry's Grog Log* (SLG, 1998), where it says that the cocktail was originally concocted by Jasper LeFranc of the Bay Roc Hotel in Jamaica. Bring on the beach.

¼ TEASPOON SUGAR

½ OUNCE FRESHLY
SQUEEZED LIME JUICE

ICE CUBES

½ OUNCE ST. ELIZABETH
ALLSPICE DRAM

1¼ OUNCES DARK RUM

1. Add the sugar and lime juice to a cocktail shaker. Swirl or stir until the sugar is dissolved.

2. Fill the cocktail shaker halfway full with ice cubes. Add the St. Elizabeth Allspice Dram and rum. Shake well.

3. Strain into a cocktail glass.

A NOTE: Sometimes seen in venerable cocktail books as "pimento dram," allspice dram is an allspice-flavored liqueur (traditionally made with Jamaican allspice berries) that also contains hints of clove, cinnamon, clover, and nutmeg.

A SECOND NOTE: If you can't find Jamaican rum, then you can sub in another rum. But Jasper might not be happy about it.

JOHNNIE MACK

S wing it, party people: "Oh the sloe gin, has tasty sloe berries, dear, and you'll taste them, oh tonight . . . mixed with oranges, from the island of Curaçao, dear, and some absinthe, that's no more out of sight. On the back deck, on Sunday morning, you'll serve a drink of chilly life. It'll come sneaking, from the shaker, could that drink perchance be Johnnie the . . . Mack?" Maybe that last lyrical bowdlerization wasn't the rhymingest, but believe me, kid, after a few of these you'll be singing songs about Johnnie Mack at full volume without a care in the world.

CRACKED ICE

2 OUNCES SLOE GIN

½ OUNCE ABSINTHE

¾ OUNCE ORANGE CURAÇAO

LEMON TWIST, FOR GARNISH

1. Fill a cocktail shaker or mixing glass half-way full with cracked ice. Add the sloe gin, absinthe, and orange curaçao. Stir well.

2. Strain into a cocktail glass. Garnish with the lemon twist.

A NOTE: Sloe gin is not, as you might think, a variety of gin that always finishes last in the 100-yard dash. It's actually a liqueur made from sloe berries, which are smaller relatives of the plum (and which are, for you trivia buffs, sometimes called blackthorn berries). Its base can be either gin or a neutral grain spirit.

---

7 Randomly Specific Excuses for a Party

GINGER BLISS & THE VIOLET FIZZ

7 Randomly Specific

Okay, it could be that you and the boss band of bossa-nova-ers you tend to imbibe with don't believe you need an excuse for a party—any old five o'clock (or ten o'clock in the morning, some days) will do. If you want to have a hoedown that stands out from the everyday though, here are some suggestions to get your party started.

1. May 8, Joan of Arc Day, cocktail of choice: Luminous Angel (page 67)

2. July 9, anniversary of the meeting of the Society of American Florists, cocktail of choice: Mexican Bouquet (page 69)

3. February 26, Victor Hugo's birthday, cocktail of choice: Hugo Special (page 236)

4. August 19, Aviation Day, cocktail of choice: Aviation (naturally) (page 55)

5. November 12, anniversary of the completion of the New York subway, cocktail of choice: Blue Train Cocktail (page 30)

6. January 15, anniversary of London's beer shortage of 1942, drink of choice: Black Fog (page 89)

7. April 19, Patriot's Day, cocktail of choice: Shooting Star (page 109)

KINGSTON HEIGHTS

Here we are, at Kingston Heights. Notice it's a classic brownstone building, brick, with three floors, two apartments on each floor, and a balcony for each apartment facing the street. You might posit that the street would be oak-lined and full of four-door sedans and minivans, but it's actually running along the beach, and mostly bare except for a few bicycles and a Saturn or two. From the Kings (which is what people sometimes call the building, when they're a little loopy), a big beat bursts from the top floor (I think it's Chicago band the National Trust), and every floor is dimly lit, and ambling up you hear the greatest sound in the world, people laughing with their friends at the silliest thing, and when passing the two front steps, and then passing the wooden front door, you see there's a small bar set up in the foyer. Don't be shy, go on up, and you'll discover there's a drink waiting, just for you. It's rummy, with a little caraway, citrus, and allspice tingle in every sip. But don't stand here stalling. Walk around, join the laughter, and enjoy the Kingston Heights. Which today is the happiest place on earth.

. . . .

ICE CUBES

1½ OUNCES WHITE RUM

¾ OUNCE KÜMMEL

¾ OUNCE FRESHLY SQUEEZED ORANGE JUICE

½ OUNCE ST. ELIZABETH ALLSPICE DRAM

1. Fill a cocktail shaker halfway full with ice cubes. Add the rum, kümmel, and orange juice. Shake well.

2. Strain into a cocktail glass. Drizzle the St. Elizabeth Allspice Dram slowly into the drink.

LADIES' COCKTAIL

Hey, ladies, this one's for you, for every single thing you do, for the wives and mothers, sisters and cousins, aunts and grandmothers, co-workers and friends, waitresses and bartenders, doctors and nurses, pilots and flight attendants, editors and writers, bloggers and beauty queens, cooks and chefs, artists and architects, poets and teachers, singers and software developers, and every other lady who's known and loved and who loves a drink with a kick and a grin. Serve it to your favorite ladies for no other reason than that you want them to know you're aware of what they do. Being aware, know whether they prefer bourbon to Canadian whisky (I've had it made with both), and switch as needed. I go Canadian because the mellow nature moves well in here, but bourbon sure won't show any disrespect.

CRACKED ICE

2 OUNCES CANADIAN WHISKY

½ OUNCE PERNOD

½ OUNCE ANISETTE

2 DASHES ANGOSTURA BITTERS

PINEAPPLE CHUNK, FOR GARNISH

1. Fill a cocktail shaker or mixing glass halfway full with cracked ice. Add the Canadian whisky, Pernod, anisette, and Angostura bitters. Stir well.

2. Add the pineapple chunk to a cocktail glass. Strain the mixture into the glass and over the pineapple.

A NOTE: Don't want to make the ladies wait for a bite of that pineapple chunk? Instead of putting it in the glass, balance it on the rim.

"Perhaps, after all, it is best to stick to Pernod, if the sartorial consequences of imbibing interest you as much as they do me. This if only for the reason that however you start off drinking the stuff, you're bound to end up more or less naked."

—PAUL HOLT, "THE WINE AND THE WAISTCOAT," *THE COMPLEAT IMBIBER 1*, 1956

MACARONI

Hold on there, champ. This drink does not, no matter what may have been whispered, contain muddled macaroni. So set down the pasta you were getting ready to pound into a paste, and put aside the muddler being palmed like a pile driver. There's no need to show off powerful pecs with this Macaroni (except when shaking), because the primary ingredient isn't a dinner pal, but anise-flavored French apéritif pastis, which contains licorice root but gets its flavor from star anise (as opposed to cousin absinthe, which gets its flavor from green anise and grand wormwood—see more about absinthe on page 225). With this in mind, search for actual pastis, and switch in absinthe only if absolutely necessary. It won't be exactly identical (call it a Macaroni-A), but it'll be better than using pasta.

. . . .

ICE CUBES

2 OUNCES PASTIS

1 OUNCE SWEET VERMOUTH

**LEMON TWIST,
FOR GARNISH (OPTIONAL)**

1. Fill a cocktail shaker halfway full with ice cubes. Add the pastis and sweet vermouth and shake.

2. Strain into a cocktail glass. Garnish with the lemon twist, if you desire.

A NOTE: While I have this shaken (so you can at least show off muscles a bit), stirring it over cracked ice is fine.

THE PANTHER'S PAW

An all-points bulletin designed to keep me free from any issues with the ASPCA: There are no actual felines involved in the assembly of this paw. Instead, it's a combination of gin, absinthe, pineapple juice, and a touch of simple syrup, accented by a lemon slice if you're feeling it. And I'm feeling it, so you should be as well, so we're in the same jungle. I make this with Aviation gin, 'cause House Spirits Distillery rocks the party and because its flavor is a touch floral and lighter, like a springtime reverie, and it doesn't overwhelm the absinthe's thunder—absinthe should stand proud as a panther. And, speaking of the absinthe, I went with Lucid originally, but I have also used Pacifique (which wasn't even out the first time I made this drink, illustrating how quickly our spirits landscape is altering—as quickly as a panther pounces, some might say), and both worked well and neither will bite. Though after a couple, you may feel slightly pawed.

ICE CUBES

1½ OUNCES GIN

1 OUNCE ABSINTHE

¾ OUNCE FRESH PINEAPPLE JUICE

¼ OUNCE SIMPLE SYRUP (PAGE 12)

LEMON SLICE, FOR GARNISH (OPTIONAL)

1. Fill a cocktail shaker halfway full with ice cubes. Add the gin, absinthe, pineapple juice, and simple syrup. Shake well.

2. Strain the mixture into a cocktail glass. Garnish with the lemon slice if that's what makes your panther purr.

RÉVEILLON

Sometimes, the path to a memorable cocktail takes a searching of the electronic kind. For example, I found this jovial number while browsing Serious Eats (which makes for awfully good reading, www.seriouseats.com) for articles by Paul Clarke (he of the essential Cocktail Chronicles blog, www.cocktailchronicles.com). He was auditioning holiday drinks and brought out this dancing sprite, which was first whipped together by Chuck Taggart, a native of New Orleans and longtime blogger at the Gumbo Pages (www.gumbopages.com). Paul says, "The Réveillon cocktail has the perfect flavors for the season without the sugary heaviness you find in so many holiday drinks." Now, that should get you in the seasonal mood, and if reading it doesn't, then by all means, go straight to the making and sipping. I sure wouldn't want to ruin any fa-la-la-ing.

CRACKED ICE

2 OUNCES CALVADOS

½ OUNCE CLEAR CREEK PEAR BRANDY

½ OUNCE ST. ELIZABETH ALLSPICE DRAM

¼ OUNCE CARPANO ANTICA

1 DASH FEE BROTHERS OLD FASHION BITTERS

CINNAMON STICK OR STAR ANISE PIECE, FOR GARNISH (OPTIONAL)

1. Fill a cocktail shaker or mixing glass with cracked ice. Add the Calvados, pear brandy, St. Elizabeth Allspice Dram, Carpano Antica, and bitters. Stir well.

2. Strain into a cocktail glass, and garnish with either the cinnamon stick or the star anise (but not both).

A NOTE: Can't find the Fee Brothers? Sub in Angostura bitters instead.

RIVIERA

This exquisite jewel of a drink brings together vanilla-spiced Italian player Tuaca with lesser-used bianco vermouth (both Martini & Rossi and Dolin brands can be employed to glamorous ends), with usual leads gin and vodka coming in as undercurrents to add more flavor bursts and a bling-y bounce, and Angostura bitters and an orange twist in place to bring a sparkle and swish. Added up, this is one cocktail you shouldn't shy away from serving to the rich relatives or regal visitors occasionally stopping by for a Sunday cocktail hour. It'll shine as bright as any worn adornments—and taste better, too.

CRACKED ICE

1½ OUNCES TUACA

1 OUNCE BIANCO VERMOUTH

¾ OUNCE GIN

¾ OUNCE VODKA

DASH OF ANGOSTURA BITTERS

ORANGE TWIST, FOR GARNISH

1. Fill a cocktail shaker or mixing glass halfway full with cracked ice. Add the Tuaca, vermouth, gin, vodka, and bitters. Stir well.

2. Strain into a cocktail glass. Twist the twist over the glass and let it slide in.

5

Brunch Bubblers

GINGER BLISS & THE VIOLET FIZZ

Sunday brunches are like bouquets of flowers: blooming with tasty dishes, pretty with people in their light-colored semi-fancy-but-not-uncomfortable outfits, and fragrant with the aromas of the following consumables.

1. Violet Fizz
(page 77)

2. Chartreuse Daisy
(page 57)

3. Mint Cooler
(page 138)

4. Eve's Garden
(page 62)

5. Mexican Bouquet
(page 69)

6. Sweet Pea
(page 73)

5

SEA FIZZ

S ay you're on vacation—say that it's a very special vacation, either the first
vacation with a new inamorata or inamorato, or a honeymoon after an
extra-long engagement, but either way you're on a remote beach in the
Caribbean where there are only bungalows, and it's that first morning near the
waves and sand and not much else, and it's a teensy, tiny smidge uncomfortable,
not in the weird unfriendly way, but in the shy, cute way, and you want to break
the proverbial ice but aren't sure how, and are so twittery inside that sentences
don't even sound right. Let me suggest making a round of Sea Fizzes. As they're
found in the "Morning" section in the exemplary *Stork Club Bar Book* by Lucius
Beebe (first published in 1946, then republished by New Day in 2004), rest
assured that they'll get rid of the awkwardness and restore the swooning.

ICE CUBES

1½ OUNCES ABSINTHE

**½ OUNCE FRESHLY
SQUEEZED LEMON JUICE**

**½ OUNCE SIMPLE SYRUP
(PAGE 12)**

**1 EGG WHITE, PREFERABLY
ORGANIC**

CHILLED CLUB SODA

1. Fill a cocktail shaker halfway full with
ice cubes. Add the absinthe, lemon juice,
simple syrup, and egg white. Shake the cob-
webs out (which means shake well).

2. Fill a highball glass halfway full with ice
cubes. Strain the sea into the glass.

3. Fill the glass almost to the top with
chilled club soda, and stir well.

A WARNING: As this drink contains raw egg, it shouldn't
be served to the elderly or to those with compromised
immune systems.

SUISSESSE HIGHBALL

On gray mornings, when it's apparent the skies won't clear before the following day at the earliest, and when the thermometer is too tired to rise above 30°F by 5 p.m., and, to add insult to injury, your head is as thick as the clouds draping the sky in that gray flannel, the last thing you want is to have to order a drink called Suissesse. Felicitously, this effervescent elixir is an early morning remedy, not a nuisance, especially with the addition of egg, which isn't in every version of this recipe but which I've come around to appreciating in the a.m. You don't even need to order it out loud—keep it written on a slip of paper, and hand it to that kind soul who'll be making your morning better.

CRACKED ICE

1½ OUNCES ABSINTHE

½ OUNCE ANISETTE

1 EGG WHITE, PREFERABLY ORGANIC (OPTIONAL)

ICE CUBES

CHILLED CLUB SODA

1. Fill a cocktail shaker halfway full with cracked ice. Add the absinthe, anisette, and egg white, if using. Shake very well.

2. Fill a highball glass three-quarters full with ice cubes. Strain the Suissesse into the glass.

3. Fill the glass almost to the top with club soda. Stir, but briefly.

A NOTE: I like shaking this with cracked ice because I think it should be extra-frothy. But if you don't feel like cracking, cubes will work without waking you up too roughly.

A WARNING: As this drink contains raw egg, it shouldn't be served to the elderly or to those with compromised immune systems.

TOUCHLESS AUTOMATIC

A loud hurrah to the many thousands of bands toiling away in garages, basements, and backyards, playing achingly beautiful pop songs, country songs, folk songs, punk rock songs, hillbilly songs, trance-y and dance-y songs, swing songs and swung songs, metal songs and mashing songs, songs that defy description and songs that are instantly hummable, songs that are played to five friends and songs played to no one but those singing them. Though most of these bands might not be heard much outside of their hometowns, the songs they're writing and singing are bound to change the world of at least one person who hears them. Because of that, and because these bands, well, rock, do the right thing and hunt down the ingredients in this cocktail: the Scotch, pineapple sage leaves (subbing in regular sage only as a last resort), the St. Elizabeth Allspice Dram made from Jamaican rum and allspice berries, and the lemon twist. This creative combination makes a harmonious melody for toasting bands from near and far.

6 OR 7 FRESH PINEAPPLE SAGE LEAVES

ICE CUBES

2 OUNCES SCOTCH

1 OUNCE ST. ELIZABETH ALLSPICE DRAM

LEMON TWIST, FOR GARNISH

1. Add the sage to a cocktail shaker. Using a muddler or wooden spoon, muddle the leaves, but don't get all drum-solo about it.

2. Fill the cocktail shaker halfway full with ice cubes. Add the Scotch and the St. Elizabeth Allspice Dram. Shake well.

3. Strain into a cocktail glass (through a fine-mesh strainer if you're worried about little bits of sage in your teeth). Garnish with the lemon twist.

A NOTE: I think a nice blended Scotch works well here, such as Famous Grouse or Grant's.

TOVARICH

There are obscure bar guides and books by bygone sages, there are strange compendiums of drinks and drink lore, there are peculiarly thin pamphlets published way back for pushing certain liqueurs and liquors and swilling sense, and then there's *Easy to Make Maidens & Cocktails: A Mixing, Swingers Bar Guide* (Enrol, 1965). This slim volume of recipes includes misogynistic (though silly, especially in hindsight) caricatures of women and quotes about certain types of drinking women (such as the "'Take me I'm yours' type . . . one drink and she wants the key to your happiness and your apartment—but will probably pass out in the cab"). It does, I must admit, have some pretty funny moments, in the "Were guys really believing this?" sense. It also does have a solid array of classic and not-as-well-known-but-darn-good drinks, including the Tovarich. History, sometimes, is a weird bar to visit.

ICE CUBES

1½ OUNCES VODKA

1 OUNCE KÜMMEL

½ OUNCE FRESHLY
SQUEEZED LIME JUICE

1. Fill a cocktail shaker halfway full with ice cubes. Add the vodka, kümmel, and lime juice. Shake well.

2. Strain into a cocktail glass.

LIQUEUR SPOTLIGHT

Kümmel

Kümmel is a mixture loved for its bit of sweet undertone and spice flavors: caraway, cumin, and fennel. The story driven by this flavor collage happened in 1696, when Russian leader Peter the Great went to Amsterdam to learn how to build ships so that he could outfit a serious Russian navy. He took a trip one day to visit the Bols Distillery, which was begun by Lucas Bols, who in 1575 (as the story goes) was the original distiller and creator of a kümmel-style liqueur. Peter fell head over heels for the kümmel he tasted, and he took a bunch of bottles and the recipe back to Russia. Once kümmel made its way east, it soon became a favorite in Russia and then throughout other parts of Eastern Europe, where the majority of it is still produced and consumed today. It's not used as much these days, which is a shame, because it's good both on its own and when mixed in cocktails such as the Weeper's Joy (page 224) and the Kingston Heights (page 207).

TROPICALIANA

This fun-and-fizzy number adds effervescence to any ol' weekend or weekday evening, or noontime, or, for that matter, breakfast (don't ever be shy about adding a new drink to the breakfast repertoire, as it's a meal too often relegated to only routine numbers, and nothing starts a day right like a good drink—unless you're about to go off to a job that involves driving heavy machinery). I believe that if bringing this to breakfast, you'll get praised from here to Tampa. If you're wearing your Tarzan costume while serving the Tropicaliana, you'll get praised from here to Tanzania. Of course, I've never been to Tanzania, so this is partially a guess. But I have seen you wearing a Tarzan costume, and it's as cute as a cheetah's spots. I mean it. Now, show a little more leg next time and we'll be in business. (Not sure what kind of business, exactly, but anytime you trot out "show a little more leg" in a sentence, you have to follow it up with a phrase like "next time we'll be in business." It's a boozer's law. Know what I mean? No? Ah, go drink your Tropicaliana.)

ICE CUBES

1 OUNCE WHITE RUM

¾ OUNCE DOMAINE DE CANTON GINGER LIQUEUR

¼ OUNCE FRESHLY SQUEEZED LIME JUICE

½ OUNCE SIMPLE SYRUP (PAGE 12)

CHILLED ROSÉ SPARKLING WINE

LIME SLICE, FOR GARNISH

1. Fill a cocktail shaker halfway full with ice cubes. Add the rum, Domaine de Canton, lime juice, and simple syrup. Shake well.

2. Strain the mixture into a flute glass. Top with the rosé sparkling wine. Garnish with that lime slice.

TUSCAN MULE

Tuaca, the liqueur that brings this mule to kicking, has an illustrious, if not footnote-able, history tracing back to Lorenzo de' Medici, also known as Lorenzo the Magnificent, during his time as the first citizen and ruler (more or less) of delightful and essential-to-visit Florence, Italy, back when Florence was *the* city in the world (we're talking late 1400s here). One of Lorenzo's lesser-known accomplishments may have been creating a recipe for a spiced liqueur with vanilla and orange accents. A recipe that (if you believe, and I do) Livorno's Tuoni and Canepa families then started producing for general consumption as Tuaca. Now, you'll be continuing the history—as long as you stop reading and start stirring, that is.

ICE CUBES

1½ OUNCES TUACA

CHILLED GINGER ALE

LIME WEDGE, FOR GARNISH

1. Fill a highball glass three-quarters full with ice cubes. Add the Tuaca.

2. Fill the glass almost to the top with ginger ale.

3. Squeeze the lime wedge over the glass, and then drop it in. Stir well.

UNDERLINED PASSAGES

Using vanilla, pistachio, and an egg white, this may seem like a dessert instead of a drink. However, reliable pal brandy balances out the cast, making this something to sip slowly while reading before bedtime, a few hours after the evening meal and sweets have been consumed. Since you'll want to time your reading and your drinking (there's no need to do one without the other), may I suggest you pick up J. Robert Lennon's book of short-short stories *Pieces for the Left Hand* (where I picked up this title, by the way)? The bursts of narrative and inspiration inside that book are short enough that you won't need to be worried about stopping mid-chapter when the drink is done.

ICE CUBES

1½ OUNCES BRANDY

1 OUNCE NAVAN VANILLA LIQUEUR

½ OUNCE DUMANTE VERDENOCE PISTACHIO LIQUEUR

1 EGG WHITE, PREFERABLY ORGANIC

1. Fill a cocktail shaker halfway full with ice cubes. Add the brandy, Navan, Dumante, and egg white. Shake exceptionally well.

2. Strain into a cocktail glass. Drink before thinking it over.

A NOTE: Navan vanilla liqueur is made by the same folks who craft Grand Marnier with such care. It's made with Madagascan vanilla combined with a neutral spirit and Cognac.

A WARNING: As this drink contains raw egg, it shouldn't be served to the elderly or to those with compromised immune systems.

WALCOTT

Perhaps it will come to pass that you'll end up one day on a raft made from logs lashed together with thick twine under a tattered sail floating on warm Caribbean currents with only a bottle of rum, a bottle of the ginger liqueur Domaine de Canton, a pineapple, and a jar of Angostura bitters, made in Trinidad and Tobago. Oh, and an ice bucket full of ice, a cocktail shaker, and a cocktail glass or two, if you like rafting with others. In this situation, I suggest you also bring along Derek Walcott's *Collected Poems: 1948–1984*. I can think of nothing to accompany the cocktails and lazy sailing as well as reading poems by this wonderful poet, originally from the Caribbean island of Saint Lucia.

ICE CUBES

2 OUNCES DARK RUM

1 OUNCE DOMAINE DE CANTON GINGER LIQUEUR

½ OUNCE FRESH PINEAPPLE JUICE

DASH OF ANGOSTURA BITTERS

1. Fill a cocktail shaker halfway full with ice cubes. Add the rum, Domaine de Canton, pineapple juice, and bitters. Shake well.

2. Strain poetically into a cocktail glass. Drink between stanzas.

Strega

There are liqueurs that are said to be magical, liqueurs that sorcerers have supposedly used in spell casting, liqueurs that lovers are rumored to have employed to enchant their inamoratos, and liqueurs that some say have mystical powers. And then there is Strega. *Strega,* which means "witch" in Italian, is, some say (myself included), the most magical of liqueurs, actual enchantment in a bottle, and beloved by both good and naughty witches. The spell of this saffron-hued liqueur started being cast in 1860, when grocer's son Giuseppe Alberti took advantage of his father's wide assortment of herbs, spices, and other ingredients to create a drink that was well balanced and glowing: strong and sweet, herbal and light on its feet, flowery and floating. After the liqueur was ready, father and son went with the name "Strega." This was in honor of both the liqueur's power and the town they lived in, Benevento, around which witches supposedly lived and danced and prepared love potions.

If visiting Benevento (which I once was lucky enough to do), you'll see that Strega is made in the same place today, and you'll see an old walnut tree in the middle of the factory—a tree the witches supposedly used to dance around. The liqueur is still made with the same family recipe (passed secretly from father to son) of 70 herbs and spices from countries worldwide, including wild mint that grows only alongside rivers in the nearby Samnite territory, and is stored in oak barrels. Today, the company also makes other liqueurs (including a Strega cream liqueur sadly not available in the United States), renowned nougats, and chocolates filled with Strega (these have to be tasted to be believed). Also, since 1947, the company has given out the prestigious Strega Prize for Italian literature, combining the art of writing with the beguiling art of creating delicious liqueur. Strega casts its spell in a variety of drinks such as the Bruja Smash (page 194) and the Warlock (page 223).

WARLOCK

I f you find yourself (as I sometimes do) singing *Ti ho stregato*, then you probably have been entranced by a Warlock. But don't get melty and weepy and head to your local coven for a magical remedy. The Warlock in this spooky situation is an Italian one, and a liquid one, whose spell comes not via incantations, dragon broth, or dancing around a pentagram in the room, but via two Italian favorites, the saffron-hued herbal liqueur Strega (which means "witch"), and the golden king of liqueurs, limoncello (with help from brandy, OJ, Peychaud's, and simple syrup). So, embrace the enchantment.

ICE CUBES

1½ OUNCES BRANDY

¾ OUNCE STREGA

½ OUNCE LIMONCELLO

½ OUNCE FRESHLY SQUEEZED ORANGE JUICE

½ OUNCE SIMPLE SYRUP (PAGE 12)

DASH OF PEYCHAUD'S BITTERS

1. Fill a cocktail shaker halfway full with ice cubes. Add everything. Shake well.

2. Strain into a cocktail glass.

WEEPER'S JOY

E very one of us has sad moments, from unfair annual meetings with sadistic bosses to a top team losing the big game to more serious sad moments. Luckily, on the other side of the shaker, everyone has joyful moments too, from seeing quitting time click in on a Friday afternoon to finding a copy of *Strange Tales* #110 in a dusty corner of a used bookstore to more serious joyful moments. And while there are drinks for both states of being, this may be the drink specifically for taking the sadness into joy—or finding the joy in sadness, if you will. This drink has been around at least since 1892, when it was published in *The Flowing Bowl*, by William Schmidt (or, as he was known, "the only William"). The knowledge that many others have made this drink for the same reason has to make things a little shinier.

CRACKED ICE

1 OUNCE ABSINTHE

1 OUNCE DRY VERMOUTH

1 OUNCE KÜMMEL

¼ OUNCE GUM SYRUP

DASH OF ORANGE CURAÇAO

1. Fill a cocktail shaker or mixing glass halfway full with cracked ice. Add the absinthe, vermouth, kümmel, gum syrup, and orange curaçao. Stir well.

2. Strain into a cocktail glass.

A NOTE: Gum syrup, or gomme syrup, is a variety of simple syrup containing gum arabic that many think has a smoother and silkier taste than regular simple syrup. It was an ingredient in many classic cocktails in days of yore, and it is now making a comeback (or a gum-back), with commercial varieties currently available from Small Hand Foods and Scrappy's.

Absinthe and Substitutes

First off, to attempt to derail the absinthe-o-philes from grumbling before we even get started, let me say that absinthe isn't, at heart, a liqueur. Most modern liqueurs today are considered to be presweetened, and absinthe isn't, so it's more a spirit. But, since a large percentage of the people drinking right now don't think of it in the same way as our base spirits, I'm going to feel okay putting it under a Liqueur Spotlight, and you should too.

To be true absinthe, the spirit must be distilled from *Artemisia absinthium*, often called grand wormwood, along with anise and fennel. Wormwood-flavored or -infused tipples have been used for drinking and as medicine for many years (we're talking thousands here), and other drinks used some of the same flavorings as absinthe, but to be in our specific category covering the drink that first became a huge hit in the eighteenth century in France and Switzerland, it has to follow the rules.

But on to what you really want to know: Does absinthe drive people mad? No more than any other drink really high in alcohol content. The supposed psychotropic and other hallucinatory powers of absinthe, though at one time legendary, have never been shown (outside of those associated with any strong liquor).

However, absinthe's reputation did lead it to being banned from many countries, including the United States, until 2007. This ban led to the creation of a number of absinthe substitutes. Perhaps the best known is Pernod (from the same company that had the first French absinthe distillery in 1805, started by Henri-Louis Pernod) or Pernod Anise, an anise-flavored liqueur created as a substitute after the ban. But though it mirrors some of absinthe's anise flavor, it is less potent, and sweeter. In the same way, Ricard Pastis, now owned by the same company and often referred to solely as pastis,or solely as Ricard, is another anise-flavored liqueur that sprang up (about 17 years later). Though it has some of the same flavors, pastis is perhaps even more related to other anise and licorice liqueurs such as Sambuca and ouzo.

There were other absinthe substitutes as well, but none contain the grand wormwood, or the mystique, of true absinthe (even if some are darn tasty). Absinthe itself does have an anise flavor, combined with fennel and an herbal-ness and bitterness provided by the wormwood (as well as traces of other herbs and flavors depending on the brand).

TROCADERO, PAGE 250

CHAPTER 8

THE JUSTICE

LEAGUE

OF VERMOUTHS

. . . .

Vermouth and the extended vermouth family, which can be said to include cousins Dubonnet and Lillet and singular siblings such as Punt e Mes and Carpano Antica, is defined both by its wine base and by its usual position as sidekick. In the Martini, to take a classic example, dry vermouth is the Jimmy Olsen to gin's Superman (or, when vodka's used, Bizarro Superman); in the Manhattan, sweet vermouth is Robin to bourbon or rye's Batman. This view is so entrenched that some folks believe that the main players in those drinks could survive without their sidekicks.

This, naturally, is wrong (even if certain movies don't contain both characters—let's stick to drinks here, kids). Without the signature aromatics and character brought from the vermouths, those famous drinks would never have become famous; they would be solely liquor, chilled, without the layers of flavors that have made them the recognizable liquid superheroes they are worldwide.

In this chapter, the vermouth family may not take the lead on every page, in every drink. Much like the ubiquitous Martini and Manhattan, the vermouth family member that's used in the Roman Cooler, or the Blackthorn Cocktail, or the Hugo Special may not be the top in terms of pure amount. It may sit behind pal gin or another friendly face. But even when it does, the vermouth rests happily, secure in its knowledge that without its presence, the drink would never make it, never triumph, never conquer the palates of those to whom it's served.

Without Dubonnet Rouge, remember, the Bentley never races through the nighttime to rescue a poor party being threatened by that insidious villain, Boring Cocktails. If Lillet leaves the terrific trio called the Great Secret, then how could the drink come to save a Saturday afternoon shindig that's slipped into the snare set by our sly old nemesis, the evil Dull Drinks? I shudder to think of the wickedness creeping from all corners without the vermouth family stepping up to save the day.

There are also, though, cocktails where vermouth does take the front role, where it gets to be the main ingredient, where it isn't a sidekick, but instead *has* sidekicks. In drinks such as the Rose, the Trocadero, and the Vermouth Cassis (which has a secret identity as the Pompier), each vermouth family member shows that it, too, should be taken as the superhero ingredient it is, and not forgotten. Without it, the world would be a much more dangerous—and much less delicious—place to drink.

5 Poetic Lines for Drinkers
. . . .

There's nothing quite as memorable as slipping in a drink- or drinking-related quote from a poem when you're shaking or stirring up a cocktail for a group of friends or (especially) a special someone. These work, but there are many more to choose from—heck, I put together a whole collection of them called *In Their Cups* (Harvard Common Press, 2010), which contains the full version of all the following—so don't stop your drink-poeticizing with these:

1. "What Elysium have ye known, / Happy field or mossy cavern, / Choicer than the Mermaid Tavern?"
—John Keats, "Lines on the Mermaid Tavern"

2. "Café au lait or coffee black / With Kirsch or Kümmel or Cognac / (The German band in Irving Place / By this time purple in the face)."
—Thomas Bailey Aldrich, "The Menu"

3. "But he'd never keep measure, if he had but the pleasure / Of washing his throat with a jug of gin-twist."
—William Maginn, "A Twist-imony in Favor of Gin-Twist"

4. "I demanded a brace / of martinis and fizzes, / called waitresses whores / and bartenders / pissants, then drained / every glass with artless / abandon."
—J. Robert Lennon, "Drinking Song"

5. "Walking seven blocks home / after four Guinness and three games of pool / the stars couldn't be any brighter."
—Dan Morris, "To the Girl with the Hair at the Club Bar, Troy, MT"

AUTUMN LEAVES

A h, autumn. Hayrides, pumpkin-carving parties, campfires, and moments spent in the backyard wondering where summer went, and why it always goes so fast, and why winter is waiting for us, gray and cold. Okay, I stumbled into the maudlin corner of the lounge, but heck, sometimes those thoughts come up between peppier party moments, in the same way that the leaves turn brown and eventually float to the ground between greener moments (and yeah, I'm sappy, but hey, I've had, like, three Autumn Leaves already, for testing purposes). You know what helps to balance out these melancholic moments? Three things. First, a good friend or two to have a drink and a joke with. Second, the perfect drink to match the moment. Third, the right person to create such a drink, a bartender of consummate skill and taste—someone like bar bright-light Jeffrey Morgenthaler (whom you can read more about on page 154, and visit at www.jeffreymorgenthaler.com). And you know what? He already created that drink. So all you need to do is call those good friends and turn the evening around.

CRACKED ICE

¾ OUNCE RYE

¾ OUNCE CLEAR CREEK APPLE BRANDY

¾ OUNCE CARPANO ANTICA

¼ OUNCE STREGA

2 DASHES CINNAMON TINCTURE (SEE A NOTE)

ICE CUBES

1 WIDE ORANGE PEEL STRIP, FOR GARNISH

1. Fill a cocktail shaker or mixing glass halfway full with cracked ice. Add the rye, apple brandy, Carpano Antica, Strega, and cinnamon tincture. Stir well.

2. Fill an old-fashioned glass with ice cubes. Strain the mix into the glass and over the ice. Garnish with the orange peel.

A NOTE: To make the cinnamon tincture, soak 4 ounces whole cinnamon sticks in 16 ounces grain alcohol or vodka for 3 weeks. Strain through a fine-mesh strainer to remove any solids, and then store in a glass bottle away from sunlight.

A SECOND NOTE: Jeffrey suggests Wild Turkey as his rye of choice here, and if you don't want your drink to fade like actual autumn leaves, I'd follow his advice.

BENTLEY

E very time I order this rich combo, I expect to hear the tooting of a little horn and to see Mr. Moneybags (the iconic Monopoly character) pulling up beside me in a miniature version of the car that shares this drink's moniker, saying, "I say, that's my drink, young man." I can understand how he wouldn't want this becoming an every-person order, because sometimes you want a signature drink to be just for you. But darnit, Moneybags, you have to share on this, because it would be a shame if regular folk (those like me who can't pony up for the car) couldn't take advantage of this combining of French apple brandy Calvados and French fortified and herbalized wine Dubonnet. So back off, rich fella, and share the bar.

ICE CUBES

1½ OUNCES CALVADOS

1½ OUNCES DUBONNET ROUGE

1. Fill a cocktail shaker halfway full with ice cubes. Add the Calvados and Dubonnet. Shake well.

2. Strain into a well-polished cocktail glass.

A NOTE: Think this is looking a little bling-less? An apple slice goes well as a garnish here.

A SECOND NOTE: Some might just stir this with ice, but I think it needs a shake.

BLACKTHORN COCKTAIL

This venerable drink has had a few permutations in the past 80 odd years (including the almost completely different variation below), and it has almost been forgotten. The former is understandable, but the latter is unforgivable. The way this drink matches up persuasive Irish whiskey with layered vermouth and important hints of absinthe, Angostura, and lemon ensures that it is a welcome guest before or after dinner.

....

ICE CUBES

2 OUNCES IRISH WHISKEY

1 OUNCE SWEET VERMOUTH

¼ OUNCE ABSINTHE

3 DASHES ANGOSTURA BITTERS

LEMON TWIST, FOR GARNISH

1. Fill a cocktail shaker halfway full with ice cubes. Add the whiskey, sweet vermouth, absinthe, and bitters. Shake well.

2. Strain into a cocktail glass. Twist the twist over the glass and let it drop in.

A VARIATION: In the 1939 Angostura pamphlet/book *For Home Use*, there's a Blackthorne Cocktail that uses equal parts sloe gin and dry vermouth shaken with 3 dashes Angostura and a touch of simple syrup. It's worth a try too, if a little less known.

....

"Besides the new bottle of gin, his cellar consisted of one half-bottle of Bourbon whisky, a quarter of a bottle of Italian vermouth, and approximately one hundred drops of orange bitters."

—SINCLAIR LEWIS, *BABBIT*, 1922

DANDY

At first when I gazed on him walking into the bumper crib (which is what I call the local), with his little boater perched on his head and that awful high-button lounge suit, I thought that he was a toke cove (a smattering like a dry bread stuck without butter), or at least a bloke ready to be cabbaged or shined by anyone whose dander is up when seeing a dandy. But then he ordered a Dandy for me, and one more for the whole of the crowd, and the next thing we're in the midst of a jolly ran-tan. We had so much fun I thought they'd call the beaks, and the next day, I hurt so much I went cagg. At least until the next Dandy, that is.

CRACKED ICE

1 OUNCE RYE

1 OUNCE DUBONNET ROUGE

¼ OUNCE COINTREAU

DASH OF ANGOSTURA BITTERS

LEMON TWIST, FOR GARNISH

ORANGE TWIST, FOR GARNISH

1. Fill a cocktail shaker or mixing glass halfway full with cracked ice. Add the rye, Dubonnet, Cointreau, and bitters. Stir well.

2. Strain into a cocktail glass. Garnish with the twists, after twisting them over the glass.

A NOTE: I've seen this made with bourbon and Canadian whisky instead of the rye. I like the rye best, but come to your own conclusions.

DUTCH CHARLIE'S

Tell me, 'cause I gotta know—is there a bar anywhere called Dutch Charlie's? A smoky joint where people show up in snazzy duds and there's a band playing (with maybe the world's snappiest snare drum, and a trumpet that, when it hits the high notes, sounds like it should be playing in heaven), and folks cutting the proverbial rug, and where the manager wears a white suit and is still completely classy, and the gorilla letting people in the door is cuddly underneath the harsh exterior, and the bartenders . . . the bartenders are swift and precise and charming and shake the drinks like paint machines. Tell me more about this bar, while we sip a drink of the same name, and let us dream it into reality.

. . . .

ICE CUBES

1½ OUNCES RYE

1 OUNCE DUBONNET ROUGE

1 OUNCE SWEET VERMOUTH

2 DASHES ANGOSTURA BITTERS

1. Fill a cocktail shaker halfway full with ice cubes. Add the rye, Dubonnet, sweet vermouth, and bitters. Shake well.

2. Strain the mixture into a cocktail glass.

FIFTH AVENUE

While it may be worthwhile to deck yourself out dashing-like any ol' time in faux fur capes, cubic zirconium necklaces, polished bluchers, and pressed trousers while swirling this sipper and playing Go Fish or Wheel of Fortune in honor of famous Fifth Avenue, you might not want to overdo the honor (the same party every day loses its luster, don't y'know). Thinking of that, and of you, I suggest donning the duds and dropping the darlings only on January 12, the anniversary of the first giant Saks sale. That way, you won't blow the whole bankroll (or bash enthusiasm among chums) by having repetitive events.

. . . .

CRACKED ICE

1½ OUNCES GIN

¾ OUNCE DRY VERMOUTH

¾ OUNCE FERNET-BRANCA

1. Fill a cocktail shaker or mixing glass halfway full with cracked ice. Add the gin, dry vermouth, and Fernet-Branca. Stir well.

2. Strain into a cocktail glass or highfalutin cordial glass.

GREAT SECRET

ould the secret be Lillet, the French apéritif made from a mix of wine, citrus lizqueurs, and undisclosed formulas? Or could the secret be that I first discovered this debonair potable in Patrick Gavin Duffy's *The Official Mixer's Manual* (Alta, 1934)? Or could the secret be that though this calls for an orange twist, the extra juice from an orange slice is also great? Or could the secret be that this particular secret, like most liquid secrets, is better when shared with at least one pal or paramour? The last is the answer I'm believing.

CRACKED ICE

2 OUNCES GIN

1 OUNCE LILLET BLANC

DASH OF ANGOSTURA BITTERS

ORANGE TWIST, FOR GARNISH

ORANGE SLICE, FOR GARNISH (OPTIONAL, USED INSTEAD OF ABOVE TWIST)

1. Fill a mixing glass or cocktail shaker with cracked ice. Add the gin, Lillet, and bitters. Stir well.

2. Strain into a cocktail glass. Twist the twist over the glass and then drop it in. Shhhhh.

HUGO SPECIAL

This pick-me-up is a pleasure, if you use fresh oranges and pineapple and aren't afraid of dropping a little elbow grease to ensure parallel tastiness. However, I have my doubts that playwright, watercolorist, poet, and all-around industrious French arty-fellow Victor Hugo ever had the happiness of muddling up a Hugo Special (though I could be wrong—if so, apologies to Victor), and my guess is he was sadder for it. If you slightly alter a quote of his, it sounds as though he at least entertained the idea: "Man does not live by bread alone. Give up the [cocktail], and you give up civilization."

. . . .

3 ORANGE SLICES

3 PINEAPPLE ROUNDS

ICE CUBES

1½ OUNCES GIN

1 OUNCE SWEET VERMOUTH

1. Add the orange slices and pineapple rounds to a cocktail shaker. Muddle well (and don't take lip from the fruit).

2. Fill the shaker halfway full with ice cubes, and then add the gin and vermouth. Shake for at least 15 seconds.

3. Strain the mixture into a cocktail glass.

A VARIATION: If you want to experience the fruit a bit more, instead of straining, pour the mix—ice, fruit, and all—into a goblet. Call it a Hugo's Messy Room.

3

Bubbly Birthday Drinks

. . . .

GINGER BLISS & THE VIOLET FIZZ

. . . .

You should want to make birthdays special days, as they're a specific celebration for someone near and dear to you (or at least someone who works in the nearest cubicle). I think making them even more special with a bubbly signature drink is one of the best presents you can give—

and having the following drinks to pick from makes the presenting easy.

1. Princess
(page 44)

2. Big Spender
(page 29)

3. Graduate
(page 95)

3

JEWEL COCKTAIL

Maybe I'm just a pitter-pattering old romantic, but I get misty at movies, books, and afternoon television specials that feature two people with starry eyes gazing at each other in the rain, two people coming into the clutch after running toward one another in a field of flowers, or two people on an old park bench as the moon glows in the sky and ducks paddle two-by-two in a passing stream. And then when one of the couple bends down on one knee and reaches slowly into a pocket to pull out a glistening, herbaceous Jewel Cocktail and proposes to the other that they drink it? A tear always comes to my eye. Ah, love, s'wonderful.

ICE CUBES

1 OUNCE GIN

1 OUNCE SWEET VERMOUTH

1 OUNCE GREEN CHARTREUSE

2 DASHES ORANGE BITTERS

LEMON TWIST, FOR GARNISH

1. Fill a cocktail shaker halfway full with ice cubes. Add the gin, vermouth, Chartreuse, and bitters. Shake well.

2. Strain into a cocktail glass, and garnish with the twist.

A NOTE: In *The Savoy Cocktail Book*, by the great Harry Craddock, this is served with a cherry, and to six people. The cherry I can't get behind, as it seems like too much fruit to me, but I'm all for making this for as many people as possible (provided the ratios remain intact).

"A medium-dry, fast-working cocktail."

—HARRY CRADDOCK, REFERRING TO THE JEWEL COCKTAIL IN *THE SAVOY COCKTAIL BOOK*, 1930

KICK-OFF

How many kick-offs do you believe happen every Friday and Saturday (and Monday night and increasing Thursdays) during fall and winter months? An unimaginable number, right? And yet, there aren't as many Kick-Off cocktail variations as this would lead one to expect—I might expect one for each collegiate and professional team, for example. I'd like to think the lack spurs from homage to this particular cocktail, one that isn't much in the modern mindset, which I found within the gorgeous *Gourmet's Guide to New Orleans* by Natalie Scott and Caroline Merrick Jones (Scott & Jones, 1933). I can see how not every tailgater would serve this, as it's a serious mascot with a rampaging host of flavor-packed ingredients, each of which scores its own points. But if you don't mind a challenge—and really, what great team dislikes a challenge?—then I say serve it up before any big game, even one that is big only to you.

CRACKED ICE

1 OUNCE GIN

1 OUNCE DRY VERMOUTH

¼ OUNCE ANISETTE

¼ OUNCE BÉNÉDICTINE

2 DASHES ANGOSTURA BITTERS

1. Fill a cocktail shaker or mixing glass halfway full with cracked ice. Add the gin, vermouth, anisette, Bénédictine, and bitters. Stir well.

2. Strain into a cocktail glass. Garnish with a tiny jersey from your favorite footballers.

"The first violinist, an expert chemist, skillfully diluted the contents of gin, rum, Scotch whisky, Bénédictine, and Cognac bottles which he bought at the crew's fifty per cent reduction from the second-class barman. (In those days of Honesty, it was 'second' and not 'cabin' class.)"

—JOSEPH WECHSBERG, "CONFESSIONS OF A BOOTLEGGER,"
THE COMPLEAT IMBIBER 2, 1958

Lillet

An aromatized wine (a cousin to vermouth, you might say) with a light orange lilt, Lillet, in its most commonly found Blanc version, tends to be consumed before dinner, either solo on ice, or mixed in cocktails such as the Great Secret (page 234). It was first made in 1887 by Paul and Raymond Lillet and sold within the Bordeaux region of France starting in 1895. At that time, Kina Lillet, as it was known, had a bit more quinine in its white wine–based makeup, and a more serious amount of the Peruvian kina kina tree's bark (a tree sometimes called the cinchona). But in 1986 the amount of quinine was reduced, which is why the Lillet most usually consumed today is lighter. Other variations have sprung up, including Lillet Dry, for the English market, and Lillet Rouge, created in 1962 (see page 241 for a bit of info on Lillet Rouge).

Of course, Lillet also has a big screen history, thanks to one James Bond, who orders a Kina Lillet Martini in *Casino Royale*, naming the drink the Vesper after one of his romantic leading ladies (and a spy). The first occurrence of Mr. Bond's recipe is in Ian Fleming's 1953 book of the same name. Bond's instructions to the bartender are to make it using "three measures of Gordon's, one of vodka, half a measure of Kina Lillet." Then, in the version of the movie released in 2006, he orders it the same way. This shows that maybe Mr. Bond—or the movie's director—had had a few too many, since Kina Lillet had stopped being produced in the 1980s. But I certainly can't fault him for needing a few drinks—making movies is tough.

LES FESSES ROUGES #2

With less international celeb panache, Lillet Rouge tends to get over-shadowed by its sibling, Lillet Blanc. But the *rouge* version of this French apéritif is worth tracking down, as its rich red wine base and echoes of citrus and herbs make for a nice pre-dinner sipper. It also makes for an intriguing component in mixed drinks, such as this one, which is adapted from a recipe I first saw on the *Food & Wine* website (www.foodandwine.com), created by Brad Farran, former bar manager at Raleigh, North Carolina's Enoteca Vin.

ICE CUBES

1½ OUNCES HANGAR ONE MANDARIN BLOSSOM VODKA

¾ OUNCE LILLET ROUGE

¾ OUNCE POMEGRANATE JUICE

½ OUNCE FRESHLY SQUEEZED ORANGE JUICE

ORANGE TWIST, FOR GARNISH

1. Fill a cocktail shaker halfway full with ice cubes. Add the vodka, Lillet Rouge, pome-granate juice, and orange juice. Shake well.

2. Strain the mixture into a cocktail glass and garnish with the orange twist.

MARGUERITE COCKTAIL

M y discovery of the Marguerite, a fitting addition to the realm of never-should-have-been-forgotten favorites, came when perusing Harry Johnson's *New and Improved Bartender's Manual*, first published by Mr. Johnson himself in 1882, with the revised version in 1900. Mr. Johnson was one of the top bartenders of his time (a peer of the more well-known Jerry Thomas), and though not a full bar's worth of information is known about him, it is known that he was a true bartender in the splendid style of the time: a fountain of knowledge and class, a well-respected member of the community, and able to make a host of cocktails, highballs, punches, and more. One thing I don't know, sadly, is whom this particular cocktail was named for. I do know that I wouldn't have the recipe for this drink without the fine folks at Mud Puddle Books, who published a facsimile of Mr. Johnson's manual in 2008, with an introduction by modern true bartender Robert Hess, who goes often by the nom de plume DrinkBoy (www.drinkboy.com).

CRACKED ICE

1¼ OUNCES GIN

1¼ OUNCES DRY VERMOUTH

¼ OUNCE ANISETTE

3 DASHES ORANGE BITTERS

MARASCHINO CHERRY, FOR GARNISH

LEMON TWIST, FOR GARNISH

1. Fill a cocktail shaker or mixing glass halfway full with cracked ice. Add the gin, vermouth, anisette, and orange bitters. Stir well.

2. Add the cherry to a cocktail glass. Strain the mixture into the glass and over the cherry. Twist the lemon twist over the glass and drop it in.

PHOEBE SNOW

Phoebe was a New York debutante and society girl, cute as a button and ready to travel—or, honestly, to advertise travel. See, friends, Phoebe was actually a lovely artistic creation, never made into a real girl by the blue fairy, used first by the Lackawanna Railroad and later by other railroads to promote trains that ran on anthracite coal. At the time (we're talking early 1900s here) most train travel would leave travelers covered in black coal dust and soot. But anthracite, believe you me, burned clean as, well, snow. And to advertise that fact: Enter Phoebe. Petticoated and rattling off a series of rhymes in pretty pictures, Phoebe helped transform how folks thought about train travel and became one of the most recognized ad icons, and figures, of her time (Mickey, eat your mousey heart out). With that fame came the following cocktail—which, with its balance of French aromatic and herbal wine Dubonnet and brandy and a wink of absinthe, would taste as good as you'd look coming off a train fueled by anthracite.

. . . .

CRACKED ICE

1½ OUNCES DUBONNET ROUGE

1½ OUNCES BRANDY

¼ OUNCE ABSINTHE

1. Fill a cocktail shaker or mixing glass halfway full with cracked ice. Add the Dubonnet, brandy, and absinthe, and stir well, as if you were a train chugging down the track.

2. Strain into a cocktail glass.

5 Historic Sippers

GINGER BLISS & THE VIOLET FIZZ

Now, there are drinks with history, and then there are drinks you should consume while watching a historic movie, reading history, or having a party where everyone comes dressed as a historical or mythological figure or as a representation of a historical moment. These cocktails are for the latter moments.

1. Washington
(page 251)

2. Persephone's Exiliar
(page 105)

3. Alaska
(page 122)

4. Zeno's Paradoxical
(page 183)

5. Hugo Special
(page 236)

THOUGH MOST OF THE CHAPTERS IN THIS BOOK ARE FOCUSED ON A CERTAIN LIQUEUR FLAVOR PROFILE, THERE'S ALSO THIS WHOLE CHAPTER, WHICH CONTAINS DRINKS HIGHLIGHTING THE PERSONALITY AND TASTE OF SPECIFIC VERMOUTHS.

While not quite the same as liqueurs (as they're wine-based, and liqueurs tend to be spirit-based), of course, they are sometimes confusing, even though they're key to probably the two most famous cocktails, the Martini and the Manhattan (which contain dry vermouth and sweet vermouth, respectively). Vermouths are serious players in many other classic and new cocktails, and they are also consumed solo in many countries.

So, what are vermouths? Like their cousins (and some would even call them variants) Dubonnet and Lillet, regular vermouths are usually referred to as "aromatized" wine. Unlike a fortified wine (such as port or Marsala), which contains an additional spirit, an aromatized wine is infused or flavored with an assortment of spices, herbs, roots, sweeteners, flowers, fairy wings, and more (okay, the fairy wings aren't usually in there, but sometimes it does seem as if magical items have been added).

The moniker "vermouth" goes back to the German *vermut*, which means "wormwood," an ingredient in many fortified and aromatized wines in the early years (which was a long, long time ago). Today, there are two main types of vermouth that are seen most often: dry (or French) and sweet (or Italian). Dry vermouth traces from most reports to the beginning of the 1900s, when it was developed by Joseph Noilly. Often referred to as white vermouth, it is clear, or sometimes has a bare tint of yellow. Sweet vermouth

is darker in color—it's sometimes referred to as red vermouth—and more herbal in flavor, though also with an underlying sweetness at different levels. Antonio Benedetto Carpano created this style of vermouth in 1786 (in Italy, naturally) using a recipe still available today as Carpano Antica. While the dry and the sweet are most prevalent, more and more often a third variety of vermouth—bianco—is becoming available from companies such as Dolin. It tends to be a little sweeter than the others, so be careful with it at first (but don't get scared off, as it can be lovely). Other vermouths sometimes seen in other countries and worth experimenting with include rosé (which is starting to become available in the United States), orange, and lemon.

You can easily find most of the well-known vermouth brands at your local and online stores, including Martini & Rossi and Cinzano (both made in Turin, Italy) and Noilly Prat (made in France). You can also find a number of newer and usually harder-to-find brands such as Vya, made in California, and the above-mentioned Dolin. Though the flavors of different brands are slightly different, you can usually use any brand of vermouth in a recipe that calls for "dry" or "sweet" vermouth and not suffer for it. However, a few vermouth brands contain such specific flavors within their bottles that they are called for by name in recipes. Be sure to track these down when called for if you want to experience maximum drinking pleasure.

ROMAN COOLER

Friends, drinkers, party people, lend me your glasses; I come to bury thirstiness, not to increase it. The parched feeling that summer brings lives after hours; the cooldown is interred within this glass; so let it be with your next party. The noble Punt e Mes hath told me gin was ambitious; if it were so, club soda will keep it from being at grievous fault.

William S. forgives me (or I believe he will when we're sitting around the big playhouse bar in the sky), as long as he knows you'll be serving this at your next hot hoedown, whether you're reading and reciting plays, poems, or movie scenes or lounging bedecked in laurel wreaths and little else. So, serve the Roman Cooler and keep me from brawling in heaven's bar.

- -

ICE CUBES

1½ OUNCES GIN

¾ OUNCE PUNT E MES

½ OUNCE FRESHLY SQUEEZED LEMON JUICE

¼ OUNCE SIMPLE SYRUP (PAGE 12)

CHILLED CLUB SODA

1. Fill a cocktail shaker halfway full with ice cubes. Add the gin, Punt e Mes, lemon juice, and simple syrup. Shake well.

2. Fill a highball glass three-quarters full with ice cubes. Strain the mixture over the ice and into the glass.

3. Fill the glass almost to the rim with club soda. Stir briefly, centurion-style.

A NOTE: I've seen this with a twist of lime. But that doesn't seem very Roman to me.

ROSE

Showing up with a dozen limp red roses picked up last-minute on Valentine's Day garners only a thumbs-down from a romantic dearest (if not a door slammed in the face, or a slap, or an invitation to spend the night on the couch). However, you can show that love how much you care and start the evening right by swapping the limp flowers for a liquid Rose and having it ready when he or she walks in the door (or when you show up at his or her door). To demonstrate your smarts (which is, naturally, also sexy), tell that paramour that this was originally made with groseille syrup, which is difficult to track down today, and that you thought about going with raspberry syrup, but because your love is so tremendous and true you decided to follow the advice of cocktail historian David Wondrich—author of the amazing *Imbibe!* (Perigee, 2007), among other books—and are making this with lush Chambord, the liqueur created from French black raspberries.

CRACKED ICE

2 OUNCES DRY VERMOUTH

1 OUNCE KIRSCH

1 OUNCE CHAMBORD

MARASCHINO CHERRY, FOR GARNISH

1. Fill a cocktail shaker or mixing glass halfway full with cracked ice. Add the vermouth, kirsch, and Chambord. Stir well.

2. Strain into a cocktail glass and add the cherry.

SANCTUARY

A triple dose of French *qualité* (it's surprising that it's not called *Le Sanctuaire*), this stirred bit of refuge combines fortified and aromatic wine Dubonnet, rich and earthy apéritif Amer Picon, and classic orange liqueur Cointreau. There's such a variety of bursting flavor in this Sanctuary that it's highly probable that you'll want to get on a France-bound plane right away (better have that passport ready before you even start to pour).

CRACKED ICE

2 OUNCES DUBONNET ROUGE

¾ OUNCE COINTREAU

¾ OUNCE AMER PICON

1. Fill a cocktail shaker or mixing glass halfway full with cracked ice. Add the Dubonnet, Cointreau, and Amer Picon. Stir well.

2. Strain into a cocktail glass.

A VARIATION: If you reduce the Cointreau to just 1 teaspoon, this turns into a Quartier Latin cocktail—a variation I found in the book *Barflies and Cocktails* by Harry McElhone and Wynn Holcomb.

A NOTE: A French apéritif, Amer Picon (sometimes just going solo as Picon) is bitter with hints of oranges. Mentioned in many older cocktail recipes, it's a bit hard to get a hold of, but it can be found online. One thing to remember: It was originally quite a bit stronger than the current version, but it still tastes darn fine. There is also a more readily available substitute called Torani Amer that is actually a bit stronger than the current Amer Picon and is worth a try.

TRILBY

his goes back to the play based on the novel of the same name and is a drink I first took notice of in this iteration when I found it in *Applegreen's Bar Book* (Hotel Monthly Press, 1909, although an earlier edition came out in 1899) by John Applegreen. Way back when, in the hopping late 1800s and early 1900s cocktail era, drinks were often named after plays and actors and actresses, so naming a drink after a play isn't so far out. Especially when it was a long-running, incredibly popular play, so popular it inspired not only this drink but also a hat (the Trilby), and started the usage of the phrase "in the altogether" to refer to being completely undressed. Does that mean that you should make two of these for you and your significant other and watch old plays (or old movies) wearing only a hip hat? Well, not necessarily. But it sure isn't a bad idea.

CRACKED ICE

2 OUNCES GIN

1 OUNCE DRY VERMOUTH

¼ OUNCE CRÈME YVETTE

1. Fill a cocktail shaker halfway full with cracked ice. Add the gin, dry vermouth, and crème Yvette. Stir well.

2. Strain into a cocktail glass.

A VARIATION: There's another Trilby (perhaps better known nowadays) that is a variation on the Manhattan, made using bourbon, sweet vermouth, and orange bitters. It's also hat-worthy.

A NOTE: Crème Yvette went out of circulation for a while, from 1969 to 2009 to be precise, but it's now available again. If you can't find it, but you can find crème de violette, then sub that in. See more on page 61.

TROCADERO

We think often of dry and sweet vermouth as being like Muhammad Ali and George Foreman fighting relentlessly in Zaire, or like two large dogs gnawing on one big bone in the backyard (the bone here would equal a bar, if you don't mind following a thinly stretched metaphor). This train of thought, though, is out of whack. We should think of the vermouths more like A.J. and Rick Simon, brother detectives who are very different in style, dress, and tone of voice but are working together to solve a crime (the crime here would be the crime of having a bad drink, instead of this tasty one).

....

CRACKED ICE

1½ OUNCES DRY VERMOUTH

1½ OUNCES SWEET VERMOUTH

DASH OF ORANGE BITTERS

¼ OUNCE GRENADINE (PAGE 14)

LEMON TWIST, FOR GARNISH

1. Fill a cocktail shaker or mixing glass halfway full with cracked ice. Add the vermouths at the same time to show no favoritism, and then the bitters and the grenadine. Stir well.

2. Strain into a cocktail glass. Garnish with the lemon twist.

VERMOUTH CASSIS

In some older books, this is called the Pompier (and oftentimes calls for equal amounts of vermouth and crème de cassis). According to the *Waldorf-Astoria Bar Book* by Albert Crockett (originally printed in 1935 and handily reprinted by New Day in 2003), it was called this "after the French term for 'firemen,' but no French fireman would understand the usual orders that were given for it."

....

ICE CUBES

1½ OUNCES DRY VERMOUTH

1 OUNCE CRÈME DE CASSIS

CHILLED CLUB SODA

1. Fill a highball glass just about halfway full with ice cubes. Add the vermouth and the crème de cassis.

2. Fill the glass with club soda. Stir briefly.

WASHINGTON

Not that you, proud patriotic person that you are, need a reason to party on February 22, the birthday of the first president of the United States. You already have the date marked in advance and have rented a wig of gray curls and Revolutionary-style regimental dress; or a combination of tricorn hat, brown breeches, woolen stockings, and thick leather footwear; or a pocket apron, mop cap, demure gown, and lace tucker. What I'm not sure of is whether the appropriate beverage to serve to other 1700s-attired attendees at the revelry has been uncovered. If not, may I offer up the following, which is named after George Washington himself (in my history lesson at least), and which contains items that he might just have had handy. (Well, maybe not the Angostura—but bittering agents were around. Aromatized wines, if not called "vermouth," were also in evidence.) One other thing to remember, my historical drinker: Have this not only on February 22, but also on December 14, which is the day our first leader of the country passed away.

....

ICE CUBES

2 OUNCES DRY VERMOUTH

1 OUNCE BRANDY

4 DASHES ANGOSTURA BITTERS

½ OUNCE SIMPLE SYRUP (PAGE 12)

1. Fill a cocktail shaker halfway full with ice cubes. Add the vermouth, brandy, bitters, and simple syrup. Shake well—for gosh sakes, you're honoring Washington.

2. Strain into a cocktail glass.

....

"My report's all tied up. He was murdered by the Communists. Perhaps the beginning of a campaign against American aid. But between you and—listen, it's dry talking, what about a Vermouth Cassis round the corner?"

—GRAHAM GREENE, *THE QUIET AMERICAN*, 1955

WEDDING BELLS OF THE QUEEN

I'm not going to insist upon it (because insisting oftentimes gets in the way of actual drinking, what with the debating and verifying of facts and such), but I want to at least go to bat for the idea that the queen referenced here should be Queen Elizabeth—the Queen Mother, that is (may she rest in peace). My reasoning comes from her supposed love of Dubonnet and gin, which happen to be the main ingredients in this very recipe. The story goes (and again, I'm not insisting you believe this story, but I'm hoping you do) that once she was getting ready to head out on a trip and said something along the lines of "I'm going to bring two small bottles of Dubonnet and gin along with me, in case it's needed." That's the kind of planning that I think deserves a toast.

CRACKED ICE

1½ OUNCES GIN (NEED I SAY BRITISH OR LONDON GIN WORKS BEST HERE?)

1¼ OUNCES DUBONNET BLANC

¼ OUNCE CHERRY HEERING

1. Fill a cocktail shaker or mixing glass halfway full with cracked ice. Add the gin, Dubonnet blanc, and cherry Heering. Stir well.

2. Strain into a cocktail glass.

A NOTE: Feel this needs a crown? Garnish it with a lemon twist.

A SECOND NOTE: Dubonnet Blanc is less familiar than the ruby-red Dubonnet Rouge and because of this sometimes isn't invited to the more fashionable parties. Which is quite a shame, because its white wine–based, drier, fortified, and herbally aromatized (it contains 50 herbs and spices) nature is as nice when chilled and served solo as when combined into this cocktail and others like it.

Dubonnet

A cousin of vermouth and Lillet (Doesn't that sound like quite a joyous family reunion to attend, by the way? How wonderful that would be!), Dubonnet is a French aromatized and flavored wine altered by the addition of an assortment of herbs, spices, and quinine. There are two Dubonnets found in the modern world: red wine–based Rouge, which is spicy and dessert-y; and white wine–based Blanc, which is dryer than Rouge. Dubonnet's history begins in 1846, when French wine agent Joseph Dubonnet wanted to construct his very own herb-and-spice-infused wine mixture. Because of the popularity of bitter tinctures and elixirs being used at the time in a medical manner, Joseph also added quinine to instill a little "healthy" hint to his mixture, and then used a sweet Greek wine to balance out the quinine. He started off filling only the glasses of his family and friends, but they praised the combination so highly and were so enamored of it that he decided to release it to the world at large. And the world at large has been very receptive, as Dubonnet is still popular today, both when shaken into cocktails such as the Bentley (page 230) and when consumed on its own.

SNOWBALL, PAGE 280

CHAPTER 9

HERE'S

TO YOU,

SWEETS

. . . .

Youse drinkers, listen up, 'cause I'm gonna shoot the works on the sweet numbers contained in this chapter. I'm not talking about a bunch of broads, neither, so don't be dragging away from your dolls (or, on the flip side, from your fellas if you thought I meant a bunch of muscle candy). And I don't care a fly's eye if some cocktail creators or chroniclers might have a beef with the sweet liqueurs and what's made from them.

Those who have no appreciation for sweet drinks can spend their time in the hash house far as I'm concerned. You and I, we have sweet business to discuss. I'm not here to flimflam you, but rather to introduce you to an assortment of beverages on the after-dinner side (I'm talking dessert favorites, y'know) that have more to bet on than any ol' bangtail, ones called Babar 'n Blitzen, Matinee, and Casual Caress.

Are youse starting to pick up what I'm shaking? I'm putting the finger on an array of fantasy players for you, and by fantasy I mean you and yours might just get taken to another plane of lovey-dovey, when you bring out the sugar hooch contained in an Alexander or a Caledonia. Heck, you may not need to play the hard guy or gal to impress anymore, and you may just get your tricks from serving up the right mixes for once.

This ain't bunk, and I'm not steering you into a clip joint, but if you want to impress, don't shirk to lifting ice (and I mean the kind in rings), but instead show up when the lights dim carrying a Snowball, and you might end up with a

Fireside, too. It may just turn your wanna-be into your Coney Island Baby, and from there, you've serving a Cara Sposa.

So don't let the wrong numbers try to shy youse away from dessert treats in liquid style. You can easily be hard-boiled while keeping a sweet side. Remember this and keep wise: Every time you end up with a Chocolate Cliffhanger, or deep in a Loch Lomond, or face to face at midnight with a full-fledged Magia Bianca, or with one of the other luscious treasures hiding in the following pages, it's much better than having a belly full of rotgut.

ALEXANDER

S it back, true believers, and listen for a second: The Alexander is the emperor of sweet liquid treats, a delish drop of chocolaty-creamy-ginny perfection, an after-dinner delight that should be savored slowly while thinking of the many Alexanders that have made mouths mad with delight since the decade starting with 1910 (or thereabouts). It's a prizewinner (when I'm giving out the prizes, at least) thanks to its three Bs: beauty, balance, and boozerificness. Anyone who says different should be sent home without an Alexander (and I shudder to think of a more horrific punishment).

ICE CUBES

1 OUNCE GIN

1 OUNCE WHITE CRÈME DE CACAO

1 OUNCE HEAVY CREAM

2 STRAWBERRY SLICES, FOR GARNISH

1. Fill a cocktail shaker halfway full with ice cubes. Add the gin, crème de cacao, and cream. Shake well.

2. Strain into a cocktail glass. Garnish with the strawberry slices.

A VARIATION: The Brandy Alexander is so widely known that it's not considered a variation but the standard in many spots (this is okay, 'cause it's a good mix—though not as good as the original), but there's also the lesser-known Alexander's Sister, made by adding crème de menthe to the gin recipe instead of crème de cacao.

ANGEL'S TIT

Sometimes sweetness needs a little wink and edge added to it, to make sure it doesn't head into saccharine territory. If this cousin of the Alexander (page 256) was just called the Angel, it might be impossible to order it for that demure or hunky someone across the bar. Not that I'm suggesting you go up to said potential paramour and say brazenly, "You have the, um, figure of an angel." But perhaps sending over one of these with a wink and a non-ogling smile would be a good way to introduce yourself.

2 OUNCES WHITE CRÈME DE CACAO

1 OUNCE CHILLED HEAVY CREAM

WHIPPED CREAM, FOR TOPPING

MARASCHINO CHERRY, FOR GARNISH

1. Add the crème de cacao to a large cordial glass. Slowly pour the cream over a spoon, floating it on top of the crème de cacao.

2. Being careful not to get too energetic about it (the crème de cacao and cream shouldn't combine much), top everything with whipped cream, and then top that with a cherry.

A VARIATION: If ordering this without whipped cream and a cherry at Seattle's Athenian Inn way back when (it was one of the first places in Seattle to have a liquor license), you would have been sipping a King Alphonse. Maybe in other spots, too, where folks weren't afraid of admitting their sweet teeth.

BABAR 'N BLITZEN

There are blogs within the drinker's blogosphere (for more on that boozy collection of bloggers, see page 25) that have a cocktail focus, and then there are blogs that focus on one specific cocktail. One of the tops in the latter category is the Pegu Blog (www.killingtime.com/pegu), which is, as blog scribe Doug Winship says, "a site about Pegus and other ramblings on the cocktail life." Okay, so maybe it's not about only one cocktail, but his devotion to the Pegu (which you can see more about on page 43) is wonderful to behold, almost as wonderful as the Pegu Blog is enjoyable to read: witty and brimming with stories, cheer, and drinks. Drinks such as the Babar 'n Blitzen, which was featured as a special winter holiday creation and is one sure to make your festivities even more festive.

ICE CUBES

2 OUNCES AMARULA CREAM LIQUEUR

1 OUNCE STOLI VANIL VODKA

1 OUNCE DARK RUM

½ OUNCE ORGEAT SYRUP

1. Fill a cocktail shaker halfway full with ice cubes. Add the Amarula, vodka, rum, and orgeat. Shake well.

2. Strain into a cocktail glass, and toast to the holiday season.

A NOTE: Made from the marula fruit, which grows on the magical marula tree in the African veld and which is supposed to have been the food of choice in ancient times for people living in South Africa, Botswana, and Namibia, Amarula cream liqueur is a smooth, sweet delight that has nutty and caramel hints to go along with its creaminess.

BLUE MOON

Okay, hum along with me (if you don't know the tune, refer to 1930s songsmiths Richard Rodgers and Lorenz Hart): "Blue Moon, I shook you up with ice cubes, alongside gin and lemon juice, with crème Yvette—just a smoosh. Blue Moon, I served you on an afternoon, with the sun in the air like a balloon, and everyone at the party swooned." Pretty, isn't it? Prettier, perhaps, is this drink, which has a lovely glow due to the music made between crème Yvette's violet-vanilla tones and gin.

ICE CUBES

2 OUNCES GIN

½ OUNCE CRÈME YVETTE

½ OUNCE FRESHLY SQUEEZED LEMON JUICE

1. Fill a cocktail shaker halfway full with ice cubes. Add the gin, crème Yvette, and lemon juice. Shake well.

2. Strain the mixture into a cocktail glass.

A VARIATION: I've seen another version of the Blue Moon that mixes equal parts rye and Bénédictine shaken together, and then it's topped with the combined amount of ginger ale. Not so bad on a spring day.

A NOTE: Be sure to go with a good dry-but-serious-in-flavor gin here, something like Washington's Voyager gin, or a classic English model like Boodles. And if you can't find crème Yvette, feel free to sub in crème de violette.

The Top Home Bar Essentials

You don't need to mortgage your house for a trip to a restaurant supply store so you can install a full ice maker and every single bar tool at your house (though this might make for some memorable parties), but a few key items will make your home entertaining more, well, entertaining (and for a few other tools you might like, see page 279).

1. A good cocktail shaker, either of the Boston or cobbler type, and being 18/10 stainless steel for the steel parts. Not all drinks in this book use a cocktail shaker, but enough do that you'll want one.

2. An assortment (matched or unmatched) or at least a good amount of clear, clean glassware. Plastic isn't nearly as classy, and it tends to bring down the delish quotient in your drinks.

3. Some good liqueurs or liquors. Well, it's pretty tough to create drinks without them.

4. A measuring device of some sort that has measurements in ounces. This way, you can be assured of balanced drinks. For punches or batches of drinks for a crowd, you'll need a larger measuring device too.

5. This book, for recipes and jolly banter.

CALEDONIA

You may wonder, when packing a backpack with such a range of ingredients, from chocolate liqueur crème de cacao to fresh milk and carefully cradled fresh eggs (you'll want a little cooler for those items) to the rich, intriguing Bittermens Xocolatl Mole Bitters to cinnamon, why anyone would be insane enough to want to lug this selection up Schiehallion Mountain in northern Scotland. (I'm taking for granted that you're already okay with lugging up brandy. There's no one out there who climbs mountains without brandy, right?) When reaching the top, and making a cocktail as the sun broaches the skyline with its first tentative streaks, and you start sipping a Caledonia in Caledonia (which is what the Romans called this part of Scotland during their occupation), and the absolute rightness of the moment hits, understanding will be far-reaching. Feel no need to thank me then—just ask me along for the next round.

ICE CUBES

1 OUNCE WHITE CRÈME DE CACAO

1 OUNCE BRANDY

1 OUNCE MILK

1 EGG YOLK, PREFERABLY ORGANIC

DASH OF BITTERMENS XOCOLATL MOLE BITTERS

FRESHLY GROUND CINNAMON, FOR GARNISH

1. Fill a cocktail shaker halfway full with ice cubes. Add the crème de cacao, brandy, milk, egg yolk, and bitters. Shake exceedingly well.

2. Strain into a cocktail glass. Sprinkle a fine dusting of fresh cinnamon over the drink.

A NOTE: Having trouble tracking down Bittermens bitters in your town? Check online at spots such as DrinkUpNY (www.DrinkUpNY.com).

A WARNING: As this drink contains raw egg, it shouldn't be served to the elderly or to those with compromised immune systems.

CARA SPOSA

S erve this sweet, frothy treat to that extra-special darling on anniversaries, birthdays, holidays, the first day of May, the last day of September, and any other day you want to remind him or her of how important he or she is, and how every day is better because your darling happens to be in it with you. Sure, there's a little sappiness in there (just as there is a little cream in this drink), but sometimes sappiness is a good thing. This Italian moniker does translate to "beloved spouse," so the sappiness and the sweetness are in the best of causes.

CRUSHED ICE

1½ OUNCES TIA MARIA

1 OUNCE ORANGE CURAÇAO

½ OUNCE HEAVY CREAM

1. Fill a cocktail shaker halfway full with crushed ice. Add the Tia Maria, orange curaçao, and cream. Shake well.

2. Strain into a cocktail glass.

A NOTE: I've seen this blended and then strained, but I think that makes it too watery. Using crushed ice and shaking like a machine gets things slushy but not overly watery.

CARIBBEAN SUNSET

W atch the big ol' ball sink down past the sand, a few reluctant rays trickling through palm trees as the ocean stretches vast and blue, a beach tableau that speaks to the contemplative side of the surf, to the moments between boisterous barbecues and moonlit dance parties. Even the most partying of spring break and summertime days needs a moment like this, to catch one's proverbial breath and soak in the scenery. Isn't it nice there's a drink to match this moment?

ICE CUBES

1½ OUNCES GIN

¾ OUNCE CRÈME DE BANANA

¾ OUNCE BLUE CURAÇAO

¾ OUNCE HEAVY CREAM

½ OUNCE FRESHLY SQUEEZED LEMON JUICE

¼ OUNCE GRENADINE (PAGE 14)

1. Fill a cocktail shaker halfway full with ice cubes. Add the gin, crème de banana, orange curaçao, cream, and lemon juice. Shake well.

2. Strain the sunset into a cocktail glass. Swirl the grenadine over the top of the glass.

CASUAL CARESS

U nlike its more wolfish cousin lust, love is at times a little languid, a little reposed, a little sleepy, with the sun sliding in slowly through the windows on a Sunday afternoon, an afternoon where the evidence of two lives is shown in their calm affection for each other while reading the paper or watching a British costume drama as the world fades into the background. With its slight sweetness and richness provided by Castries peanut liqueur and Crema de Alba and underlined by bourbon's deep connection balanced out by the lightness of sparkling wine, this may be the only drink that can make a casual Sunday even better for two. • SERVES 2

ICE CUBES

3 OUNCES BOURBON

2 OUNCES CREMA DE ALBA

1 OUNCE CASTRIES PEANUT RUM CRÈME

CHILLED CHAMPAGNE OR SPARKLING WINE

1. Fill a cocktail shaker halfway full with ice cubes. Add the bourbon, Crema de Alba, and Castries liqueur. Shake well.

2. Strain equally into two cocktail glasses. Top each with just a splash of Champagne.

A NOTE: Crema de Alba is a brandy-based cream liqueur that is becoming more available. It features flights of coffee, nut, and sherry fancies on the tongue.

A SECOND NOTE: Castries is a rum-based peanut liqueur that's a bit creamy but with a touch of rum bite.

CHOCOLATE CLIFFHANGER

Sometimes, brain-teasing mysteries should be less about bloodthirsty, depression-driven detectives and more about playing Clue after a nice dinner, where the real danger comes only from choosing Colonel Mustard in the library with the candlestick, because you should have known it was Mrs. Peacock (it's always Mrs. Peacock). For the Clue marathons, or post-dinner hours when you want a little something sweet while snacking on milder mystery novels—say, Charles Ardai's "Hard Case" good-timer *Fifty-to-One*—this is the whodunit whistle-wetter you'll want to discover.

ICE CUBES

1½ OUNCES BAILEYS IRISH CREAM

1 OUNCE CRÈME DE MENTHE

½ OUNCE GIN

DASH OF ORANGE BITTERS

1. Fill a cocktail shaker halfway full with ice cubes. Add the Baileys, crème de menthe, gin, and bitters. Shake well.

2. Strain into a cocktail glass. Garnish with a tiny noose.

"She shut the door behind us and turned up the radio. Jump music jumped at us. She made a vague gesture in the direction of the bottle of gin."

—GEORGE BAGBY, *THE CORPSE WITH STICKY FINGERS*, 1952

What Does "Crème de" Mean?

The world of liqueurs (and booze in general) can be a confusing place. Take, for example, the phrase *crème de*. Just looking at it, you might think it referred to something creamy, as the French translation is "cream of." So, the popular minty liqueur (and key ingredient of the Chocolate Cliffhanger, page 264) crème de menthe you might think is a cream-based mint mixture. But it's actually clear or occasionally green, and contains no dairy products at all, though it does often contain Corsican mint. Okay, once you get that down, you see the classic blackcurrant liqueur crème de cassis, and think that it must be related in some way to crème de menthe, or at least be cream-based (outside of being a hit in the Cassisco on page 91). But it has no cream either, and it shares only that "crème de" moniker in common with our minty friend. When you add in crème de banana, crème de cacao, crème de mûre, crème de gingembre, crème de noyaux, crème de pêche, crème de violette, crème de framboise, and others, it could get really confusing. But, just realize that most often the "crème de" is used to refer to the liquid being a liqueur of something, and you'll be set: liqueur of mint, liqueur of peach, and so forth. It doesn't ensure a shared brand, or even a shared quality, but instead refers to the liquid being a particular flavor infused with a base spirit and a sweetening agent. If a liqueur actually has a *cream* base, it will almost always say that up front (as an example, consider Baileys Irish Cream liqueur).

CONEY ISLAND BABY

L es Appleton knew, way back in 1945, that Coney Island can be both romantic and sweltering, which is why he wrote a barbershop ditty about this very drink, as its crafty combining of chocolaty crème de cacao, peppermint, and chilled club soda is bound to cool down and enthrall anybody's baby. Wait, Les wrote a song about *losing* his Coney Island Baby, you say? Well, I'll believe you, but only if you believe me when I say he left her because she walked off with his Coney Island Baby highball, the one depicted here. 'Cause that's enough to cause any summertime split-up.

CRACKED ICE

2 OUNCES WHITE CRÈME DE CACAO

1 OUNCE PEPPERMINT SCHNAPPS

ICE CUBES

CHILLED CLUB SODA

FRESH PEPPERMINT SPRIG, FOR GARNISH

1. Fill a cocktail shaker or mixing glass halfway full with cracked ice. Add the crème de cacao and peppermint schnapps. Stir well.

2. Fill a highball glass three-quarters full with ice cubes. Strain the mixture over the ice. Fill the glass almost to the top with club soda. Stir, and garnish with the peppermint.

EL POSTRE ➤

Gather round, cowpokes, and let me spin out a yarn. It's about an after-dinner drink—one whose name comes from the Spanish for "dessert," one that I wrassled from and adapted from within the pages of Grady Spears and Brigit L. Binns' saddlebag special, *Cowboy Cocktails* (Ten Speed, 2000). In that dusty, delicious tome, they say, "This drink is much easier to make than peach cobbler when you feel a hankering for something sweet after supper." I couldn't have said it better myself, even with a backing choir of coyotes and cattle to support me.

ICE CUBES

1½ OUNCES TEQUILA

1 OUNCE BAILEYS IRISH CREAM

½ OUNCE BUTTERSCOTCH SCHNAPPS

¼ OUNCE HEAVY CREAM

1. Fill a cocktail shaker halfway full with ice cubes. Add the tequila, Baileys, and schnapps. Shake well.

2. Fill an old-fashioned glass three-quarters full with ice cubes. Strain the mixture over the ice. Swirl the cream over the top of the drink.

FIRESIDE

Certain occasions lend themselves to a little spice, a pinch of pep, a thimbleful of tang—maybe even to reclining on the proverbial bearskin (faux, naturally, because nothing brings down an evening like a dead animal) rug in front of a roaring fire. *Spicy* has a number of definitions, mind. On these occasions, turn to a spiciness you can rely on, which I think is the spiciness of the cocktails populating Kara Newman's zippy book *Spice & Ice: 60 Tongue-Tingling Cocktails* (Chronicle, 2009). That's where I found this jazzy liquid affair, which combines chai tea, Baileys Irish cream liqueur, and Goldschläger with, ahem, spicy results.

5 OUNCES HOT WATER

1 TEABAG VANILLA CHAI TEA

1 OUNCE BAILEYS IRISH CREAM

1 OUNCE GOLDSCHLÄGER CINNAMON SCHNAPPS

1 TOASTED MARSHMALLOW, FOR GARNISH

1. Add the hot water to a teacup, and then add the teabag to the cup. Steep for 2 minutes, and remove the teabag.

2. Add the Baileys and the Goldschläger to the cup, and stir briefly. Garnish with the marshmallow.

FRIAR UNTUCKED

O oh, Friar, what a long robe you have on—but why is it so ruffled? I'd say it's because this affectionate cocktail is probably favored by the more rakish members of the various orders (or of the various dinner parties). More the Friars in the vein of Tuck, those who appreciate a flagon of something on the luscious side after their meager meals (or even after their five-course meals), those who might have ruffled robes over their good hearts (and a bottle of crème de cacao in the cupboard). And I, for one, sure won't blame them. On the contrary, I'm going to join them—and if I'm preaching anything, it's that others do the same.

ICE CUBES

1½ OUNCES PRALINE PECAN LIQUEUR

1½ OUNCES DARK CRÈME DE CACAO

1½ OUNCES HEAVY CREAM

CINNAMON STICK, FOR GARNISH

1. Fill a cocktail shaker halfway full with ice cubes. Add the Praline liqueur, crème de cacao, and cream. Shake well.

2. Strain into a cocktail glass. Garnish with the cinnamon stick.

VARIATIONS: I've seen this made with Frangelico (the Italian hazelnut liqueur originally made by monks, now in the monk-y bottle) and called just Friar Tuck. It's tasty, but adding the Praline instead gives this drink a bit of a Southern flair that adds a lot to an evening. I've also seen a drink called the Friar Tuck made with vodka, coke, and blackberry cordial. Which seems so unholy I would suggest not even mentioning it.

A NOTE: Dark crème de cacao is simply a brown version of the more typically used white (clear, really) crème de cacao.

LILY

Serve the Lily alongside its namesake flower, a well-made omelet, and a bowl of fruit on Mother's Day (as long as Mom likes gin). The light and fresh flavors are sure to show off an appreciation for all she's done, and your shaking and straining ability will show off your skill—which will make your mother proud. All in all, you might end up being the top child in the land (not that it's a contest, but hey, being the best isn't ever bad, especially when it's in the service of Mom).

ICE CUBES

1½ OUNCES GIN

½ OUNCE CRÈME DE NOYAUX

½ OUNCE LILLET BLANC

½ OUNCE FRESHLY SQUEEZED LEMON JUICE

LEMON TWIST, FOR GARNISH

1. Fill a cocktail shaker halfway full with ice cubes. Add the gin, crème de noyaux, Lillet, and lemon juice. Shake well.

2. Strain into a cocktail glass. Garnish with the lemon twist after twisting it over the drink.

A NOTE: Crème de noyaux is a pink-tinged, almondy liqueur made from apricot and/or peach kernels.

LOCH LOMOND

Whoever U. Walton was, he must have had quite a wee bit of imagination to bring together Drambuie, made from Scotch, honey, herbs, and gold, and Cointreau, an orange liqueur made in France with bitter oranges from the world over, and tropical favorite fresh lime, and to name it after a lake in Scotland made famous by a song penned in 1841 called the "Bonnie Banks o' Loch Lomond." (Okay, I'm guessing a little on that last fact, but someone named U. Walton has to have loved music, right?) How, you ask, do I know about U. Walton and his Loch Lomond cocktail? My thanks (and yours) must be fourfold, and go not only to U. Walton but also to bartender W.J. Tarling, who originally compiled the recipes in the *Café Royal Cocktail Book* in 1937; to Pall Mall Ltd. of London, which originally published the book; and to Jared Brown, whose Mixallany Books imprint reprinted the book in 2008.

ICE CUBES

1½ OUNCES DRAMBUIE

¾ OUNCE COINTREAU

¾ OUNCE FRESHLY SQUEEZED LIME JUICE

1. Fill a cocktail shaker halfway full with ice cubes. Add the Drambuie, Cointreau, and lime juice. Shake well.

2. Strain into a cocktail glass.

MAGIA BIANCA

Let's see, there's Merlin; but then also Gandalf; Albus Dumbledore and his students (most famously Harry Potter); Dr. Strange, his teacher the Ancient One, and his disciple (and lady friend from another dimension) Clea; Zatanna and her father Zatara; not to mention Glenda. Now, that's nowhere near a complete list of the heroic, helpful, and generally good magicians out in the world (or the world of literature and imagination, at least). But it is a solid list of folks worth raising a thaumaturgic toast to (while wearing a robe, or a pointy hat, or at least carrying a wand or stirring stick with a star on it) when making Magia Biancas with fellow magical friends.

ICE CUBES

1½ OUNCES STREGA

1 OUNCE WHITE CRÈME DE CACAO

½ OUNCE HEAVY CREAM

FRESHLY GRATED NUTMEG, FOR GARNISH

1. Fill a cocktail shaker halfway full with ice cubes. Add the Strega, crème de cacao, and cream. Shake well.

2. Strain into a cocktail glass. Garnish with a thin dusting of magic powder or freshly grated nutmeg.

MATINEE

I believe this cocktail has a bit more in common with the origins of the word *matinee* than with the current meaning, since the word derives from the Latin goddess of the dawn, Matuta, and the drink contains a well-shaken egg white, which makes me associate it with morning drinks. Does this mean I wouldn't be happy to watch a matinee of a Billy Wilder movie or a Thornton Wilder play while consuming one or two Matinees? On the contrary, I think it would be a delectable experience. Much like words change over time, we have to be ready for change, even if it means drinking an egg drink in the afternoon.

ICE CUBES

2 OUNCES GIN

¾ OUNCE SAMBUCA

¼ OUNCE FRESHLY SQUEEZED LIME JUICE

¼ OUNCE HEAVY CREAM

1 EGG WHITE, PREFERABLY ORGANIC

1. Fill a cocktail shaker halfway full with ice cubes. Add the gin, Sambuca, lime juice, cream, and egg white. Shake exceedingly well.

2. Strain into a cocktail glass.

A WARNING: As this drink contains raw egg, it shouldn't be served to the elderly or to those with compromised immune systems.

MOOD INDIGO

I sing, because I revere: "You ain't been blue, no, no, no, you ain't been blue, till you've had a Mood Indigo. That gin goes stealin', down to my cognac, while Parfait Amour sighs, 'Go 'long, egg white. . . .'"

This colorful cocktail shouldn't be seen as available for only one occasion (feeling blue), though having one might help remove those somber sentiments, and I wouldn't want to hold you back from chippering up. By all means, then, shake yourself out of the blues if needed. Once out, though, don't think you can't have another of these to celebrate. Because it goes down as good with a grin as with a frown.

ICE CUBES

1 OUNCE GIN

¾ OUNCE COGNAC

¾ OUNCE PARFAIT AMOUR

1 EGG WHITE, PREFERABLE ORGANIC

1. Fill a cocktail shaker halfway full with ice cubes. Add the gin, Cognac, Parfait Amour, and egg white. Shake very well (not moodily at all).

2. Strain into a cocktail glass.

A NOTE: Once thought to be a mystic type of love potion (and, who knows, maybe it actually is), Parfait Amour is a violet-colored liqueur that has floral hints (roses and violets) surrounded by slight nutty and vanilla flavors.

A WARNING: As this drink contains raw egg, it shouldn't be served to the elderly or to those with compromised immune systems.

ONCE IS ENOUGH

Once upon a time, I discovered what looked to be a brunchy-time cocktail in one of my fairy tale favorites (I may read a slightly different type of fairy tale than most kids), Crosby Gaige's *Cocktail Guide and Ladies' Companion* (M. Barrows, 1941). I thought the name was coolly captivating, reminding consumers to drink just one, which is what a brunch drink should do, and I saw that it had an egg yolk, which lent it a relationship to omelets and scrambles. So I took the plunge and found out, as happens more than you'd think, that my assumptions were way off. First, once is not enough. Second, the time for this is almost flip-flopped from brunch, as it sways on the sweet side, and falls more into after-dinner-ing than drinking in the a.m. And, finally, not to stand at odds with my old friend Mr. Gaige, but I liked the egg white in here more than the yolk, due to the frothy component it brings. One facet didn't change, luckily: The ending of the tale is still "happily ever after."

ICE CUBES

1 OUNCE BRANDY

1 OUNCE ORANGE CURAÇAO

1 OUNCE ANISETTE

1 EGG WHITE, PREFERABLY ORGANIC

1. Fill a cocktail shaker halfway full with ice cubes. Add the brandy, orange curaçao, anisette, and egg white. Shake exceptionally well.

2. Strain into a cocktail glass.

3. If once isn't, actually, enough, repeat steps 1 and 2.

A WARNING: As this drink contains raw egg, it shouldn't be served to the elderly or to those with compromised immune systems.

PING-PONG COCKTAIL

Older cocktails such as this, that have gone through some permutations and that have a few variations out there, lead me (and maybe you, too, if I'm guessing right about you) to wonder what exactly tied the name to the list of ingredients. And is it because the name is a keen one that there are variations? These theoretical questions can be almost as much fun as playing Ping-Pong, with theories jumping the table like Ping-Pong balls—as long as there are a couple of cocktails made, that is. So, take this as a lesson: Always make the drinks before starting the questions and before taking that first swing with a paddle. Both activities (like so, so many others) are only enhanced with cocktails. Oh, one more lesson here: If the sloe gin and violet-y crème Yvette combo is too cuddly for your taste, try experimenting with another base spirit instead of sloe gin (like gin, for example). But to keep any more confusion from arriving, call the new drink Gossima or Whiff-Whaff, both being one-time names for the Ping-Pong.

ICE CUBES

2 OUNCES SLOE GIN

1½ OUNCES CRÈME YVETTE

½ OUNCE FRESHLY
SQUEEZED LEMON JUICE

1. Fill a cocktail shaker halfway full with ice cubes. Add the sloe gin, crème Yvette, and lemon juice. Shake well.

2. Strain into a cocktail glass.

LIQUEUR SPOTLIGHT

Anisette

Anisette is the basic name for a colorless liqueur made by a distillation of the seeds of the Mediterranean anís plant (a relative of parsley) or by a blending of these seeds with a neutral grain spirit and sugar syrup. Though it is often consumed solo, it may be best when mixed in cocktails such as the Ladies' Cocktail (page 208), where its sweeter notes shine. This sweetness sets it apart from many other anise-flavored liqueurs (such as pastis and Pernod), as does its lower alcohol content. Also, anisette differs from pastis and others through its use of anise seed as opposed to star anise (which comes from a tree of the same name). Anisette is especially popular in Spain and Italy, where you'll see a number of different brands, but other countries also produce and export it.

POOR HARRIET

L et me assure you in my most forceful manner (which isn't too forceful, unless my local liquor store is out of Prosecco—then I get awfully uptight) that this is not a bubbler to be served in sadness over a string of calamities that have befallen Harriet (whoever she may be). Oh no, it's the complete flip-flop of that. It should be served as a way of letting Harriet know that things aren't that bad. That she should cheer up even if she might have to miss one party, as Harriet does in Jane Austen's *Emma*, leading the leading character to say, "The delightful family party which Emma was securing for herself, poor Harriet must, in every charitable caution, be kept at a distance from." Remind Harriet that there will be more parties, and she can show at the majority of them, and even if she misses one, here's a dreamy drink for her right now that puts a lavender glow on the situation. If you don't actually know a Harriet, then sub in any needed name. But don't sub in another ingredient for the Italian sparkling wine Prosecco. You know how that irritates me—think what it'll do to Harriet.

ICE CUBES

1 OUNCE GIN

½ OUNCE PARFAIT AMOUR

½ OUNCE SIMPLE SYRUP
(PAGE 12)

½ OUNCE FRESHLY
SQUEEZED ORANGE JUICE

DASH OF PEYCHAUD'S
BITTERS

CHILLED PROSECCO

1. Fill a cocktail shaker halfway full with ice cubes. Add the gin, Parfait Amour, simple syrup, orange juice, and bitters. Shake well.

2. Strain into a flute glass. Top with chilled Prosecco. Start turning frowns upside down.

RUSTY NAIL

A perfect union of big, gruff-voiced, smoky Scotch and its naiad-like neighbor Drambuie, made from Scotch, honey, and an herbal combination of anise, saffron, nutmeg, and more. It's this magical, but simple, combination that makes the drink a prize from small-town lounges to glitzy big-city clubs. It turns out that to be a classic drink, there's no need to go overboard with ingredients or wackiness. Great ingredients that work together do the trick, with the Drambuie's feathery touch softening the sharp edges of the Scotch, while the Scotch rolls up its tight T-shirt to reveal muscles ready to support the more delicate Drambuie. Whew, musing about it that way, this is one nail no one minds cuddling up with on a stormy evening.

ICE CUBES

2 OUNCES SCOTCH

1 OUNCE DRAMBUIE

**LEMON TWIST,
FOR GARNISH (OPTIONAL)**

1. Fill an old-fashioned glass halfway full with ice cubes. Add the Scotch and then the Drambuie to the glass.

2. Stir briefly and garnish with the lemon twist.

A VARIATION: I recently heard that if you substitute rye for Scotch in this, and you are in Canada, it's called a Donald Sutherland. Not to take anything away from my astounding neighbors to the north, but I gotta take this worldwide. It's genius.

"Generally, I don't like to consume liquor before lunch, but drinking with a man is a good recipe for getting on his right side. Muir was in the mood to talk and I ordered double Scotches to help loosen his tongue. The time of day meant nothing to him."

—HAROLD Q. MASUR, *SO RICH, SO LOVELY, AND SO DEAD,* 1952

YOU HAVE THE BASIC NECESSITIES (THOSE FIVE MENTIONED ON PAGE 260) FOR YOUR HOME BAR, AND THE RIGHT ATTITUDE (WHICH EQUALS FUNTASTICGOODTIMES-NESS), AND NOW YOU WANT TO EXPAND YOUR BAR-TOOLING AND DRINK-MAKING CAPABILITIES.

The following five tools will help you along your path, young bar Jedi:

1. A muddler, preferably one that's wooden, to be used for muddling fruits and herbs and anything else that needs it, as well as for turning ice cubes into cracked ice in a muscular manner.

2. At least one reliable, long, thin, somewhat cool-looking (it never hurts) bar spoon. Many drinks in this book are stirred rather than shaken, and while a normal spoon (or chopstick, I suppose) can be used for this purpose, having a dedicated bar spoon is a better idea.

3. While your cocktail shaker might have a built-in strainer, and while your regular bar set might have a julep or Hawthorne strainer, it's nice having a fine-mesh strainer for straining out fruit or for presenting drinks of maximum clarity.

4. A dedicated mixing glass, for stirring drinks. You can make stirred drinks in a cocktail shaker, but having a mixing glass that boasts classic lines and grace helps keep you organized and provides a dose of smooth.

5. For larger gatherings, and to take a little stress off your position as host or hostess, having a sparkling punch bowl is key. Besides letting you make a few fewer single drinks, a punch bowl lends itself to more happening happenings.

SNOWBALL

This is not the creative chiller expected when one sees the title, which has led many throughout history to believe that this drink was pitch-perfect for sweatier moments, those afternoons when all soiree sojourners desire an icy libation. But we, intrepid party throwers, know that planning involves testing at times, or at least having me do some testing for you—to step in front of the Snowball, as it may be. And I'm just the type of guy who is happy to step up for you—yes, *you*—and deliver the information in plenty of time for the party: The Snowball isn't, actually, ideal for the summer's day, but it would be dandy for a very late summer night, after a large dinner or before bed, when it's dessert-y nature and layered flavors are sure to shine (and not with the glow of sweat).

ICE CUBES

2 OUNCES GIN

½ OUNCE CRÈME DE VIOLETTE

½ OUNCE WHITE CRÈME DE MENTHE

½ OUNCE ANISETTE

½ OUNCE HEAVY CREAM

1. Fill a cocktail shaker halfway full with ice cubes. Add the gin, crème de violette, crème de menthe, anisette, and cream to a cocktail shaker. Shake well.

2. Strain into a cocktail glass.

A VARIATION: There is another drink called the Snowball that's very popular in some locales. It mixes advocaat (a liqueur made from egg, sugar, and brandy) and sparkling lemonade.

A SECOND VARIATION: There is a third drink called the Snow Ball that isn't just different in spelling, but also in ingredients: It contains brandy, simple syrup, an egg, and ginger ale.

"This is woman's work."

—HARRY CRADDOCK, REFERRING TO THE SNOWBALL IN *THE SAVOY COCKTAIL BOOK* (1930)

TI PENSO SEMPRE

The Italian title of this coquetter translates as "I always think of you," and if that doesn't influence your serving it at your next tête-à-tête, then perhaps the players within the drink will: brandy, for history and experience; Italian aperitivo Aperol, for flavor and continental appeal; simple syrup, for smoothness and sugar; and an orange slice, for a touch of tang and style. Now if that arrangement doesn't influence you, then I suggest a deep immersion into Al Green's greatest hits, because friend, your romance meter needs a jump start.

ICE CUBES

1½ OUNCES BRANDY

1 OUNCE APEROL

½ OUNCE SIMPLE SYRUP (PAGE 12)

ORANGE SLICE, FOR GARNISH

1. Fill a cocktail shaker halfway full with ice cubes. Add the brandy, Aperol, and simple syrup. Shake lovingly.

2. Strain into a cocktail glass and garnish with the orange slice.

6 Rereleases You'll Want to Read
....

So, as far as I know, no one has invented a time machine. Which means we can't go back in time to visit all those fantastic bartenders who slung drinks way back when, or visit the bars where they served up drinks. Luckily, we now have a little insight into past happy hours, thanks to a few bubbly publishers who have brought out in reprinted form some of the best books from the past, including the following:

1. *Bariana: A Practical Compendium of All American and British Drinks*, by Louis Fouquet, translated and annotated by Charles Vexenat (originally published in 1894, reprinted in 2009 by Mixellany Books)

2. *Cocktail Boothby's American Bar-Tender*, by William T. "Cocktail" Boothby (originally published in 1891, reprinted in 2008 by Anchor Distilling)

3. *The New and Improved Illustrated Bartenders' Manual or: How to Mix Drinks in the Present Style*, by Harry Johnson (originally published in 1882, reprinted in 2008 by Mud Puddle Books)

4. *The Stork Club Bar Book*, by Lucius Beebe (originally published in 1946, reprinted in 2003 by New Day Publishing)

5. *The Café Royal Cocktail Book*, by W.J. Tarling (originally published in 1937, reprinted in 2008 by Mixellany Books)

6. *Barflies and Cocktails*, by Harry McElhone and Wynn Holcomb, with slight contributions from Arthur Moss (originally published in 1927, reprinted in 2008 by Mud Puddle Books)

MEASUREMENT EQUIVALENTS

Please note that all conversions are approximate.

Liquid Conversions

U.S.	Imperial	Metric
1 tsp		5 ml
1 tbs	½ fl oz	15 ml
2 tbs	1 fl oz	30 ml
3 tbs	1½ fl oz	45 ml
¼ cup	2 fl oz	60 ml
⅓ cup	2½ fl oz	75 ml
⅓ cup + 1 tbs	3 fl oz	90 ml
⅓ cup + 2 tbs	3½ fl oz	100 ml
½ cup	4 fl oz	120 ml
⅔ cup	5 fl oz	150 ml
¾ cup	6 fl oz	180 ml
¾ cup + 2 tbs	7 fl oz	200 ml
1 cup	8 fl oz	240 ml
1 cup + 2 tbs	9 fl oz	275 ml
1¼ cups	10 fl oz	300 ml
1⅓ cups	11 fl oz	325 ml
1½ cups	12 fl oz	350 ml
1⅔ cups	13 fl oz	375 ml
1¾ cups	14 fl oz	400 ml
1¾ cups + 2 tbs	15 fl oz	450 ml
2 cups (1 pint)	16 fl oz	475 ml
2½ cups	20 fl oz	600 ml
3 cups	24 fl oz	720 ml
4 cups (1 quart)	32 fl oz	945 ml
		(1,000 ml is 1 liter)

Weight Conversions

U.S./U.K.	Metric
½ oz	14 g
1 oz	28 g
1½ oz	43 g
2 oz	57 g
2½ oz	71 g
3 oz	85 g
3½ oz	100 g
4 oz	113 g
5 oz	142 g
6 oz	170 g
7 oz	200 g
8 oz	227 g
9 oz	255 g
10 oz	284 g
11 oz	312 g
12 oz	340 g
13 oz	368 g
14 oz	400 g
15 oz	425 g
1 lb	454 g

Oven Temperature Conversions

°F	Gas Mark	°C
250	½	120
275	1	140
300	2	150
325	3	165
350	4	180
375	5	190
400	6	200
425	7	220
450	8	230
475	9	240
500	10	260
550	Broil	290

INDEX

Note: Page references in *italics* indicate photographs.